POLLUTION CONTROL IN MEAT,

POULTRY AND SEAFOOD PROCESSING

POLLUTION CONTROL IN MEAT, POULTRY AND SEAFOOD PROCESSING

Harold R. Jones

NOYES DATA CORPORATION

Park Ridge, New Jersey   London, England

1974

Published in the United States of America by
Noyes Data Corporation
Noyes Building, Park Ridge, New Jersey 07656

FOREWORD

Slaughtering and meat processing produce a highly loaded, but biologically degradable wastewater, containing dissolved, suspended and dispersed blood, bile, grease and fibrous animal matter with high nitrogen content, bringing with it also serious air pollution and odor removal problems. This is especially true of plants where fat is rendered.

All of these problems were stated in detail by A.J. Steffen in a paper before the Meat Industry Research Conference in 1969.

Since animal slaughter is the primary source of enormous wastewater volumes and pollution loads, it was necessary to examine the size and structure of the meat packing industry. A meat packing plant usually is both a slaughterhouse and a meat processing plant, where edible and inedible fats are also processed.

In this book are condensed vital data from government sources that are unusually difficult to pull together. Important pollution removal processes are interpreted and explained by examples from recent U.S. patents.

Poultry and seafood wastes are also considered in detail in this volume. These industries have pollution problems all their own, to which solutions are offered. One should have to go no further than this condensed information to establish a sound background for action towards combating pollution in the meat, poultry and seafood industries.

A previous volume in this series covers the related food industry area of *Waste Disposal Control in the Fruit and Vegetable Industry.* A subsequent volume will cover *Pollution Control in the Dairy Products Industry.*

Advanced composition and production methods developed by Noyes Data are employed to bring our new durably bound books to you in a minimum of time. Special techniques are used to close the gap between "manuscript" and "completed book." Industrial technology is progressing so rapidly that time-honored, conventional typesetting, binding and shipping methods are no longer suitable. We have bypassed the delays in the conventional book publishing cycle and provide the user with an effective and convenient means of reviewing up-to-date information in depth.

The Table of Contents is organized in such a way as to serve as a subject index. Other indexes by company, inventor and patent number help in providing easy access to the information contained in this book.

CONTENTS AND SUBJECT INDEX

Contents and Subject Index

PART I.

THE MEAT PROCESSING INDUSTRY

STRUCTURE OF THE MEAT PACKING INDUSTRY

There are three different types of plants which are included in the category described in this report as meat packing: the slaughterhouse or abattoir, the meat packing plant, and the meat processing plant.

1. A slaughtering plant is a killing and dressing plant which does almost no processing of by-products.
2. A meat packing plant is both a slaughtering house and a meat processing plant. Packing houses will often be involved in the cooking, curing, smoking and pickling of meat, the manufacture of sausage, the rendering of edible fats into lard and edible tallow, and the rendering of inedible fats into greases.
3. A meat processing plant does no slaughter at all.

Since animal slaughter and/or meat production are the primary factors determining wastewater volumes and pollution loads of the meat packing industry, it will be necessary to examine the size and structure of the meat packing industry in order to estimate the total wasteload of the industry. Neither value-added nor sales are adequate measures of plant or industry size from which to estimate plant or industry wasteload because these measures may not reflect pollution loads.

For example, those plants and/or areas with high beef sales may have a low beef packing wasteload because there is little slaughtering. Thus animal slaughter data are more relevant measures of plant and industry size than meat production or value-added statistics, as pollution loads are related primarily to the slaughtering aspect of the production process. Technically, data pertaining to meat production or value-added may include

2

the processing of imported dressed carcasses and, hence, overstate the
pollution load. Total liveweight, then, is the measure of size which will
be utilized in this study, primarily because this measure makes possible
the meaningful addition of unlike species. Two cattle plus two hogs is
not as meaningful an aggregate as two thousand pounds of cattle plus five
hundred pounds of hogs. Total liveweight killed per year will be used as
the measure of meat packing size as well as of the industry size.

The three types of slaughter data available which can be used to measure
industry size are shown in Table 1. The most inclusive category is total
slaughter which is composed of farm slaughter and total commercial slaughter and state or locally inspected slaughter constitute total commercial
slaughter. The preferred category for measuring industry size is total commercial slaughter.

Total commercial slaughter is preferred to total slaughter as a measure of
industry size related to pollution load. Total slaughter is only slightly
larger than total commercial slaughter, the difference being the amount
of farm slaughter. Farm slaughter in all cases is a very small and continually decreasing proportion of total slaughter. In 1965 less than 2-1/2%
of all animal slaughter took place on farms. Such an insignificant proportion of the total can be ignored without affecting the results. Even more
important, however, is the fact that farm slaughter is not geographically
concentrated and, therefore, poses no significant pollution problem.

Total commercial slaughter is also preferred to federally inspected slaughter as a measurement of size. Although more information is generally
available about federally inspected slaughter than about total commercial
slaughter, the latter is a more acceptable indicator of size because federally inspected slaughter represents only about 85% of total commercial
slaughter.

Table 2 shows the number of plants by type of inspection and total liveweight killed by type of inspection for the years 1960, 1965 and 1971.
Notice that less than 20% of commercial slaughter plants are federally
inspected, yet these plants kill almost 85% of the liveweight slaughtered.
These statistics are a clear illustration of the dangers of basing meat packing statistics upon the number of plants.

Commercial slaughter data by type of animal are available on a regional
or national basis in two forms: the number of animals killed and the total
liveweight of animals slaughtered.

Many conclusions about meat packing industry activity which are based
upon the number of plants will be misleading because of the structure

TABLE 1: TOTAL ANIMAL SLAUGHTER, UNITED STATES, 1971

	Thousands of Animals					Millions of Pounds of Liveweight				
	Cattle	Hogs	Sheep	Calves	Total	Cattle	Hogs	Sheep	Calves	Total
Federally Inspected	31,419	86,667	10,256	2,806	131,148	32,680	20,771	1,067	579	55,097
Other	4,166	7,771	473	883	13,293	3,908	1,764	45	340	6,057
Total Commercial	35,585	94,438	10,729	3,689	144,441	36,588	22,535	1,112	919	61,154
Farm	312	1,112	238	132	1,794	303	277	23	52	655
Total	35,897	95,550	10,967	3,821	146,235	36,891	22,812	1,135	971	61,809

Sources: U.S. Department of Agriculture, Livestock and Meat Statistics, Supplement for 1971 to Statistical Bulletin #333, Washington, D.C.: U.S. Government Printing Office, 1972.

U.S. Department of Agriculture, Livestock Slaughter: 1972, Statistical Reporting Service, Washington, D.C.: U.S. Government Printing Office, 1973.

TABLE 2: NUMBER OF PLANTS AND LIVEWEIGHT SLAUGHTERED BY TYPE OF INSPECTION

Type of Inspection	No. of Plants			Liveweight Slaughtered, millions of lbs.			Percent of Total Commercial Slaughter Plants by Type of Inspection			Percent of Total Liveweight Slaughtered by Type of Inspection		
	1960	1965	1971	1960	1965	1971	1960	1965	1971	1960	1965	1971
Federally Inspected	530	570	766	38,319	44,569	55,097	16.9	19.3	19.5	80.9	84.3	90.1
Other Commercial	2,614	2,387	3,144	9,062	8,319	6,057	83.1	80.7	80.5	19.1	15.7	9.9
Total Commercial	3,144	2,957	3,910	47,381	55,888	61,154	100.0	100.0	100.0	100.0	100.0	100.0

Sources: Same as Table 1.

of this industry. Even the most casual analysis of the data shown in Table 2 will illustrate the misleading nature of these data. General information based upon the number of plants is misleading because of the extremely large number of very small meat packing plants. Meat packing plants range in size from plants whose annual kill is less than one million pounds to those plants whose annual kill is over 800 million pounds. 20% of all meat packing plants in 1966 belonged to the size category in which annual kill was less than 10 million pounds, for example.

DEFINITION OF SMALL, MEDIUM AND LARGE PLANTS

In the meat packing industry itself, there exists a lack of agreement as to the correct size designation of a plant in terms of small, medium, or large. National packers will define small differently than independent packers will. Firms are designated as national packers who have national systems of distribution, widely known brand names, and national programs of advertising and promotion. National packers would include such firms as Armour & Co., Swift & Co., Wilson & Co., and eight or ten others, such as Cudahy, Hormel, Morrell, Oscar Mayer, and Rath.

A national meat packer would probably specify any plant killing less than 100 million pounds per year as small. Thus, the national packer tends to estimate size in terms of the national meat packing industry. National meat packers define the size of plants differently, depending upon the type of animal killed. In general, a plant engaged in the killing of cattle and classified as a medium-sized plant, will handle two times the liveweight as a similarly designated plant killing hogs. A small plant in terms of cattle would be one whose annual kill is less than 25 million pounds. A small plant in terms of hogs would be one whose annual kill is 12 or 13 million pounds.

In spite of the lack of consistency concerning size definition on the part of the national packer, in this volume the size of plants will be defined in terms of annual liveweight slaughter. This definition of size allows for a meaningful comparison between a plant killing four species of animals and a plant killing only one species.

A small meat packing plant will be defined as one in which the annual liveweight kill is less than 25 million pounds, a medium plant as one in which the annual liveweight kill is approximately 100 million pounds, and a large plant as one in which the annual liveweight kill is 200 million pounds or more. See Table 3. Table 4 summarizes the characteristics of the federally inspected meat packing industry by the size classes to be utilized in this discussion, that is, small, medium, and large.

TABLE 3:   DEFINITION OF PLANT SIZE — SMALL, MEDIUM, LARGE
MEAT PACKING INDUSTRY

Plant Size in Annual Liveweight Killed[a] (Mil. lbs.)	Equivalent Size in Terms of Daily Kill				
	Liveweight (Thou. lbs.)	Cattle[b] (No. head)	Hogs[c] (No. head)	Cattle & Hogs[d] (No. head)	
Small 25	95,000	95	380	48	190
Medium 100	379,000	379	1,156	190	758
Large 200	758,000	758	3,032	379	1,516

[a]In terms of a range in Annual Liveweight Killed, plant
sizes would be as follows:
            Small: 0 - 25 millions of pounds
            Medium: 25 - 200 millions of pounds
            Large: 200 - up.

[b]Cattle average 1000 lbs. per head.

[c]Hogs average 250 lbs. per head.

[d]Liveweight divided equally between cattle and hogs.

Source: FWPCA Publication IWP-8

TABLE 4:   NUMBER OF PLANTS AND TOTAL LIVEWEIGHT KILLED BY
SIZE GROUP FEDERALLY INSPECTED PLANTS, U.S., 1966

Size Class TLWK/Year (Mil. of lbs)	No. of Plants	Per Cent of Plants	TLWK/Year (Mil. of lbs)	Per Cent of Total Slaughtered
0- 24.9	239	38.0	2,437	5.2
25-199.9	335	53.3	24,718	53.0
200 and up	55	8.7	19,399	41.8
All Plants	629	100.0	46,555	100.0

Source: U.S. Department of Agriculture, unpublished data quoted in
FWPCA Publication IWP-8

This section has defined the medium-sized plant in such a manner that the range includes both the average-size and median-size plant under federal inspection. The average-size plant under federal inspection is one whose annual kill is 74 million pounds. The median-size plant under federal inspection is one whose annual kill is 38 million pounds. To the extent that the definition of medium-size is such that it includes both the average and median-size plants, it is a reasonable definition.

MEAT PACKING PROCESSES AND POLLUTANTS

A general flowchart of the meat packing industry showing products, processes and waste generation is presented in Figure 1.

Six fundamental industry processes which can be carried out in several ways have been identified. The method by which a fundamental process is executed is defined as a subprocess. Those processes whose subprocess choice determines its pollution contribution have been identified in Table 5. Table 5 further shows the percentage distribution of the subprocesses among meat packing plants. Only those distributions of plants by subprocess in the Killing, Washing, and Cleanup sections include all meat packing plants. The remaining categories should be interpreted as the distribution of plants among the subprocesses when that fundamental process is part of the packing plant's operation. The fundamental process of Paunch Handling will serve to illustrate this interpretation.

In 1972, according to Table 5, of all plants handling paunch material, (that is, those plants killing cattle and/or calves) 25% employed the dry dumping method, 71% used wet dumping, and the remaining 5% allowed paunch material to be dumped into the sewer. The projected percentage distributions for 1977 assume continued efforts on the part of industry to reduce wastewater flow and/or wastewater strength.

Many conclusions about meat packing industry activity which are based upon the number of plants, will be misleading because of the structure of this industry. As mentioned earlier, even the most casual analysis of the data shown in Table 2 illustrates the misleading nature of these data. General information based upon the number of plants is misleading because of the extremely large number of very small meat packing plants. Meat

7

FIGURE 1: FLOWCHART FOR PACKINGHOUSE

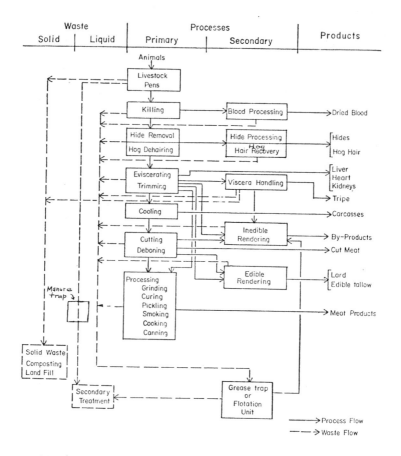

Source: North Star Research & Development Inst., "Final Report,
Industrial Waste Study of the Meat Products Industry,"
EPA Contract No. 68-01-0031

packing plants range in size from plants whose annual kill is less than one
million pounds to those plants whose annual kill is over 800 million pounds.
20% of all meat packing plants in 1966 belonged to the size category in
which annual kill was less than 10 million pounds, for example. These
124 plants together handled only 1% of total liveweight slaughtered that
year. To the extent that an estimate of industry participation is based
upon the percent of plants participating, the participation is likely to be
understated. The extent of the understatement will, of course, depend
upon the number of very small plants in the estimate.

TABLE 5

Production Process and Significant Subprocesses	Estimated Percentage of Plants Employing Indicated Subprocess				
	1950	1963	1967	1972	1977(est.)
I. KILLING AND BLEEDING					
1. Recovery of all blood	70	80	83	90	99
2. Recovery of no blood	30	20	17	10	1
II. WASHING OF CARCASS					
1. Interruptable water flow (Lever type valves on water hoses and/or automated washing mechanisms causing water to shut off when no animals are present)	0	5	25	80	90
2. Continuous water flow (In washing mechanisms or hoses)	100	95	75	20	10
III. PAUNCH REMOVAL					
1. Dry dumping of paunch material followed by off-site disposal	0	5	16	25	35
2. Wet dumping of paunch material followed by off-site disposal	50	70	71	70	65
3. Dumping of all paunch material into sewer	50	25	13	5	0
IV. EDIBLE RENDERING					
1. Dry rendering	20	30	40	50	60
2. Wet rendering with no evaporation of tank water	40	30	26	10	0
3. Low temperature rendering	0	10	19	25	30
4. Wet rendering followed by evaporation of tank water	40	30	15	15	10
V. INEDIBLE RENDERING					
1. Dry rendering	70	74	80	80	80
2. Wet rendering with no evaporation of tank water	15	13	9	5	0
3. Continuous rendering	0	3	5	10	19
4. Wet rendering followed by evaporation of tank water	15	10	6	5	1
VI. CLEANUP					
1. Dry cleanup followed by wet cleanup	0	5	10	30	60
2. Wet cleanup	100	95	90	70	40

Source: FWPCA Publ. IWP-8

Three levels of technology may be specified in terms of the process or sub-processes. The latest method of performing a fundamental process may be categorized as "advanced" technology. The oldest methods still utilized may be designated as "old" technology. The most widely used method may be characterized as "typical" technology. In general, the different methods of paunch handling, edible rendering, inedible rendering, carcass washing and cleanup can be designated as "typical," "old" or "advanced" technology.

An old plant is one in which all rendering is wet with no evaporation of stick water; paunch material is washed into the sewer and cleanup is wet. A typical plant is one in which rendering is either wet with evaporation of stick water or dry. Paunch material will be dumped wet but screened and disposed of offsite. An advanced plant is one whose edible rendering is low temperature and whose inedible rendering is dry. Paunch material will be dumped dry and conveyed dry to trucks for offsite dumping. Cleanup will be dry followed by wet. Any plant which does not collect blood is automatically listed as old technology, regardless of the type of rendering, paunch handling, etc.

When the method of edible rendering was a different technology from that of inedible rendering, the assignment of technology was based upon the animal mixture. If only cattle were killed, the inedible rendering was felt to be the determining factor. If hogs dominated, then the edible rendering method became the deciding factor.

Table 6 shows the percentage distribution of plants by technology level for 1967 as published in the results of a questionnaire study by the Federal Water Pollution Control Administration in Publication IWP-8, "Meat Products." This table further shows the percentage distribution within a given technology level by size of plant. In the data shown, 80% of all plants employed subprocesses classified as typical. Half of these plants were medium size plants. Or it could be stated that 40% of all plants were medium sized using typical technology.

It is interesting to note that of those few plants with advanced technology only 6% are small plants, while close to 30% of those plants with old technology are small.

KILLING

In the meat packing industry cattle, hogs, sheep, and calves are first brought to the packing house. There they are held for a few hours before stunning and sticking. Animals are taken from the holding area, and

TABLE 6

Technology Levels and the Associated Typical Subprocesses	Estimated Per Cent of Plants by Type of Technology	1967 Proportion of Plants of this Type by size			Size Range of Plants by Type of Technology Mil. Lbs. LWK/yr.
		Sm.	Med.	Lar.	
"TYPICAL TECHNOLOGY"	80	.05	.50	.45	1-800+
1. Recovery of all blood 2. Wet dumping of paunch material followed by hauling away of the gross paunch material 3. Edible rendering--dry rendering or wet rendering with evaporation of tank water 4. Inedible rendering--dry rendering 5. Wet cleanup					
"OLD TECHNOLOGY"	10	.28	.36	.36	1-500
1. Recovery of all blood 2. Washing of all paunch material down the sewer 3. Edible rendering--wet with no evaporation of tank water 4. Inedible rendering--wet with no evaporation of tank water 5. Wet cleanup					
"ADVANCED TECHNOLOGY"	10	.06	.47	.47	15-500
1. Recovery of all blood 2. Dry dumping of the paunch material followed by the hauling of the gross material away from the plant premises 3. Edible rendering--low temperature 4. Inedible rendering-- continuous 5. Dry cleanup followed by wet cleanup					

Source: FWPCA Publ. IWP-8, Questionnaire Data.

immediately prior to their entering the kill area are immobilized by chemical, mechanical, or electrical means. Cattle are suspended by their hind legs from an overhead rail for sticking and bleeding. The immobilized hogs are positioned on a conveyor, so their heads are over the bleeding trough, which is a drain constructed underneath the conveyor for collection of blood.

BLOOD RECOVERY

Because blood is one of the major sources of BOD, the recovery of blood is an important subprocess to the process of killing. Failure to recover blood increases the BOD by 72%. In other words, blood recovery can cause the BOD to decrease by 42% according to J.A. Macon and D.N. Cote in "Study of Meat Packing Wastes in North Carolina," N.C. State College Ind. Extension Service (1961).

By 1967, according to survey results by the Federal Water Pollution Control Administration, four out of every five packing plants in the United States recovered blood. Plants which allow blood to escape directly into the sewer are usually small in size. Of all plants that do not recover blood, 70% are small plants. 24% are at the lower end of the range of medium sized plants, and 6% fall in the middle of the range of the medium sized plants. As shown in Table 6, only 83% of meat packing plants attempted to and/or accomplished recovery of all blood.

This statistic on blood recovery provides an excellent example of understatement of the meat packing industry's adoption of waste reducing subprocesses. On a total liveweight basis more than 96% of the meat packing industry is practicing blood recovery. Since failure to recover blood is a major source of BOD, face value acceptance of Table 6 percentages will overestimate the pollution load.

The consensus of opinion among national packers is that although medium and large sized plants would have attempted to recover blood as early as 1950, recovery methods were less than they are today. Improvements in the design of the kill area have increased the percentage of blood recovered from the animals. In 1950 it was estimated that 70% of all plants recovered blood. This percentage represents two factors: a larger proportion of packing plants not recovering blood, as well as a less efficient recovery on the part of those packers who did attempt to recover blood.

It seems likely that concern with the water pollution effects of no blood recovery will force the adoption of blood recovery upon all meat packers in the near future.

HIDE REMOVAL

Mechanical hide-removers are used in most meat packing plants to separate the hide from the carcass. These mechanical devices are designed
to handle approximately fifty to sixty head per hour or approximately one
hundred million pounds per year. The introduction of the mechanical hide-
remover appears to be an important factor in the determination of plant
size.

Most new cattle plants will be killing an even multiple of the fifty to
sixty head per hour. That is, the high cost of the mechanical hide-remover
dictates that if it is desired to increase the rate of kill to more than 60
head per hour, the increase will necessarily be to 100 or 120 per hour.
In terms of a liveweight equivalent, this means that the size of cattle
plants will be 100 million pounds per year, 200 million pounds per year,
300 million pounds per year, etc.

HOG DEHAIRING

Hair is removed from the hog carcass without skinning. Hair is loosened
in a scalding vat or tub where the water is kept at about 140°F. The hair
is then removed by scraping. In larger plants this hair is removed by
mechanical scrapers. After removal, hair may be sold, hauled to offsite
disposal, or dissolved in a caustic solution. The trend seems to be towards
sale of the hog hair because it can be used in the manufacture of foam
rubber.

EVISCERATION

Viscera are removed and distributed to the proper channel, depending
upon whether they will become an edible or an inedible product. Hearts,
stomachs and lower digestive tracts are usually the edible items.

PAUNCH HANDLING

In ruminants (cattle, calves, and sheep) the paunch or first stomach contains a large amount of undigested material. The paunch content of a
1,000 lb. cow might weight from 60 to 90 pounds, and at the packing
house the paunch is opened and its contents removed. The method by
which the contents of the paunch are removed and the ultimate disposal
of the contents will affect the wasteload of a particular packing plant.
Combinations of the various methods of removing the undigested material

from the paunch with those methods of ultimate disposal have led to the differentiation of three alternative subprocesses.

Dry Dumping: The first subprocess is designated as dry dumping of paunch material and offsite disposal. This method of paunch handling is one in which the undigested material (hay, corn, straw, and grain) is dumped into a hopper and conveyed by mechanical means to a truck. The hauling of this material to its offsite disposal may be at the expense of the packer or may be provided free-of-charge in exchange for receipt of the paunch material. Paunch material may be used as land fill or soil conditioner. Recent attempts to process paunch material into animal feed have met with only partial success.

Dry dumping and offsite disposal represents advanced technology in the handling of paunch material. The use of this method of handling may in part be dictated by waste treatment practices. After the gross material has been removed from the paunch, the paunch itself is cleaned with water. In some plants, the paunch is saved for tripe; in other plants where tripe is not processed, the paunch probably is used for inedible rendering.

Wet Dumping: The second subprocess is designated as wet dumping of paunch material and offsite disposal of the gross paunch material. This process involves the use of water under pressure to flush the entire paunch or the dumping of the paunch contents into a flowing stream of water which will be passed over vibrating or rotating screens. Screening separates the coarse material from the fine. The gross material is then trucked away. The solution containing the suspended fine material plus any dissolved matter passes into the sewer.

This subprocess is most typical of the meat packing industry today, and probably represents an intermediate stage in terms of technology. The introduction of screens for separation of gross material was probably pollution oriented in that their use was caused by the desire to lower the total solids content of the wastewater.

Dumping Into Sewer: The third alternative subprocess is one in which all paunch contents are washed down the sewer. This subprocess represents the oldest form of technology and probably would have been practiced primarily by packers located along major rivers who in earlier times were less concerned with this polluting characteristic of meat packing wastewater than the inland packers.

Paunch material is troublesome primarily because it increases greatly the total solids concentration in packing plant effluent. Should all plants now dumping all paunch material directly in the sewer abandon this practice,

50 to 60 pounds of solids per thousand pounds of liveweight killed would
be eliminated from the wastewater. Paunch material presents a waste
treatment problem because this undigested material is not readily handled
by a bacteriological treatment facility. For some reason the bugs do not
like paunch material. The difficulty in handling this material at end-of-
line treatment plants dictates that this material be separated from other
waste material and disposed of separately.

In those cases where the paunch is wet dumped, elimination of the wet
dumping and wet transfer of this material should reduce the BOD content
by at least 5%. It is the elimination of the paunch fines from the effluent
that should cause the 5% reduction.

RENDERING

In general, there are two types of rendering: edible and inedible. Edible
rendering is the process by which fats are converted into lard and edible
tallow. Edible rendering is applied primarily to hog fats but also to some
beef fat. Inedible rendering is the process by which scraps, trimmings,
and inedible organs (heads, feet, etc.) are converted into inedible fats,
which are used in soap, in the manufacture of grease, and in animal feeds.
Inedible rendering also provides an outlet for those parts of an animal
which have been condemned by federal meat inspectors. Through rendering, condemned material is sterilized and converted into a recoverable
product.

Edible Rendering

There are five basic edible rendering processes: dry rendering, wet rendering, low temperature rendering, caustic rendering, and enzyme rendering. The latter two types are insignificant relative to the others and will
not be included in the tabulations. Very few rendering operations rupture
fat tissues with a caustic, and it is therefore excluded. Enzyme rendering
is excluded because it is still in the development stage.

Because of differing effects upon the waste loading, four subprocesses
will be included in this study. These are (1) dry rendering, (2) wet rendering without evaporation of tank water, (3) low temperature rendering,
and (4) wet rendering followed by evaporation of tank water. Each subprocess will be discussed in detail.

Dry Rendering: Dry rendering refers to the process in which fats are cooked
in steam-jacketed tanks under a vacuum. A dry rendering system is usually
more advantageous than a wet rendering one because of the increased

recovery of protein material. Also, the dry rendering process does not contribute directly to water pollution, although the vapors from a dry rendering process may contribute to air pollution through the resulting unpleasant odors. These odors may be removed by washing the vapors. If washwater for this process is not recirculated it will contain some small amounts of pollution material, but compared with other sources of polluting material, this seems to be rather insignificant.

Wet Rendering: This process is often referred to as steam rendering because it is a process in which a large tank is loaded with fat and the tank sealed. Steam is introduced at some 40 to 60 pounds gauge pressure and kept at the particular level chosen until the fats are completely freed from the tissues. On standing, three layers form in the tank. Fats are on top, water is largely in the middle of the tank, and slush is in the bottom. After the fats are drawn off, the water and slush are either run through some kind of centrifuge or press to separate the suspended solids from the liquid. This liquid is the tank water, which when concentrated to about 35% moisture is known in the trade as liquid stick.

It has been estimated that 75% of the total protein content of the rendering inputs is dissolved in tank water. Tank water before evaporation is therefore a major source of BOD, and it has been estimated that tank water will contain on the average 32,000 ppm BOD. The most polluting subprocess of edible rendering would be wet rendering without evaporation of tank water. This process is typical of older technology.

Wet Rendering Followed by Evaporation of Tank Water: Because of the relatively high protein and solids content of the tank water, it is usually economically desirable to concentrate the tank water. The concentrated material, which is the by-product of edible rendering, can be sold to pharmaceutical houses for use in some products. The high protein content of the evaporated tank water in any case would be a source of protein which could be used to upgrade tankage, but even though this tank water is evaporated, it is estimated that as much as 50% of the protein content will be lost to the sewer. Therefore, this subprocess is the second highest polluting method of rendering edible materials. This subprocess is a modification of the older technology, and it is doubtful if a new packing plant would install this type of edible rendering equipment.

Low Temperature Rendering: This name is applied to the edible rendering process which produces a mechanical breakdown of the fatty tissues. No water is added, and the maximum temperature is 118°F. Because no water is added to the fat-yielding tissues, there is a minimum of water pollution arising from this subprocess. This process represents the latest technology in edible rendering.

The unevaporated tank water, which is a by-product of the wet rendering system, is a main source of BOD. The installation of evaporating equipment should reduce the BOD of the wastewater by approximately 50%. Even when great care is taken to evaporate this tank water, it is estimated by those in the meat packing industry that some BOD will be lost to the sewer. Therefore, it was estimated that the substitution of the process of dry rendering for one of wet rendering without evaporation would result in a 60% reduction in BOD.

Inedible Rendering

There are four subprocesses or methods of rendering inedible material: dry rendering, wet rendering with no evaporation of tank water, continuous rendering, and wet rendering followed by evaporation of tank water.

Dry Rendering: See description of this subprocess under Edible Rendering.

Wet Rendering: See description of this subprocess under Edible Rendering.

Continuous Rendering: There are several processes for continuous rendering of inedible material. Almost all of the continuous rendering processes are considered dry rendering.

Wet Rendering Followed by Evaporation of Tank Water: See description of this subprocess under Edible Rendering.

MEAT PACKING WASTELOADS

In the Federal Water Pollution Control Association publication designated Industrial Waste Profile No. 8 (IWP-8), Meat Products (Sept. 30, 1967), it was decided to use organic load as the measure of wastewater strength. Organic load will be measured in terms of biochemical oxygen demand (BOD). To be more specific, the organic load was measured in five day, 20°C. BOD. The five day designation refers to the usual incubation period and the 20°C. to the temperature maintained during incubation. This particular form of the BOD test, as well as the BOD test itself, was chosen because it is the one most generally used.

The reliance upon one measure of wastewater strength (BOD) does not imply that this indicator is the only one or even the best one. In many instances total solids may be an equally important measure of meat packing wasteload. BOD was chosen because it is one of the most important, commonly used measures of wastewater strength. Additional studies of meat packing wastewater should include analysis at least of total solids and suspended solids. The BOD test is a time consuming, expensive and delicate test of wastewater strength. These characteristics of the test may be one explanation of the lack of information concerning the strength of industrial wastewater.

RELATIONSHIPS BETWEEN BOD, WASTEWATER VOLUME AND PLANT SIZE

There is no discernible pattern relating BOD per thousand pounds of liveweight killed to plant size. If one were to eliminate those plants whose wastewater averages above 3,000 gal./1,000 lbs. of liveweight, there seems to be a pattern in which the wastewater per unit of product increases with plant size. This relationship is to be expected in that larger plants will tend to have more processing which would increase their water and wastewater use per 1,000 lbs. of liveweight. The visually obvious direct relationship between wasteload and wastewater per unit of product is unexpected from a theoretical point of view. The formula by which the wasteload per unit of product is obtained is as follows.

$$\text{BOD in lbs./1,000 lbs. LWK*} = \frac{(\text{BOD in mg./l.})(8.34)(\text{wastewater in MGD})}{(\text{TLWK in 1,000 lbs./day})}$$

$$*\text{LWK} = \text{Liveweight killed.}$$

As wastewater per unit of product increases, one would simply expect the BOD concentration in mg./l. to be lowered but the BOD in lbs./1,000 lbs. to be unaffected. The empirical study of over 60 plants indicates that there is a direct relationship between BOD/1,000 lbs. liveweight and wastewater per 1,000 lbs. liveweight. As wastewater use per unit increases, so does the wasteload per unit.

This relationship is reasonable if the amount of wastewater per unit of product is some kind of index of the plant's wastewater consciousness. "Wastewater consciousness" would probably mean that greater attention is given to dry cleanup and to the recovery of all scraps and trimmings for by-product manufacture. On this basis then, the direct relationship between wastewater per unit and wasteload per unit seems reasonable.

WASTELOADS AND WASTEWATER VOLUMES BY TYPE OF TECHNOLOGY

The number of plants, the range, and average values of the waste characteristics by type of technology are shown in Table 7 as determined in the survey conducted by the Federal Water Pollution Control Administration and reported in Publication IWP-8.

Once the sample plants had been identified by technology level, the plants in each technology group were analyzed to determine the average pounds of BOD/1,000 lbs. liveweight killed. A simple average BOD per unit of product was obtained as well as a weighted average with total liveweight killed serving as the weight. In all cases the weighted average BOD was slightly larger than the simple average.

It should be noted that all wasteloads in Table 7 are post-catch basin wasteloads. These wasteloads must be increased by a factor of 1.33 in order to represent the gross wasteload/1,000 lbs. liveweight killed. Table 8 shows

TABLE 7: WASTELOAD AND WASTEWATER/1,000 LBS. LIVEWEIGHT KILLED BY TYPE OF TECHNOLOGY, 1966* (POST-CATCH BASIN WASTELOADS)

Type of Technology	No. of Plants	Size of Plant in Annual Liveweight Killed (mil. of lbs.)		Wasteload lbs. BOD/1000 lbs. Liveweight Killed			Wastewater gal./1000 lbs. Liveweight Killed		
		Range	Ave.	Range	Ave.	Wt. Ave.**	Range	Ave.	Wt. Ave.
Typical Technology	22	12-800	235	2.2-24.6	13.9	14.4	375-3668	1352	1294
Old Technology	14	8-500	164	8.6-36.4	19.4	20.2	937-2694	1960	2112
Advanced Technology	17	8-700	194	1.9-25.2	8.9	11.3	125-2507	923	1116

*Technology is defined by the subprocess mix as indicated in Table 6. There will be a higher proportion of single specie plants in the category Advanced Technology than in the other two categories.

**Weighted by annual liveweight killed.

NOTE: Since all questionnaire data BOD values were measures of effluent strength, the above BOD values must be adjusted to eliminate the pollution reducing effect of the catch basin. It will be assumed that catch basins, on the average, will reduce BOD by approximately 25 per cent. To adjust the above BOD values to a gross BOD value, increase each BOD value in the above table by thirty-three per cent.

TABLE 8: WASTELOAD AND WASTEWATER/1,000 LBS. LIVEWEIGHT KILLED BY TYPE OF TECHNOLOGY, 1966* (PRECATCH BASIN WASTELOADS)

Type of Technology	No. of Plants	Size of Plant in Annual Liveweight Killed (mil. of lbs.)		Wasteload lbs. BOD/1000 lbs. Liveweight Killed			Wastewater gal./1000 lbs. Liveweight Killed		
		Range	Ave.	Range	Ave.	Wt. Ave.**	Range	Ave.	Wt. Ave.
Typical Technology	22	12-800	235	2.9-32.8	18.5	19.2	375-3668	1352	1294
Old Technology	14	8-500	164	11.4-48.5	25.9	26.9	937-2694	1960	2112
Advanced Technology	17	8-700	194	2.5-33.6	11.9	15.1	125-2507	923	1116

*Technology is defined by the subprocess mix as indicated in Table 6. There will be a higher proportion of single specie plants in the category Advanced Technology than in the other two categories.

**Weighted by annual liveweight killed.

NOTE: Since all questionnaire data BOD values were measures of effluent strength, the above BOD values were adjusted to eliminate the pollution reducing effect of the catch basin. It was assumed that catch basins, on the average, reduced BOD by approximately 25 per cent. The above wasteloads were obtained by multiplying the wasteloads in Table 7 by 1.33.

Source: FWPCA Publication IWP-8

the precatch basin wasteloads per unit of product. The precatch basin wasteload per unit of product should be used to estimate all gross wasteloads. All estimates of gross wasteloads should be based upon the weighted average BOD and wastewater values per unit of product. An assumed distribution of slaughter by technology is also necessary to determine a gross wasteload.

Table 9 shows the effect of technology upon wasteload and wastewater volume per unit of product in an index form. Old technology is the base. Advancing technology has a slightly greater effect upon wastewater volume than upon BOD, according to Table 9.

TABLE 9:   WASTELOAD AND WASTEWATER INDEX BY TECHNOLOGY

	Waste Characteristics Per 1000 lbs. LWK		Index of Waste (Old = 100)	
	BOD in lbs.	Wastewater in gals.	BOD	Wastewater
Old Technology	20.2	2112	100	100
Typical Technology	14.4	1294	71	61
Advanced Technology	11.3	1116	56	53

Based on questionnaire data in which plants were classified as old, typical, or advanced on the basis of their subprocess mix. (See Tables 7 or 8)

Source: FWPCA Publication IWP-8

EFFECT OF PLANT SIZE AND TECHNOLOGY ON WASTEWATER USE

Table 10 shows wastewater volume per unit of product by level of technology and by plant size. As explained earlier, wastewater per unit of product declines as technology advances. According to Table 10 this relationship applies to small and to medium plants but not to large plants. The paucity of large plants classified as having advanced technology in the questionnaire sample probably accounts for the wastewater use per unit of product being higher at the advanced level of technology than at the typical level of technology. Small plants used the least amount of wastewater per unit of product, probably because small plants tend to do less processing than medium or large plants.

TABLE 10: WASTEWATER USE PER UNIT OF PRODUCT BY TYPE OF TECHNOLOGY AND PLANT SIZE, 1966 (GALS./1,000 LBS. LIVEWEIGHT KILLED)

Plant Size	Old Technology	Typical Technology	Advanced Technology	All Plants*
Small	1,529	760	356	1,320
Medium	1,756	1,340	855	1,486
Large	2,262	1,293	1,990	1,326
All Plants*	2,112	1,294	1,116	1,410

*Average weighted by total liveweight killed.

Source: FWPCA Publication IWP-8

Medium sized plants use the largest amount of wastewater per unit of product. Large plants, according to Table 9, use slightly less wastewater per unit than medium sized plants but more than small plants. It is probable that this relationship is due in part to the distribution of plants by technology and size in the sample.

Most of the sample firms had typical technology and most of these firms were medium or large in size. There was almost no difference in the wastewater use per unit of product between large and medium plants of typical technology. There is little reason to expect that there should be. Until the percentage of large plants with advanced technology increases, there is not sufficient evidence to predict the effect of size upon wastewater use in this category.

GROSS WASTELOAD AND WASTEWATER VOLUMES: 1963 TO 1977

Gross wasteloads and wastewater volumes have been estimated from meat production data for selected years between 1963 and 1977 by the Federal Water Pollution Control Administration as reported in Publication IWP-8. Production or slaughter projections by type of animal are shown in Table 11. For reasons described earlier, value added is not a satisfactory measure of production upon which to base pollution estimates. Slaughter projections were based upon assumed rates of population growth and per capita consumption of meat which in turn were based upon assumed elasticities of demand for meat and assumed changes in per capita income and meat prices.

The weighted average post-catch basin wasteloads shown in Table 7 were used in making the projections of gross wasteloads shown in Table 12.

TABLE 11: TOTAL COMMERCIAL SLAUGHTER IN THE U.S. (BILLIONS OF POUNDS)

Year	Total	Cattle	Hogs	Sheep	Calves
1950	37	18	16	11	2
1955	45	24	18	1	2
1960	46	25	18	1	2
1965	52	32	17	1	2
1970	61	36	22	1	2
1975 est.	68	42	23	1	2

TABLE 12: PRODUCTION, GROSS WASTELOADS AND WASTEWATER VOLUMES WITH PROJECTIONS TO 1977 (POST-CATCH BASIN WASTELOADS)

Year	Total Comm. Slaughter Bil. of Pounds Per Year	Wasteload per unit[a] lbs BOD/ 1000 lbs LWK	Wastewater per unit[a] gals/1000 lbs LWK	Total Wasteload Per Year Mil. lbs BOD	Total Wastewater Per Year MGY
1963[b]	50.8	15.99	1531	812	77,806
1966[c]	54.9	14.05	1322	771	72,578
1967[c]	57.0	14.05	1322	801	75,354
1968[c]	60.2	14.05	1322	846	79,584
1969[c]	61.4	14.05	1322	863	81,171
1970[c]	62.8	14.05	1322	882	83,022
1971[c]	63.9	14.05	1322	898	84,476
1972[c]	65.2	14.05	1322	916	86,194
1977[d]	71.6	12.85	1205	920	86,278

a. Wasteload or wastewater per unit is the weighted average BOD per thousand pounds liveweight killed shown in Table 7 by type of technology, which has been averaged according to the assumed distribution of technology levels.

b. 1963 Assumes 65 per cent of the industry has Typical Technology. 30 per cent of the industry has Old Technology. 5 per cent of the industry has Advanced Technology.

c. 1966-1972 Assumes 60 per cent of the industry has Typical Technology. 30 per cent of the industry has Advanced Technology. 10 per cent of the industry has Old Technology.

d. 1977 Assumes 50 per cent of the industry has Typical Technology. 50 per cent of the industry has Advanced Technology. 0 per cent of the industry has Old Technology.

Source: FWPCA Publication IWP-8

The weighted average precatch basin wasteloads shown in Table 8 were used in making the projections of gross wasteloads shown in Table 13.

TABLE 13: PRODUCTION, GROSS WASTELOADS AND WASTEWATER VOLUMES WITH PROJECTIONS TO 1977 (PRECATCH BASIN WASTELOADS)

Year	Total Comm. Slaughter Bil. of Pounds Per Year	Wasteload per unit[a] lbs BOD/ 1000 lbs LWK	Wastewater per unit[a] gals/1000 lbs LWK	Total Wasteload Per Year Mil. lbs BOD	Total Wastewater Per Year MGY
1963[b]	50.8	21.32	1531	1083	77,806
1966[c]	54.9	18.73	1322	1028	72,578
1967[c]	57.0	18.73	1322	1068	75,354
1968[c]	60.2	18.73	1322	1128	79,584
1969[c]	61.4	18.73	1322	1151	81,171
1970[c]	62.8	18.73	1322	1176	83,022
1971[c]	63.9	18.73	1322	1197	84,476
1972[c]	65.2	18.73	1322	1221	86,194
1977[d]	71.6	17.13	1205	1227	86,278

a. Wasteload or wastewater per unit is the weighted average BOD per thousand pounds liveweight killed shown in Table 8 by type of technology which has been averaged, according to the assumed distribution of technology levels.

b. 1963   Assumes 65 per cent of the industry has Typical Technology. 30 per cent of the industry has Old Technology. 5 per cent of the industry has Advanced Technology.

c. 1966-1972
Assumes 60 per cent of the industry has Typical Technology. 30 per cent of the industry has Advanced Technology. 10 per cent of the industry has Old Technology.

d. 1977   Assumes 50 per cent of the industry has Typical Technology. 50 per cent of the industry has Advanced Technology. 0 per cent of the industry has Old Technology.

Source: FWPCA Publication IWP-8

UNIT WASTE LOADINGS

A detailed discussion of wasteloads from the meat packing industry has been presented by Bell, Galyardt and Wells, Architects and Engineers of Rapid City and Omaha in a seminar on pollution control for the meat packing industry held at Kansas City, Missouri on March 7 and 8, 1973. The following paragraphs are drawn from the manual published for that seminar.

A definite analysis of the waste characteristics of the meat packing industry
is not a simple matter. It is difficult to characterize a typical plant and
its associated wastes, due to the many procedures and facets of meat processing operations. A single plant may perform just a few or many of these
procedures. However, for all practical purposes, the industry may be divided into three categories.

   (1)   Slaughterhouses (killing and dressing)
   (2)   Packinghouses (killing, dressing, curing, cooking, etc.)
   (3)   Processing plants (processing with no killing operation)

Typical slaughterhouse and packinghouse wastes are generally high in biochemical oxygen demand (BOD_5), total suspended solids, floatable material, and grease. Furthermore, the waste is generally at an elevated temperature and contains blood, bits of flesh, fat, manure, dirt and viscera.

Important processes such as blood recovery, grease recovery, separate
paunch manure handling, and efficient rendering operations can substantially reduce wasteloads and may also produce salable by-products. Furthermore, a well managed program of in-plant housekeeping practices is desirable both from a sanitary and wasteload standpoint. Wasteloads which have
been found through extensive study to be typical of various types of meat
processing plants are given in Table 14.

TABLE 14:   STANDARD RAW WASTELOADS

Type	Flow (gal)	BOD_5 (lb)	SS (lb)	Grease (lb)
Slaughterhouse Per 1000 lb LWK	696	5.8	4.7	2.5
Packinghouse Per 1000 lb LWK	1046	12.1	8.7	6.0
Processing Plant Per 1000 lb Product	1265	5.7	2.7	2.1

Source: Industrial Waste Study by North Star Research and Development
          Institute for Environmental Protection Agency

The values listed for slaughterhouses apply only to medium sized plants which
slaughter from 95,000 to 750,000 lbs./day and do very little or no processing of edible by-products, perform dry inedible rendering and do no
blood processing or dry blood in such a manner as to produce no blood water.
The values listed for packinghouses apply to most medium or large plants

which carry out all processes associated with slaughtering, cutting, rendering, and processing. Values for processing plants represent plants which
cut and process meat, but do no slaughtering or rendering.

These values are in general agreement with other values found in the literature although the variations may have a wide range. Table 15 shows the
characteristics of the wastes from numerous cattle and hog packing plants,
illustrating a typically wide variation from plant to plant. In general, the
processes which are undertaken at a packing plant have a far greater effect on the waste load factors than the size of the plant.

TABLE 15: UNIT WASTELOADINGS FOR MEAT PACKING PLANTS (LBS./1,000 LBS. OF LIVEWEIGHT)

Type of Animal Slaughtered	BOD	Suspended Solids	Nitrogen	Grease
Hogs	18.0	12.0	2.67	0.90
Hogs	15.0	9.1	1.29	2.30
Mixed	12.7	4.6	2.02	1.44
Hogs	13.1	9.8	1.25	2.83
Cattle	20.8	14.8	2.24	.68
Hogs	15.7	14.8	2.01	1.79
Hogs	10.5	10.0	1.02	1.00
Mixed	19.7	9.4	2.59	.60
Hogs	9.8	7.2	1.46	.27
Mixed	16.7	15.0	2.18	2.00
Cattle	10.0	11.0	1.08	.55
Mixed	14.7	13.2	1.70	1.5
Mixed	6.5	6.2	.79	.5
Mixed	19.2	11.2	2.10	2.1
Mixed	8.9	10.8	.89	---
Mixed	21.6	21.7	1.82	6.0
Average	14.6	12.0	1.70	1.63

Source: EPA Technology Transfer Report by Bell, Galyardt and Wells of
Rapid City and Omaha (March 1973).

A limited number of studies have attempted to analyze the component parts
of the process. The fact that such wide variations in raw waste loads do
exist make data obtained from actual sampling of wastes similar to those
anticipated extremely useful and often economically beneficial in designing waste treatment facilities.

Table 16 presents a typical source breakdown of hog packinghouse wastes.
Packing plant wastes are of an organic nature and treatment may be accomplished by many different systems of biological treatment.

TABLE 16: ANALYSES OF MAJOR COMPONENTS OF WASTE FROM
HOG PACKINGHOUSES

| Source of Flow | Concentration in mg/l | | | | | | |
| | Solids | | Nitrogen | | | | |
	Total	Sus-pended	Organic	NH_3	Cl as Na Cl	BOD	pH
Killing Department	1,840	220	134	6	435	825	6.6
Blood and Tank Water	44,640	3,690	5,400	205	6,670	32,000	9.0
Scalding Tub	13,560	8,360	1,290	40	640	4,600	9.0
Hog Dehairing	1,540	560	158	10	290	650	6.7
Hair Cook Water	4,680	80	586	30	290	3,400	---
Hair Wash Water	7,680	6,780	822	18	230	2,200	6.9
Meat Cutting	2,840	610	33	2.5	1,620	520	7.4
Gut Washer	22,600	15,120	643	43	360	13,200	6.0
Curing Room	26,480	1,800	83	12	19,700	2,040	7.3
Curing Room Showers	34,100	1,720	255	25	29,600	460	6.7
Cured Meat Wash	9,560	920	109	17.5	6,200	1,960	7.3
Pickle	140,000	------	2,750	37	77,800	18,000	5.6
Sausage & Miscellaneous	11,380	560	136	4	880	800	7.3
Lard Department	820	180	84	25	230	180	7.3
By-Products	4,000	1,380	186	50	1,330	2,200	6.7
Laundry	18,620	4,120	56	5	-----	1,300	9.6

Source: An Industrial Waste Guide to the Meat Industry, U.S. Department
of Health, Education and Welfare.

REDUCTION OF GROSS WASTELOADS

Gross pollution loads can be reduced in three ways: (1) change of subprocess; (2) use of industry owned waste treatment facilities; and (3) use of
municipal waste treatment facilities. Any of these three methods can be
used singly or in combination with one or both of the other methods. Each
of these methods will be discussed in turn.

IN-PLANT MEAT PACKING WASTE TREATMENT

The importance of in-plant modification to reduce pollution needs no emphasis here. It is a simple economic fact that conservation and in-plant waste saving, along with water recycle and reuse must be considered before any plant undertakes to build pretreatment facilities for discharge to a public sewer, pays a municipal charge for wastewater treatment or builds a complete treatment plant for discharge to a watercourse.

Table 17 shows the percentage reduction in BOD which could be expected with the specified change in subprocess.

TABLE 17:   CHANGES IN SUBPROCESSES AND THEIR EFFECT UPON
WASTELOAD AND WASTEWATER VOLUME*

Subprocess Change	Percent Wasteload Reduction with Indicated Change
Killing and Bleeding	
Change subprocess from recovery of no blood to recovery of all blood.	42
Washing of Carcass	
Change from a system of continuous water flow to one of "interruptable" water flow.	See Text
Paunch Removal	
Change subprocess of dumping all paunch material into sewer to wet dumping of paunch material with offsite disposal.	See Text
Change subprocess of wet dumping of paunch material with offsite disposal to dry dumping of paunch material with offsite disposal.	5
Change subprocess of dumping all paunch material into the sewer to dry dumping of paunch material with offsite disposal.	10

(continued)

TABLE 17:   (continued)

Subprocess Change	Percent Wasteload Reduction with Indicated Change
Edible Rendering	
Change subprocess of wet rendering with no evaporation of tank water to one in which tank water is evaporated.	50
Change subprocess of wet rendering with no evaporation of tank water to subprocess of dry rendering	60
Change from a system of wet rendering with no evaporation of tank water to subprocess of low temperature rendering.	60
Inedible Rendering	
Change subprocess of wet rendering with no evaporation of tank water to one in which tank water is evaporated.	50
Change subprocess of wet rendering with no evaporation of tank water to continuous rendering.	60
Change subprocess from wet rendering with no evaporation of tank water to continuous rendering.	60
Cleanup	
Change subprocess of primarily wet cleanup to one of dry cleanup followed by wet cleanup.	10

*Only those subprocess changes which will alter wasteload are considered.

Source: FWPCA Publ. IWP-8

A manual has been issued by the Environmental Protection Agency entitled In-Plant Modification to Reduce Pollution and Pretreatment of Meat Packing Wastewaters for Discharge to Municipal Systems. This was prepared as part of EPS's Technology Transfer Program and was presented at a Design Seminar for Upgrading Meat Packing Facilities to Reduce Pollution held at Kansas City, Missouri on March 7-8, 1973 by A.J. Steffen, Consulting Environmental Engineer from West Lafayette, Indiana.

Wherever possible, that manual deals with waste conservation in existing plants. However, many of the methods discussed are applicable largely to new plants and can not readily be retrofitted into existing plants because of space limitations and layout. Thus each manager and engineer can make use of that manual as a guide and check list, evaluating each waste conservation concept as it applies to his particular plant.

Section II of the above-cited manual was prepared by A.J. Steffen in conjunction with W.H. Miedaner, Chief Environmental Engineer of Globe Engineering Co. of Chicago, consultants serving the food industry. The following paragraphs are drawn from that section of the manual.

PRACTICES IN WASTE CONSERVATION

Except for very small slaughtering plants, most plants recover blood, screen-able solids and grease by various in-plant systems and devices. Many small packers without blood drying facilities or inedible rendering departments recover such materials for local tank truck pickup operated by specialized by-products plants in the area.

The quantity of water used varies widely, based on waste conservation prac-tices, blood and solids handling methods and the amount of processing done in the plant. It may range from about 0.5 to 2.0 gallons per pound of live weight killed.

The degree of wastewater conservation, recycle and reuse, and solids and blood recovery in each individual plant depends upon many factors: the age of the plant; the views of management on the subject; whether markets or final disposal facilities for recovered blood, solids and grease are readily available; market prices of the recoverable materials; the local regula-tions regarding effluent quality and surcharge costs for plants discharging to public sewers; and the first cost, and operating costs of independent treatment if the packer discharges to a watercourse.

The low market price for recovered inedible grease in some localities has forced many packers to dispose of it as feed-grade grease. If the meat packing plant is conveniently located near a soap plant, the possiblities of an improved price will provide special incentives for grease recovery.

Variations in economics in disposing of the solids and concentrates such as paunch manure, blood, hair, casing slimes and concentrated stick (in wet rendering) inevitably affect the diligence with which these pollutional solids are kept out of the sewer.

However, the limitations and surcharge regulations for wastes discharged to city sewers, or the cost of complete treatment if the plant discharges to a watercourse must be carefully evaluated to establish the level of waste conservation appropriate to the packing plant. For example, a plant dis-charging to its own anaerobic-aerobic pond system may find that some floatable inert solids such as stock-pen bedding can improve the insulating scum blanket on the anaerobic lagoon. Then, neglect in recovery of such materials would not be important. On the other hand, a packing plant in Springfield, Mo., faced with a municipal waste treatment charge of $1,400 a month, modified its production processes (including solids recovery), so that the monthly payment dropped to $225.

SEGREGATION OF WASTE STREAMS

In meat packing, it has been common practice to provide separate sewer systems for grease wastes; nongrease (variously termed "manure" sewer or "red" sewer); clear waters from chilling, condensing and cooling operations; surface and roof water (surface drainage); stock-pen wastes and sanitary wastes. However, for new plants, further segregation is often desirable in order to permit removal of pollutional ingredients before the wastewaters mingle with other plant waters. Screening equipment can be smaller and can be designed for the special solids present. In some cases, such segregated waters may be sufficiently dilute to use for recycling.

In the interests of dry or semidry manure separation, a separate manure sewer should be provided in new plants for all sources of manure. This waste can be pretreated by screening, followed by dissolved air flotation. The floated solids can be analyzed for fats and wet rendered if warranted.

The grease sewer should receive only those wastes that contain grease. If the color of the rendered tallow is a factor, special diligence must be exercized that all manure-bearing wastes be kept out of the sewer. The settled solids should be discharged over a screen, dried and utilized in feeds, if possible. They contain an appreciable amount of grease. Basically, the grease sewer should receive wastes from boning, cutting, edible and inedible rendering, casing washing (after manure and slime have been removed), canning, sausage manufacturing, slicing, prepackaging, smoking and smoked meats hanging, cooking, tank car loading and washing, carcass coolers, lard and grease storage areas, equipment washrooms, pickling areas and the like.

The conventional nongrease sewer receives wastes from hog scalding, dehairing, tripe washing, chitterling washing, and kill drains up to and including the polisher. It also receives the flow from manure recovery systems when a separate manure screen is not provided. Hide processing waters are commonly recirculated either with or without screening for solids reduction. If these waters must be dumped, they should be screened separately and then discharged to the nongrease sewer.

Vapors from cooking and rendering operations can be cooled and condensed through heat exchangers and recycled to dryers, or sent to the grease sewer. All clear water (jacket cooling water, air conditioner water, steam condensate and chill water) should be carefully separated for reuse.

Curing pickle (undiluted) has a very high BOD and should be reused whenever possible. Run-off pickle from processing should be caught in recycling pan systems as part of the injection equipment. In a recent study,

it was found that only 25% of the pickle produced was retained in the product, the rest was lost by general leakage and spilled from the injection
machines. The BOD of pickle varies but the dextrose alone has a BOD of
about 660,000 mg./liter. Sanitary wastes are, of course, discharged directly to the city sewer or to a separate treatment system, and should not
enter any pretreatment elements.

PLANT WASTE CONSERVATION SURVEY

The first step in waste conservation is a well-organized and well-executed
waste conservation survey, backed by management. First the engineer
should collect data on the volume, nature and general facilities of the
business. If he is a company employee, he already has this information.
In addition, he should know all plans for future construction. He should
attempt to develop a 10 year forecast of business. If the wastewaters discharge to a city sewer, he should know something about populations trends
in the area and the possibilities of industrial growth and whether such
growth will add load to the municipal plant. Whether the wastewaters discharge to a public sewer system or to the packer's private treatment plant,
he should be familiar with the system and the sewage treatment plant and
the requirements for the receiving stream.

The approach to wastewater control need not be complicated or expensive.
The principal effort applied should be in the direction of preventing product (and contaminants) from entering the waste stream and to reduce water
use to a minimum. High waste load areas should be probed first. Accurate
sampling, chemical analysis and flow measurements need not be performed
initially, but can be deferred until after the gross problems have been
solved.

Since most suspended solids in meat wastewaters are organic, their removal
results in a reduction of BOD. Suspended solids concentrations (after
screening) are a rough measure of BOD and can be easily and quickly
measured. Dissolved solids can be measured with a conductivity meter.
Red color indicates the presence of blood, a very large contributor of BOD.
A simple jar test will give some information. During the initial phase of
in-plant waste control, approximate figures are sufficient. Flows must be
measured at the time of sampling. Flows can be estimated or simply catch
the flow in a pail or 50 gallon drum for a period of time. The gallons per
minute can be calculated. In some instances, it may be necessary to break
into a sewer line or disconnect a pipe to obtain a sample or flow measurement.

Solids per unit volume, with associated water consumption will give a measure of the pounds of organic wastes generated. Problem areas can then be studied for methods of control. In many cases, a small outlay of money will effect substantial waste control. Records should be kept to follow progress. The following waste load ranges are listed to provide a rough guide line. They cover a broad range because they include small and large operations; some small plants with no inedible rendering and no blood recovery, and others with a broad line of meat processing, with inedible rendering and blood recovery.

Typical Plant Waste Generated per
1,000 lbs. LWK (Live Weight Kill, All Species)

BOD	4 to 18 lbs./1,000 lbs. LWK
Suspended Solids	3 to 17 lbs./1,000 lbs. LWK
Grease	1.5 to 12 lbs./1,000 lbs. LWK
Flow	600 to 2,000 gal. of water per 1,000 lbs. LWK

The following equation can be used to convert laboratory analyses and flow to pounds per 1,000 pounds LWK.

$$\text{lbs. of pollutant/1,000 lbs. LWK} = \frac{\text{Flow in gallons} \times 8.34 \times \text{mg./l.}}{1,000 \text{ lbs. LWK} \times 1,000,000}$$

where mg./l. = milligrams per liter (from laboratory data)

Values for typical flow, BOD, suspended solids and grease from various processing operations vary widely from plant to plant; thus it will be most useful to cite methods of correction without attaching specific values to each process or process change. The order of priorities for in-plant waste conservation will vary depending upon the results of the waste conservation survey in each individual plant.

RECOVERY OF SOLIDS AND BY-PRODUCTS

Blood: This has the highest BOD of any liquid material emanating from meat processing. It has an ultimate BOD (approximately 20 day) of 405,000 mg./liter. Customary analytical methods of 5 day BOD are not sufficiently accurate in these high ranges, but are estimated to average from 150,000 to 200,000 mg./liter. Considering that one head of cattle contains approximately 49 lbs. of blood, the 5 day BOD of blood from a single animal is about 10 lbs., as against about 0.2 lbs. 5 day BOD discharged per person per day.

Thus, if the blood from a single animal killed in a day is discharged to the sewer, its pollutional load would be equivalent to that of 50 people.

Clotted blood (about 70% of the total) has a BOD (ultimate) of about 470,000 mg./liter while the liquid portion is about 200,000 mg./liter. Comparing these figures with the ultimate BOD of domestic sewage of about 300 mg./liter, it is evident that blood conservation pays. The curbed bleeding area that discharges to the blood tank should be as long as possible and the blood should be squeegeed to the blood tank before the valves are switched to drain to the sewer for the cleanup operation.

The floor and walls should then be cleaned with a minimum of water by use of small diameter hoses. If the water used in the first rinse is held down to 30 to 50 gallons, it can be discharged to the blood tank as an added con-servation measure. The additional cost of evaporating this quantity of water will, in most cases, be far less than the cost of treating it as waste-water.

Water is sometimes mixed with blood to facilitate transportation in pipes. The evaporation of this added water in the dryer is an added expense and can often be eliminated if the drain from the bleeding area to the blood tank is large enough and the blood tank is located to permit a straight drop into it. If the blood is pumped to the tank, the piping layout should be checked. If sewer alignment cannot be improved to prevent drains from clogging, decoagulating electrodes can be installed to prevent coagulation. Troughs to catch and convey blood should be pitched and curved to facili-tate squeegeeing before washing.

Blood processing methods are important in waste conservation. For lowest losses to the sewer, continuous dryers are most common, using a jacketed vessel with rotating blades to prevent burn-on. Continuous ring dryers are also popular. They produce a relatively small amount of bloodwater that, in small plants, is usually discharged to the sewers. This bloodwater can be further clarified by discharging it through a small settling tank. This is a waste conservation problem that warrants further study.

The older steam coagulation systems are more serious problems in waste conservation, since a substantial amount of fines can be lost when the co-agulated blood is screened. A combination of paunch manure solids and bloodwater can be cooked to produce a hydrolyzed hair stick but the process economics should be explored before a packer embarks on such a project. Casing slimes can be added to the blood dryer if desired or can be dried with other products in conventional inedible dry rendering.

Paunch Manure: This is either wet or dry dumped for recovery of tripe. Wet dumping consists of cutting the paunch open in a water flow, dis-charging to a mechanical screen and then to the manure sewer. This wash-ing action carries a large fraction of the BOD from the paunch waste solids into the water phase. Paunch solids are about 75% water, weigh about 50 to 60 lbs. per animal and have a "dry dump" first-stage BOD of over 100,000 mg./liter (5 day BOD, slightly less). 80% of this BOD is soluble.

Dry dumping consists of dry discharge of the manure solids down a chute to an inedible area for ultimate disposal as a waste solid or blending to produce a marketable solid. After dry dumping, fines are removed by washing and are discharged into the manure sewer. Stomach and peck contents may contain undigested grains which contain proteins and fats. An investigation may disclose that these materials can be routed directly to a dryer, unopened, if the resulting product is acceptable as an ingredient in the end product.

Casing-Saving Operations: These contribute substantially to pollution. Waste from the deslimer should be passed directly to cookers in inedible rendering or dried with the blood. A small catch basin in the immediate casing area will recover sizable amounts of good quality fats. Water should be kept at a minimum. Sprays should be checked for efficiency in volume of water used, proper design, proper direction and maximum spacing.

Stockpen Wastes: They are high in nutrients and should be segregated in a manner to allow alternate methods of disposal. Pens should be dry cleaned and the waste should be hauled away for land disposal. Usually runways and pens are hosed down periodically. Consideration should be given to segregation of this strong liquid waste for disposal by trucking or piping for disposal directly on farm land, within the limits of regulations regarding land disposal.

Scraps and Bone Dust: Plant operations in cutting and trimming should be carefully examined for opportunities to intercept waste solids before they enter the sewer. Scraps and liquids from the hog-neck washer should be caught in a container directly beneath the washer. Some form of grease trap can suffice. Collected contents should be routed direct to rendering. Bone dust from sawing operations is an important source of pollution and contains a high concentration of phosphorus. Bone dust is of fine texture and when diluted with water is difficult to recover. It should be recovered intact by catching directly in containers or sweeping up and hauling to the inedible rendering department.

Hide Curing: These operations are becoming increasingly involved as segments of tanning operations are transferred from tanneries to beef slaughtering plants. During winter months, a single hide can contain 60 pounds of attached lumps of manure, mud and ice. In addition, salt, caustic acids and fleshing waste enter the sewage stream. The washwater should be recycled, or retained for separate treatment (usually screening) if considerable volumes are involved.

Disposal of Tankwater: If lard is wet rendered or if any inedible wet rendering is in service at the plant, the disposal of tankwater may be a problem (BOD about 22,000 mg./liter). In processing lard by low or medium temperature continuous rendering, one process uses about 150 lbs. of water (as steam) per 230 lbs. wet rendered product.

However, there is a market in some areas for 50 to 60% edible stickwater produced by evaporating this tankwater. In another process, less water is used and it goes out with the cracklings. In contrast, inedible tank-water is evaporated and is commonly blended with animal feed as inedible stickwater. Under no circumstances can this high BOD waste be discharged to the sewer. In some cases the tankwater can be trucked to a central processing plant for evaporation. It can also be dried with inedible solids.

WATER CONSERVATION

In processing and in quality control, the meat industry finds water an es-sential tool to help cleanse the product and to convey and remove unwanted materials. But in wastewater handling, water becomes a problem — a di-luter that flushes and dissolves organic matter and carries it to the sewer. Wastewater treatment is basically nothing more than a processing system to again separate the organic and inorganic matter from the water that picked it up. The goal of every wastewater engineer is to remove organic solids "dry" without discharging to the sewer, and then use an absolute minimum of water for the essentials of sanitation. The closer one comes to this goal, the simpler becomes the wastewater problem. This goal provides the pattern in waste conservation in the plant, and can be briefly summarized in the following axioms:

(1) Use water wisely — only enough to get the job done.
(2) Keep waste solids in bulk whenever possible, for disposal
       as a solid or as a concentrated sludge, without dis-
       charging to the sewer.
(3) Clean with high pressure and minimum water volume
       (small hoses). Use the right detergents in the right
       proportions to clean well with minimum rinsing.
(4) Recycle water as much as possible, within the limits
       of USDA regulations. Some reconditioning, such as
       cooling or screening, may be necessary for recycling
       in some instances.
(5) Use the minimum pressure and volume for washing prod-
       uct, consistent with quality control. High pressure

in washing product may drive soil into the product and
also wash away valuable edible protein and fat.
(6) Control volume, temperature and pressure automatically.
Dependence upon manual regulation can lead to waste.
(7) Use valves that shut off automatically when the water is
not needed. For example, photo-electric cells are
used in Japan to turn water on when product is in a
washing position.
(8) Study each process independently. General rules alone
will not do the job.

Water conservation is thus an essential part of an in-plant wastewater control program. It has been shown that packing plants using the most water
per animal generate the most waste per animal. Excessive washing, especially with hot water, removes juices and tissues from product and flushes
them into the sewers. Water usage can be reduced at many locations.

The viscera pan sterilizer and the final carcass washer are large water users.
These washing operations should be modified so that when the carcass chain
stops, the water automatically shuts off. This can be done with solenoid-
operated valves under control of the conveyor-chain motor starter. The
viscera pan sterilizer uses large amounts of 180°C. water. This often runs
continuously during the work day (and during the clean-up period). Thought
should be given to engaging the services of those skilled in spraying techniques — not only to design the sterilizer for economy in water use, but
also to design cleaned-in-place (CIP) cleaning systems for the viscera pans.
The sprays on the final carcass washer should be checked for proper spacing,
direction, shape of spray, pressure and water consumption.

Old-fashioned cleanup operations usually use excessive amounts of water,
hot and cold. Many cleanup hoses discharge 10 to 20 gpm of high velocity
140° to 180°C. hot water. Some operators believe that a flood of hot water
for cleaning floors and equipment is necessary. Indiscriminate use of hot
water is not only undesirable from a wastewater control standpoint, but
erodes floors, walls, removes lubrication from equipment, and can cause
electrical failures.

It is altogether too common for cleanup men to remove floor drain grates
and flush meat scraps down the drain, believing that a screen or catch basin
will trap all solids. By the time the scraps are recovered, they have been
broken up in the flow and much of the organic matter has been dissolved or
suspended in the wastewater to the extent that it cannot be removed without
complete treatment — by the packer or by the city. What started as a re-
movable scrap has then become a part of a wasterwater treatment load.

Floors and equipment should be dry cleaned before hosing and scraps taken to the inedible rendering. This first step in cleanup requires rigid surveillance. Smaller nozzles on smaller hoses and application of modern cleaning methods will reduce water. For example, a kink-type valve, that is inserted in the hose and opens only when the hose is bent, will automatically stop the water when the operator drops the hose. Water should be automatically controlled to maintain the lowest temperature, lowest volume and highest pressure consistent with each cleaning job. Effective detergents to emulsify fats and lift proteins and soil will reduce the quantity of rinse water required. Well-qualified cleaning consultants are available for guidance. The use of automated cleaned-in-place (CIP) systems will reduce and control water use.

SELECTION AND MODIFICATION OF PROCESS EQUIPMENT

Chitterling washers can be improved by fitting them with limiting orifices and spray nozzles rather than drilled pipes. Water consumption can be reduced from 130 to 70 gpm by proper design of sprays and control of water and pressure on these units.

Hog-casing cleaning machines can be modified to recover the slime from the stripper, which amounts to 0.2 lbs. of dry solids per hog.

Scalding tub — A means of slow drainage of the scalding tub and separate removal of the sludge will reduce the waste concentration materially. It is reported that 100 hogs, at maximum slaughter rate, produce 11.2 lbs. of BOD and 23.5 lbs. of suspended solids. It may be expected that as much as 30% of the BOD and 80% of the suspended solids will settle in the tub. The scalding tub can be fitted with a perforated riser pipe in the drain, extending about 6 inches above the floor of the tub. The residual sludge can then be squeegeed through a 12" x 12" square sluice gate at tank floor level and discharged to a truck for disposal as waste solids.

Low or medium temperature continuous edible rendering can be accomplished with a limited amount of water discharged to the sewers. This factor should enter the cost analysis when a new system is purchased.

Hasher-washer screen — It is not uncommon to eliminate the hasher-washer screen. The entire product can be dry rendered if the quality of the rendered product is not a sensitive consideration. The added bulk in dry rendering is small when balanced against increased yield and the elimination of the hasher-washer screen drainage.

Automated (CIP) Cleaning — For daily cleaning, consideration should be given to automated cleaning of viscera pans, tank trucks, continuous rendering systems, conveyor tables, piping, cookers and dryers. Systems that will conserve water and labor are available from detergent manufacturers.

Heart washers — A considerable amount of raw water is used to chill hearts in modern heart washers. A study of this operation may prove that the use of refrigerated chill water will conserve water and result in a better shelf life product.

Offal areas — In the offal areas, continuous streams of water are sometimes used to aid in moving product down chutes. Special sprays or redesign of chutes will reduce water usage at these points. Any sprays made up of a pipe with drilled orifices are usually inefficient and should be replaced with engineered sprays, designed for minimum water consumption, proper pressure and maximum effective coverage. Master shut-off valves can be used to shut groups of sprays during rest periods. Ball type valves are effective for this service.

Knife and sterilizing boxes are often operated with excessive amounts of water and temperature. The use of electric temperature-controlled knife boxes should be considered — particularly in coolers where steam causes condensation problems and refrigeration losses.

Sanitary facilities for personnel — Press-to-open valves (foot or knee-operated) should be used on all lavatories. Drinking fountains should not run continuously. Refrigerated water fountains will conserve water.

Animal drinking water should be minimal but consistent with satisfactory yields. In the past, it was believed that abundant drinking water was necessary for good yields; consequently, drinking troughs flowed continuously. Recent information indicates that animals can go one or two days without water and show negligible yield reduction. Time clock control of the master valve for drinking water supply, programmed for one minute on and four minutes off will reduce water use by 80%.

Once-through raw water in refrigeration condensers and compressor cooling jacket water is expensive. Such water should be either reused in plant processes or recycled through a heat exchanging device — cooling towers or evaporative condensers. Evaporative condensers are usually the most feasible.

If possible, blowdown water should be returned to the soil because of its high mineral content. Generally, regulated quantities can be discharged to the city sewer directly without violating limiting regulations. Boiler

blowdown water is soft water and can be reused in cleanup operations
or in fabric wash machines. This requires some experimentation to develop
a proper blend of plant water supply with the blowdown water, particularly
relating to temperature.

Manual washing of meat and offal products can be improved. Washing
operations requiring "under-the-spray" time of less than 50%, should have
press-to-open sprays. On-site observations have disclosed many hand-
washing operations (particularly offal) with time under the spray of not
more than 10%. Sprays should not flow unattended at work tables. In
addition to press-to-open spray valves, efficient redesign of spray heads
will improve product cleaning and conserve water. Pressures and volume
of flow should be controlled with pipe restrictions or locked valves to establish a minimum consistent with quality results. Photoelectric cells could
serve well as automatic control.

In dry rendering systems, many plants mix raw cold water with cooking
vapors from rendering dryers to condense vapors and reduce odors. The
mixture of vapors and water is discharged to the sewer. A recent study
of a typical operation disclosed that each dryer used 120 to 130 gpm of
water and the mixture contained 118 mg./liter of BOD and 27 mg./liter
of grease. The BOD and grease were likely due to carryover from overloaded dryers. The water consumption represented 40% of the entire plant
water. A heat exchanger was recommended for direct water condensing
to eliminate the cooling water loss. Heat extracted from the vapors can
be removed by means of a cooling tower or returned to the plant hot water
system. Commonly, cooking operations closely follow killing operations;
thus, the recovered heat can be reused.

In some instances a portion of dissolved air flotation cell effluent is routed
to the inedible cooker vapor condensers. Condensed cooking vapors from
dry rendering operations should be routed to the fat-bearing stream if they
contain a significant amount of recoverable solids.

PRETREATMENT OF MEAT PACKING WASTEWATERS
FOR DISCHARGE TO MUNICIPAL SYSTEMS

The importance of the pretreatment of meat packing wastewaters for discharge to municipal systems becomes evident when we note that a 1967
survey by the Federal Water Pollution Control Administration showed that
70% of the wastewater from the meat packing industry was discharged to
municipal facilities. It seems likely that this percentage may now be
slightly lower with the continuing trend towards decentralization into
small plants discharging into independent lagoon systems in semirural areas.

ADVANTAGES OF PRETREATMENT

Although compliance with municipal regulations regarding the quality of
a meat packer's wastewater for discharge to the city's sewer will usually
determine the degree of pretreatment, there are some factors that may encourage pretreatment beyond the levels required by ordinance:

(a) A higher quality of pretreatment may be economically
    justified if the city's charges and subcharges are at
    a level where some additional pretreatment becomes
    economically advantageous.
(b) The meat packer may prefer to assume treatment respon-
    sibilities to avoid complaints from the municipality.
(c) There may be indications that the future will bring in-
    creases in the city's rate structure.
(d) Grease and solids may have a good market in the area.
    Proximity of a soap plant or similar grease market
    may produce economic advantages for grease recovery
    or may warrant some expense in improving quality of

41

the finished inedible grease or tallow. Such improvements
will also improve the wastewater effluent.

DISADVANTAGES OF PRETREATMENT

The pretreatment will be placed on the property tax rolls unless state regulations permit tax-free waste treatment for industry. The maintenance,
operation and record-keeping may be expensive or burdensome. The bur-
den of good operation increases as the treatment becomes more complex and
extensive.

EVALUATING NEEDS

After the plant has been completely surveyed and all possible waste conservation and water reuse systems have been cataloged, the necessary pretreatment system must be designed and the cost estimated. Those parts of
the treatment attributable to flow (such as grease basins and dissolved air
flotation) should be totaled and reduced to a cost per 1,000 gallons. Similar break-outs in costs per pound can be carried out for grease, suspended
solids and BOD.

Then each major in-plant expense for waste conservation, water recycle
and reuse can be evaluated based on the estimated reduction in flow, BOD,
suspended solids and grease. From such data, priorities can be established
for each in-plant waste conservation measure suggested in the survey.

The future planning for the meat packing plant should serve as a guide to
determine piping arrangements and suitable locations (and sizes) for projected facilities.

COSTS

Waste-saving and treatment costs should be charged back to the department
from which the flow, BOD, suspended solids and grease emanated.

PRETREATMENT BY FLOW EQUALIZATION

Equalization facilities consist of a holding tank and pumping equipment
designed to reduce the fluctuations of waste streams. They can be economically advantageous whether the industry is treating its own wastes or discharging into a city sewer after some pretreatment. The equalizing tank

will store wastewater either to recycle or reuse the wastewater or to feed the flow uniformly to treatment facilities throughout the 24-hour day. The tank is characterized by a varying flow into the tank and a constant flow out. Lagoons may serve as equalizing tanks or the tank may be a simple steel or concrete tank, often without a cover.

Advantages of equalization for the meat packer discharging to a city sewer are: (a) in-plant pretreatment can be smaller, since it can be designed for the 24-hour average, rather than the peak flows; and (b) the city may have penalties for high peaks which can be avoided by equalization.

Disadvantages are few: (a) more equipment to maintain and operate; and (b) additional fixed costs.

PRETREATMENT BY SCREENING AND CENTRIFUGING

Since so much of the pollutional matter in meat wastes is originally a solid (meat particles and fat), or sludge (manure solids), interception of the waste material by various types of screens and centrifuges is a natural step.

Unfortunately, when these pollutional materials enter the sewage flow and are subjected to turbulence, pumping, and mechanical screening, they break down and release soluble BOD to the flow, along with colloidal and suspended grease solids. Waste treatment, that is, the removal of soluble, colloidal and suspended organic matter, is expensive. It is far simpler and less expensive to keep the solids out of the sewer entirely.

But, because in-plant conservation is, at best, imperfect and people are fallible, final organic solids separation in the main effluent sewer is generally employed. Various combinations of facilities for pretreatment may be selected, including screening, gravity grease and solids separation, dissolved air flotation and biological treatment of various types.

The information in this discussion of screening and centrifuging can be applied both for in-plant waste conservation and waste treatment. Screens might be used throughout the plant. Whereas vibrating screens are common, other types of screens could be suitable for service. Whenever feasible, pilot scale studies are warranted before selecting a screen, unless specific operating data is available for the specific use intended, in the same solids concentration range and under the same operating conditions.

MUNICIPAL MEAT PACKING WASTE TREATMENT

Many meat packing plants use municipal waste treatment facilities for the treatment of wastewater. Some plants will pretreat the wastewater before disposing of it into municipal sewers; other plants have no pretreatment.

Table 18 shows the estimated annual wastewater discharge of meat packing plants into the municipal sewerage system by size class. These estimates were based upon information obtained from the questionnaire data reported by the Federal Water Pollution Control Administration in Publication IWP-8. The total gallons discharged by medium and large plants were approximately equal. The 25 billion gallons from large plants represented a much higher proportion of their total discharge than did that from medium plants. 70% of all meat packing wastewater is discharged to the municipal sewerage system.

Table 19 contains estimates of the percent of wastewater discharged to municipal treatment facilities in selected years. The projected percentages for 1977 show increased use of municipal treatment facilities.

TABLE 18:   QUANTITY OF WASTEWATER FROM MEAT PACKING PLANTS, QUANTITY AND PERCENT DISCHARGED TO MUNICIPAL TREATMENT FACILITIES, BY PLANT SIZE, 1967

Plant Size	Gross Wastewater Emerging From Plant (mil. gal. per year)	Wastewater Discharged to Municipal Facilities (mil. gal. per year)	Percent of Gross Wastewater Discharged to Municipal Facilities
Small	3,768	2,449	65
Medium	42,198	24,897	59
Large	29,388	25,568	87
Total	75,354	52,914	70

Source: FWPCA Publ. IWP-8

TABLE 19:   PERCENT OF MEAT PACKING WASTEWATER DISCHARGED TO MUNICIPAL TREATMENT FACILITIES

Year	Percent
1950	35
1963	50
1966	70
1972	80
1977 (est.)	85

Source: FWPCA Publ. IWP-8

PLANNING, DESIGN AND CONSTRUCTION
OF WASTEWATER TREATMENT FACILITIES

SAMPLING THE WASTE

When a meat packing plant undertakes the task of providing treatment for its wastewater, one of the first steps is to determine the characteristics of the waste flow, as noted in a paper by Bell, Galyardt and Wells before an EPA Technology Transfer Seminar at Kansas City, Missouri, March 7-8, 1973.

As mentioned previously, meat packing wastes vary considerably from plant to plant. Consequently, it is important to set up a sampling program to determine the specific nature of the flow for which the treatment facilities are to be designed. Sampling stations should be established at all accessible points of waste discharge, and samples should be taken at half-hour intervals continuously for three days, and preferably one week. These samples should be combined for every 24-hour period to provide an accurate composite of the waste.

A weir or similar measuring device should be installed at each sampling station in order to provide a means of determining the rate of flow when each sample is taken. The sampling bottle must be kept chilled during the sampling period, and should be delivered to the testing laboratory as quickly as possible at the end of each 24-hour interval. It is important that the laboratory selected to perform the tests be experienced in the analyzing of wastewater samples. The most frequently performed determinations are BOD_5 (5-day Biochemical Oxygen Demand), COD (Chemical Oxygen Demand), settleable solids, suspended solids, volatile suspended solids, grease, Kjeldahl nitrogen, and pH.

46

DEVELOPMENT OF DESIGN CRITERIA

Once the results of the sampling program have been fully reviewed and analyzed, the design engineer is able to establish the design criteria. These factors are usually determined on the basis of 1,000 pounds of live-weight kill or per head. Any anticipated change in slaughtering or processing operations must be considered, as it will affect the current waste characteristics. If flows and BOD appear to be excessively high as sampled, a conscientious review of waste conservation and in-plant housekeeping programs should be made, with the goal of reducing these values to more generally acceptable values.

The following design factors are determined from sampling data:

Design average flow (gallons/1,000 lbs. liveweight/day)
Design maximum flow (gallons per day)
Design BOD (pounds/1,000 lbs. liveweight kill)
Design suspended solids (pounds/1,000 lbs. liveweight kill)
Design work week (days/week)

DEVELOPMENT OF ALTERNATE TREATMENT METHODS

Once design criteria and effluent requirements have been established, various methods of waste treatment which will provide an effluent meeting those standards are investigated by the design engineer. Several additional factors must be considered in making a choice. They include land availability, proximity to residential or commercial areas, initial construction cost, operation and maintenance costs and ease of operation.

Meat packing plants which are located in a built-up area will have less options to consider, since available space will be at a minimum. It is wise to be in contact with state regulatory agencies at this stage of the design. Preliminary submittal of the selected treatment scheme for approval of design criteria and layout will facilitate later review by these agencies.

DESIGN OF THE TREATMENT SYSTEM

Preparation of final plans and specifications for construction is begun by the design engineer once the selection of the treatment system is made. At this stage, it is important that reliable topographical information is obtained, providing ground elevations, location of existing property lines, building and sewers, sewer invert elevations, and a benchmark elevation on which to base proposed construction. Where a large area is involved, an aerial survey is often the most efficient way to obtain this information. The design engineer must also check the availability of utilities and electrical service at the site, as well as the power characteristics which should be used in specifying equipment.

Once the treatment units have been sized, an overall site layout can be developed, leaving adequate room between structures for access and maintenance. This layout will include utilities and wastewater piping, site grading and other site improvements. It is essential that future expansion of the system be considered in making the layout, permitting additions to be made to the facilities with minimum disruption of the existing treatment system. Sewer outfall lines can often be designed with extra available capacity at little additional cost.

Final plans and specifications will include all structural, electrical and mechanical work required to complete the project. Equipment drawings and specifications are generally prepared in such a manner as to permit various manufacturers to bid on the units, and installation details are provided with shop drawings furnished after award of contract.

When the plans and specifications are complete, the design engineer prepares for the owner an estimate of the construction cost. The final design documents are then submitted to the state environmental regulatory agency for review and approval leading to issuance of a permit for construction.

CONSTRUCTION OF THE TREATMENT SYSTEM

As soon as a permit has been granted by the state, the project can be advertised for bids. A notice describing the project is made available to any qualified contractor in the vicinity, and plans and specifications are issued to any of these contractors upon request for a period of three weeks to a month. Sealed bids are then opened by the owner or his representative on a specified letting date. Award of contract is usually made to the low bidder, contingent upon the recommendation of the engineer.

The construction phase of the project should be subject to periodic inspection by the design engineer or other qualified personnel hired by the owner. Careful conformance of construction with plans and specifications is essential to correct and reliable functioning of the system. Any deviation from the contract documents should be made only with the approval of the design engineer. Equipment shop drawings should also be routed to the engineer for review and approval.

When construction has been completed, the contractor should put the facility into operation for a brief period of observation, during which time the owner and the design engineer should inspect the project for final acceptance.

TYPES OF WASTEWATER TREATMENT FACILITIES

The secondary treatment methods commonly used for the treatment of meat processing waste flows as outlined by Bell, Galyardt and Wells of Rapid City-Omaha before an EPA Technology Transfer Symposium at Kansas City, Mo., March 7-8, 1973 include (1) anaerobic processes; (2) aerobic lagoon systems; (3) variations of the activated sludge process; (4) high rate trickling filters; and (5) rotating biological discs.

All of these treatment processes are capable of providing complete treatment and can achieve BOD reductions of 70 to 95% and suspended solids reductions of 80 to 95%. Each system has advantages and disadvantages, and generally, the degree of treatment required, together with site location and limitation, capital costs and operational costs will dictate the selection of the treatment system. The following discussion of such systems describes the treatment process, equipment utilized, as well as advantages and drawbacks.

Treatment by the anaerobic process is often used for wastes originating from meat processing plants, since the nature of the waste lends itself to this type of biological activity. Elevated temperatures (85° to 95°C.), and high concentrations of BOD and suspended solids — typical characteristics of the waste flow from a meat packing plant — are necessary for successful anaerobic treatment.

As previously discussed, anaerobic bacteria, which function in the absence of free oxygen, break down organic waste into gases (primarily methane and carbon dioxide) through production of intermediate acids. When compared to aerobic processes, the rate of removal and sludge yield are small. Nevertheless, anaerobic treatment often proves to be a highly economical

50

method for removing substantial amounts of BOD and suspended solids. Two types of anaerobic treatment are commonly utilized: (1) anaerobic lagoons, and (2) anaerobic contact units.

Treatment of domestic and industrial wastes, including those from meat packing plants, is frequently accomplished in aerobic lagoons. Two types of lagoons are generally classified as being aerobic: (1) aerated lagoons, which mechanically introduce oxygen by aeration; and (2) oxidation ponds which are lightly loaded and rely on sunlight and wave action to accomplish biooxidation and photosynthesis. Aerobic lagoons are frequently utilized to provide additional treatment to the effluent from an anaerobic lagoon system.

CATCH BASINS

Catch basins are gravity settling tanks with grease skimming. Larger packing plants have utilized catch basins because of the economic value of the recovered grease. The effectiveness of this means of treatment will depend upon the size of the tank and the detention time. Several years ago the meat packing industry made a study of the detention time which maximized the economic return of use of the catch basins. The detention time was about 20 minutes. From a waste reduction standpoint the detention time should be twice as long for maximum efficiency. To the extent that meat-packers are still following the 20 minute guide in designing catch basins, full waste reduction potential is not realized.

BENTONITE TREATMENT

A process developed by E.E. Pittman and R.R. Bottoms; U.S. Patent 2,261,924; November 4, 1941; assigned to The Girdler Corporation is one in which packing house waste from a composite waste storage tank may be pumped into any convenient mixing apparatus into which a slurry of a bentonite in colloidal suspension may be added, after which the mixture is thoroughly agitated and heated when desired.

The thus treated mixture of waste liquid and colloidal bentonite slurry may then be directed into any suitable separating means, such as a settling basin, vacuum or other types of filter apparatus, or any desired type of centrifugal apparatus. In this apparatus a filter cake or precipitate of an agglomerate of bentonite and organic solids from the waste will be recovered and a liquid effluent will be discharged which is suitable for reciruclation as plant wash water.

ELECTROLYTIC TREATMENT

A process developed by H.T. Anderson; U.S. Patent 3,673,065; June 27, 1972; assigned to Swift & Company is one in which fat-water emulsion systems are deemulsified by impressing direct current electrical energy therethrough and positioned such that a carefully defined anolyte stream is formed. The anolyte stream, having low pH values, breaks the emulsion, enabling the fat to rise to the surface and to be skimmed off.

It has been the usual practice in the past to run the waste water from the packinghouse to a settling tank or basin having baffles wherein the water would set for about 1/2 hour or more and the free fat would rise to the top and be skimmed off. The emulsified fat would of course remain in the water and would accompany it to the sewers. Various means such as aeration and complex apparatus have been employed in attempts to deemulsify the waste-waters. Usually, however, unless the emulsified oil was very valuable, no effort was made to separate it from the water that was passed to the sewers and hence to the rivers and seas. The following are some specific examples of the operation of the process.

Example 1:   A steel tank of about 60 feet long by 10 feet wide and 6 feet deep was approximately 3/4 filled with packinghouse wastewater containing principally fat, proteins and cellulose. Ten high silica-iron anodes, each 1 1/2 inches in diameter and 5 feet long, were connected in parallel and positioned below the water surface in 2 rows parallel to the longitudinal walls of the tank. The anodes were 2 1/2 feet from the longitudinal walls and were inclined progressively upward from inlet end to outlet end with the two anodes nearest the inlet end positioned so as to be slightly below the point of entry of the incoming wastewater.

An electrical wire was connected to a high point of the tank wall, which acted as the cathode, and grounding this to the rectifier completed the circuit. Using a rectified DC current to energize the anodes, various voltages were applied. Voltages between about 6 volts and about 9 volts and a current of between about 20 amps. and about 35 amps. resulted in an anolyte stream with fat particles and other solids floating to the surface where they were removed by mechanical sweeps.

Example 2:   Wastewater from a meat packing plant was clarified in an electrical setup similar to that used in Example 1. A current of 20 amps. and a potential of 9 volts was impressed on the system. Solids quickly rose to the surface and were skimmed off after 1/2 hour and 1 hour. After 1/2 hour there was about 25% reduction in total solids in the wastewater effluent and about 35% reduction in 1 hour.

Example 3:   Two steel catch basins side by side and equipped with mechanical sweeps were filled with the same packinghouse wastewater. One of the
tanks was equipped with an impressed current system. In this tank, which
is about 60 feet long by 10 feet wide and 6 feet deep were positioned two
rows of 5 anodes each made from high silica iron and being 1 1/2 inches in
diameter and 5 feet long. The anodes were placed parallel to the longitudinal wall and inclined upwardly toward the exit end of the tank. The
anodes were placed approximately 3 feet from and parallel to the longitudinal walls.

Using a potential of about 5.8 volts and a current of 22 amps., a definite
difference was noted between the two basins. Fat and other solids rose to
the top in the basin equipped with anodes. In order to increase the amount
of solids, about 300 ppm of sulfuric acid, 50 ppm of ferric sulfate and 2
parts of a cationic flocculant were added. Skim bars supporting rails 3/4
inch below the surface area were not visible in the control unit. However,
not only were rails visible in the test cell but the water was clear to such
an extent that one could see the moving parts near the bottom of the catch
basin.

ION EXCHANGE TREATMENT

A process developed by R.A. Grant; U.S. Patent 3,697,419; October 10,
1972; assigned to Tasman Vaccine Laboratory Limited, New Zealand involves the use of a particulate ion exchange material for the purification
of waste effluents, such as washings obtained from slaughter houses, which
contain protein or fat, or both. The use of the material can provide effluent
with a sufficiently low contamination level for it to be readily disposed of,
or even reused for further cleaning purposes. By suitable elution of the
material, the protein or fat can be released and isolated for use, for example, as animal food. The ion exchange material can be regenerated
for reuse.

Preferably, the ion exchange material comprises a cross-linked regenerated
cellulose (such as viscose) modified by the introduction of cationic or an-
ionic exchange groups. The exchange groups may be capable of anion exchange, such as amino, alkylamino, guanidino and quaternary ammonium
groups or capable of cation exchange, such as sulfonic acid, phosphate
and carboxyl groups.

The cross-linking may be provided by aldehyde residues, such as formaldehyde residues, produced by treatment of the regenerated cellulose with an
aldehyde under acid conditions. Alternatively the cross-linking may be a
achieved by treatment with epichlorhydrin under basic conditions or

physically, by exposure of the cellulose to high intensity ionizing radiation. The preparation and properties of such ion exchange materials are set out in U.S. Patent 3,573,277. Figure 2 is a block flow diagram showing the essentials of effluent treatment according to the process.

FIGURE 2:   BLOCK FLOW DIAGRAM OF OVERALL ION EXCHANGE
                      PROCESS FOR EFFLUENT PURIFICATION

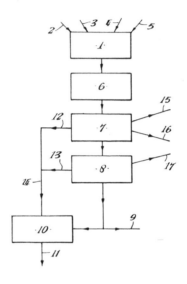

Source: R.A. Grant; U.S. Patent 3,697,419; October 10, 1972

Referring to the drawing, a receiving vessel (1) is provided, adapted to receive waste effluents. For example, the effluents may be from a slaughter board drain (2), a casing drain (3), a skin wash drain (4), or paunch washing drain (5). However, it is to be understood that in practice, it may be necessary or desirable to treat departmental wastes separately. From the receiving vessel (1), the washing or effluent are passed through a mechanical pretreatment section (6) where, for example, the treatment merely consists of passing the material through a 60 mesh sieve, the sieve being provided with suitable means whereby the collected material may be removed either continuously or from time to time.

Alternatively, on a larger scale a rotary vacuum filter could be used. Following mechanical treatment, the effluent passes to a filter bed (7) in which the filter bed comprises a particulate resin material capable of taking up at least the major portion of protein and fat remaining in the effluent.

After such treatment it is preferable that the effluent be further treated by a fibrous resin in a scavenger bed (8). Following this, the effluent may pass either directly through conduit (9), to a waste discharge station, or may be passed through a percolating filter or bone char filter (10) whereupon the outgoing effluent from conduit (11) leading from filter (10) may be chlorinated and reused.

Both the filter bed (7) and scavenger bed (8) may be backwashed when desired to dislodge solid matter from the resins. The backwash waters may be also conducted to the filter (10) by means of conduits (12), (13) and (14). During the regeneration of the resin in the filter bed (7), the effluent containing the released protein may be collected through conduit (15). Similarly, during regeneration of the fibrous resin in the scavenger bed (8), released protein may be collected through conduit (17). Waste liquors which do not need to go through the filter (10) may be withdrawn from the filter bed (7) and scavenger bed (8) through conduits (16) and (9) respectively. Figure 3 is a diagram of an experimental filter bed complex using the particular filter of the process.

FIGURE 3:   DETAIL OF FILTER BED COMPLEX USING PARTICULATE FILTER

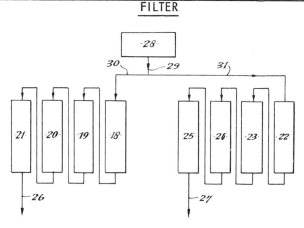

Source: R.A. Grant; U.S. Patent 3,697,419; October 10, 1972

The equipment shown in the block diagram under reference (7), may take the shape of a series of tanks (18) to (25), the first groups(18) to (21) being connected in series, and the second group (22) to (25) being also connected in series, the first group supplying an output (26), the second group supplying an output at (27), and both groups leading to beds of fibrous resin.

The two groups of tanks are supplied from a supply tank (28), which may be the pretreatment tank (6) shown in the block diagram (or may be an alternative tank), through leads (29), (30) and (31). Tanks may be of any suitable size, for example, for experimental purposes, these tanks have been made in 4 inch diameter glass columns, and the settled heights or resin have been about 12 inches high in each tank.

The flow rate in this case, is approximately 8 gallons per hour, and the dead volume in each tank, about 1 gallon per tank. For a pilot plant, the tanks could be approximately 3 feet in diameter and 10 feet high, holding a total quantity of approximately 1 ton of resin. For a full scale plant, an input of 1 million gallons per day, which indicates the size of beds required, would be equivalent to a bed 70 feet in diameter, and 5 feet deep. Of course, the area of the bed could be spread over several tanks. These figures are based on ion exchangers described in U.S. Patent 3,573,277, using the very simplest form of operation.

In view of the fact that the effluent contains a wide range of proteins with different isoelectric points, it may not be possible to take up the protein and fat material in an ion exchange bed in a single state with acceptable efficiency. Accordingly, a more complete taking up of protein from the effluent may be obtained by passing the effluent through two types of bed in series one in the hydroxide form, and the other in acid form. Various arrangements have been used experimentally. For example, an arrangement has been used wherein bed (18) was in the acid condition, beds (19) to (21) in the basic form, beds (22) to (24) in the acid form, and bed (25) in the basic form.

AIR FLOTATION

Air flotation is a treatment process in which a coagulation agent such as ferric chloride or alum is added to the wastewater, which is then subjected to air pressure in an enclosed chamber. The wastewater is left in the chamber for a few minutes and then released to atmospheric pressure. This method is supposed to be especially good for treatment of wastes which contain quantities of fat and protein.

The introduction of the air aids the oxidation of the organic material with the iron salts acting as catalyst. The air further aids by bringing flock and colloidal matter to the surface where it can be skimmed off. There is lack of agreement within the meat packing industry as to the success of this method of treatment; however, one of the "national" packing companies has installed this method of treatment in approximately half of its plants.

A process developed by E.A. Rubin; U.S. Patent 3,314,880; April 18, 1967; assigned to AB Purac, Sweden involves flocculation of contaminants and removal of the flocculated contaminants by air flotation. A method has earlier been suggested for purifying wastewater containing proteinaceous substances by being first precipitated in special flocculation plants, whereupon the precipitate is flotated by means of air bubbles obtained from a water-air dispersion supplied to the precipitate. The flocculation plants are relatively complicated and make the purification more expensive, while the separation effect cannot be considered quite satisfactory.

The special flocculation plants may be avoided, and the purification of the liquid improved by the utilization of the process, which is characterized by the fact that the contaminated quantity of liquid is passed into a flotation apparatus provided with a dispersion sprayer and that, at least in respect to the substances to be flocculated, substantially pure liquid is mixed with a precipitant and a gas for obtaining a dispersion which is passed through the dispersion sprayer so as initially to come into contact with the contaminated quantity of liquid in the flotation apparatus, flocculi of precipitated contaminations being formed, and the gas supplied together with the precipitant adhering in the form of small air bubbles to the flocculi formed and lifting the latter towards the surface.

As already mentioned, there has earlier been suggested a method of purifying proteinaceous wastewater by a flotation process. The purification has taken place in two stages having acid and basic precipitation products, respectively. A similar process may advantageously be accomplished by combining a plant according to the process with a previously known device. Figure 4 shows a suitable form of apparatus for use in the process.

The device includes a riser shaft (1), which the liquid to be treated enters through the channel (2). The dispersion plant includes an input of water (3), the water being conveyed by a pump (4) to an air supply device (5), to which air is supplied through a conduit (6). A receptacle (7) contains a precipitant and a substance, acid or base, for the purpose of giving the liquid to be purified a suitable pH value. The precipitant and the substance are moved by a pump (8) through the conduit (9) to the air supply device (5), for example, via the conduit (10) between the pump (4) and the air supply device or through the dashed conduit (9') to the dispersion holder (11) via the conduit (12) between the air supply device (5) and the dispersion holder (11).

In the dispersion holder (11) all the substances are mixed well into a homogeneous air-liquid dispersion, the air being dissolved in the liquid mixture. At the bottom of the riser shaft (1) a dispersion sprayer (13) is provided. As already mentioned the untreated water enters the riser shaft (1) through the channel (2). The water is assumed to be proteinaceous and fairly neutral, i.e., a pH value of approximately 6.5 to 7. An acid should therefore be added to give the liquid a suitable pH value, i.e., approximately 4 to 4.5. The acid, for example H_2SO_4, is mixed with the precipitant in the receptacle (7). A suitable precipitant is a lignin sulfonic acid product or other cation active substance. In the way described an air-liquid dispersion is produced, which is supplied to the liquid to be floated in the riser shaft (1) through the dispersion sprayer (13).

Then flocculi of precipitated contaminations are momentarily produced in the shaft. The dissolved air is transformed by the pressure reduction into small air bubbles (14), which adhere to the flocculi formed in the water, whereby these flocculi are subjected to a lifting force towards the surface. The proteins (15) accumulated in this way at the surface are removed by a scraper (16) or other means and are transported to a collection basin (17). After this first purification process the water (18) has a pH value of about 4 to 4.5. The water purified in respect of acid substances is passed through the channel (19) to the next basin for further purification.

FIGURE 4:   FLOTATION TANK FOR EFFLUENT PURIFICATION

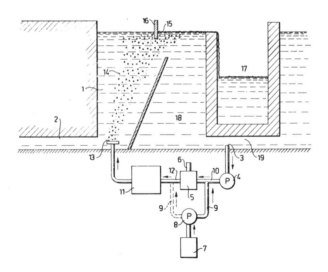

Source: E.A. Rubin; U.S. Patent 3,314,880; April 18, 1967

Figure 5 shows a plant design in which a device according to the process is combined with a previously known device. Before water enters the riser shaft (20) a basic substance, for example NaOH or slaked lime, is added to increase the pH value to a suitable value on the alkaline side. To obtain a thorough mixture of the added basic substance with the acid water a special precipitation or flocculation takes place. The precipitant consists for example of a neutral salt. Other precipitants are of course also conceivable. One of these is the substance which is known as Fixanol.

FIGURE 5:   TWO-STAGE FLOTATION PROCESS FOR EFFLUENT
PURIFICATION

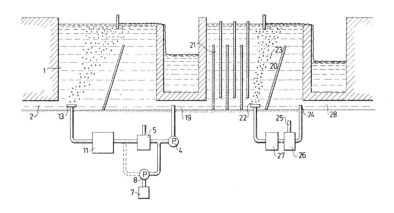

Source: E.A. Rubin; U.S. Patent 3,314,880; April 18, 1967

When the water arrives at the dispersion sprayer (22), accordingly the precipitation is already completed. In the same way as before the precipitate is floated by means of air bubbles (23) in the riser shaft (20). However, the dispersion now consists only of water with air dissolved therein and is produced by passing water through the conduit (24) and air through the conduit (25) to an air/water mixer (26) and further to a dispersion holder (27) in which the air is dissolved in the water. From the dispersion holder (27) the dispersion is conducted to the dispersion sprayer (22) and out into the riser shaft (20). The collection of the floated contaminations is effected in a similar way as before. The pure water is discharged through a channel (28).

A process developed by W.H. Hoffman; U.S. Patent 3,350,301; Oct. 31, 1967 involves the purification of wastewater containing fat, oil, greases, or the like in emulsion which process includes the step of treating the water in a flotation vessel in the presence of lime and air bubbles and the step of recycling partially purified water to the flotation vessel. The improvement comprises the step of diluting the wastewater entering the flotation vessel with a sufficient volume of the recycled water to break the emulsion. More particularly, the improvement comprises the steps of diluting each volume of wastewater before entering the flotation vessel with a first dilution stream which consists essentially of about an equal volume of water containing a substantial proportion of the soil-lime agglomerates which form in the flotation vessel; diluting each volume of wastewater entering the flotation vessel with a second volume of recycled water for each 1,000 parts/million impurities in the wastewater, the second dilution stream being substantially purer water than the first dilution stream; and adding the air and lime to the second dilution stream.

TRICKLING FILTERS

A trickling filter is a bed of coarse, rough impervious material over which wastewater is sprayed or distributed. The wastewater trickles downward through the filter in contact with the air. Organisms attached to the material of the filter oxidize the organic matter in the wastewater. It is necessary to see that solid materials are screened or settled out before the wastewater is distributed onto the filter in order to prevent clogging of the filter. Very cold weather may interfere with the working of this system. When operating efficiently, a 90% BOD removal can be expected.

Trickling filters are commonly used for biological wastewater treatment. With this system, wastewater which has undergone primary settling is sprayed over beds of rock or other media to achieve contact between microorganisms present on the surface of the media and organic material in the wastewater. A trickling filter is composed of three main components: (1) the rotary distribution arms; (2) the media; and (3) an underdrain system.

Where ample head is available, rotary distribution arms are turned by the reaction of water leaving nozzles in the arm. Distribution arms are used to uniformly distribute the wastewater flow over the filter media. Where sufficient head is not available, water must be pumped to the distributor. The filter media provides both a surface for the biological growth and also voids for movement of air and water through the filter bed.

Because of its low cost, durability and availability, stone or crushed rock has been the most popular filter media in the past. New materials have recently been developed and are on the market. They include various plastic media and also redwood slats. Advantages of the newer media include lower weight, chemical resistance, and a high specific surface area with a

large volume of void spaces. Thus the synthetic media will require significantly less space to accomplish the same degree of treatment. The underdrain system provides the means to carry away the filter effluent, allows
circulation of air through the filter bed and provides structural support for
the filter media.

Filters utilizing light weight plastic media are able to utilize much deeper
beds (up to 21.5 feet) than for rock filters. The high rate filter and the
roughing filter are the most common trickling filter systems presently used.
Flow diagrams for the high rate and roughing filter systems are shown in
Figure 6.

FIGURE 6:   FILTER SYSTEM FLOW DIAGRAMS

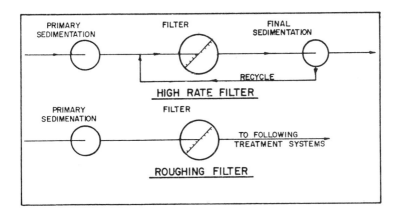

Source: Bell, Galyardt and Wells, EPA Technology Transfer Seminar,
           Kansas City, Mo. (1973)

BOD loadings to trickling fliter systems are generally expressed either as
pounds of BOD per 1,000 cubic feet of filter media or as pounts per acre-
foot of media. Hydraulic loadings are expressed as million gallons per acre
per day of filter area or gallons per minute per square foot of filter area.
The hydraulic loading is computed using both the raw wastewater flow plus
the recirculated flow.

The high rate trickling filter is capable of achieving BOD reductions as
high as 90% with proper recycle and loading rates. Removals in the
roughing filter are considerably less than those in the high rate system.

The major use of trickling filters in the meat processing industry involves their use as roughing filters. Roughing filter systems operate at hydraulic and BOD loadings much higher than those of conventional trickling filter systems. Their major function is to smooth out influent shock loads and provide some initial reduction of BOD. In most cases roughing filters are used prior to some type of the activated sludge system.

ROTATING BIOLOGICAL DISCS

The use of rotating biological discs is a new approach to the treatment of meat processing wastes. The discs were first developed in Europe in 1955 for the treatment of domestic wastes. Today there are approximately 1,000 domestic installations located primarily in West Germany, France and Switzerland. Development work on the rotating biological discs in the United States began in 1965. Utilization of the discs in the treatment of meat processing wastes is recent, and to date, no operational data is available except on a pilot plant scale. A large treatment facility, using these discs, for the Iowa Beef Processors plant at Dakota City, Nebraska, is under construction.

The rotating biological discs system consists of large diameter, light weight plastic or high density styrofoam discs, which are mounted on a horizontal shaft and placed in a semicircular shaped tank containing wastewater. Organisms present naturally in the wastewater adhere to the rotating surfaces and begin to multiply. As the discs rotate through the wastewater, wastewater adheres to the discs and then trickles down the discs absorbing oxygen. The aerobic organisms present in the wastewater then utilize the oxygen to reduce the organic matter in the wastewater.

As the discs continue to rotate through the wastewater, the organic material is further reduced. The discs support a growth of organisms, provide aeration of wastewater, and also provide contact of organisms with the wastewater. Excess growths of organisms slough off the discs. This minimizes clogging problems and maintains a nearly constant growth of organisms on the discs. The mixing action of the discs in the wastewater prevents the solids that have sloughed off from settling in the tank. These solids are removed in a final clarifier following the discs.

BOD removal and oxidation of ammonia nitrogen has been found to be directly proportional to the hydraulic loading on the disc units. At a specific hydraulic loading, a given percentage of BOD is generally removed even with fluctuation of the influent BOD. As a result, the principle design criterion is hydraulic loading.

Wastewater temperature will affect rotating biological disc efficiency, but this affect is negligible for normally encountered ranges of temperature. Wastewater temperatures in the range of 60° to 80°F. have little affect on disc treatment efficiencies. Waste temperatures from packing plants will generally average from 80° to 95°F.; thus the treatment efficiency would be higher than normally experienced.

The arrangement of biological media (organisms) in a series of stages has been shown to enhance the overall treatment of a wastewater, because the organisms that develop on each successive stage (disc) are adapted to treat the characteristics of the wastewater in each stage. Generally the organisms present in the first stages remove the organic (carbonaceous) material present in the wastewater while the last stage organisms are adapted to converting ammonia nitrogen to nitrate nitrogen (nitrification). Nitrogen in the ammonia nitrogen form is toxic to aquatic life.

The rotating biological discs should be enclosed to protect the organisms from cold temperatures and to help control odor emissions. As previously discussed, waste treatment efficiencies are reduced considerably when temperatures fall below 55° to 60°F. The enclosure helps to prevent winter weather from adversely affecting the treatment system. The enclosure will also help to control odor problems which may occur, by confining the odors in the building. Adequate ventilation is imperative, however, particularly if the waste flow is anaerobic when it enters the system. An odor control system may be required.

The type of enclosure that is generally used for a rotating biological disc system is a timber or concrete building with a poured concrete floor. Steel construction is not generally suitable since the air within the rotating biological disc building has a high degree of humidity. To protect any steel equipment from corrosion, due to this high moisture content, air in the enclosure would have to be heated. Heating may be necessary during the winter months.

A simplified typical flow schematic illustrating the treatment of a meat processing waste using rotating biological discs is shown in Figure 7. The raw wastewater flows into anaerobic lagoons or a pretreatment facility where suspended solids and BOD are removed and where flows are equalized. The partially treated flow then goes to the rotating biological discs where the organic material is converted to a biological floc which can be settled in the final clarifiers. The wastewater is then disinfected by chlorination, prior to discharge to the receiving stream.

Rotating biological discs can also be used in completely aerobic systems. The discs must be preceded by adequate grease removal. The number of stages of discs required will depend upon the desired degree of treatment. The sytem will also include a final clarifier and chlorination. A system of this type is currently treating poultry wastes with the effluent discharged to the municipal sewer system. With four stages, 98% BOD reduction is achieved.

FIGURE 7:   TYPICAL SCHEMATIC FOR ROTATING BIOLOGICAL DISCS

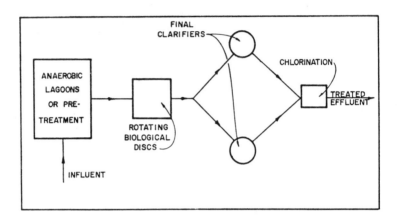

Source: Bell, Galyardt and Wells, EPA Technology Transfer Seminar, Kansas City, Mo. (1973)

LAGOON SYSTEMS

There are three types of lagoons: aerobic ponds, facultative ponds, and anaerobic ponds.

Aerobic Ponds

The aerobic pond depends upon algae to supply oxygen to satisfy the BOD. Because the algae are dependent upon sunlight to produce oxygen the pond must be shallow; that is, less than 18 inches. This type of pond has often been used to treat meat packing waste. An 80% BOD reduction can be obtained in some cases. Other aerobic lagoon designs mechanically intro- duce oxygen. Aerated lagoons are usually designed with detention times of of 2 to 10 days, have liquid depths of 8 to 15 feet, and utilize some type of aeration equipment, either fixed mechanical turbine type aerators, float- ing propeller type aerators, or a diffused air system.

In most cases, not enough turbulence is maintained in the basin to maintain the solids in suspension and those solids which settle may be degraded
anaerobically on the bottom. In those instances where sufficient turbulence
does exist, the system approaches the conditions of an extended aeration
system without sludge return.

BOD removal in aerated lagoons is dependent upon temperature, detention
time and influent waste characteristics. Treatment efficiency decreases as
temperature decreases. In northern climates, lower BOD reduction is experienced during the winter months. Aerated lagoons treating meat packing wastes are generally designed to achieve an average BOD reduction of
50 to 60%.

Power requirements are a major consideration and treatment facilities
handling a high industrial flow may utilize several hundred horsepower.
Facilites for small meat processing plants may use no more than 20 horsepower. When aerated lagoons are used in series with anaerobic lagoons,
sufficient oxygen is added to restore the waste to an aerobic state, including
oxidation of sulfides, and to provide for the additional biological treatment.

The most significant advantage of an aerated lagoon system is its relatively
small land requirement. The high cost or unavailability of land can easily
offset the higher operational cost of the aerated lagoon system. There is,
however, only a minimum reduction of ammonia nitrogen in an aerated
lagoon. Furthermore, aerated lagoons must always be followed by an oxidation lagoon to capture the suspended solids and to provide additional
treatment.

Oxidation ponds consist of relatively shallow, lightly loaded lagoons (20
to 40 lbs. of BOD per acre) with detention times often as long as several
months. They will provide a high degree of BOD reduction and have been
widely used for both domestic and industrial wastes. There are, however,
some drawbacks to their use. The water depth in oxidation ponds varies
usually from 4 to 8 feet. Frequently a level control system is provided to
permit rapid discharge of the effluent during periods of higher flow in the
receiving stream, dropping the water level to a minimum of 2 feet prior to
cutoff of discharge and temporary storage.

Oxidation ponds which treat wastes from the meat processing industry are
frequently preceded by anaerobic lagoons or anaerobic lagoons in conjunction with aerated lagoons. Even with this prior treatment, the BOD
remaining in the flow entering the oxidation pond may still be substantial.
Since the loading rate to oxidation ponds is generally kept quite low in
order to minimize odor problems and to provide for a high degree of treatment, large areas of land are necessary to provide adequate surface area

for the wastewater. Loadings for oxidation ponds are expressed in pounds of BOD per acre of water surface. Generally accepted values for industrial ponds range from 20 to 40 pounds per acre, with 25 to 30 pounds per acre being a commonly used design loading. Loadings as high as 100 and 150 pounds of BOD per acre have been used for meat processing wastes with reasonably high initial treatment efficiencies; however, odor problems have usually occurred and the quality and efficiency of the lagoons have frequently deteriorated after a period of several years. Because of this, state and federal health officials are increasingly reluctant to approve these high loading rates, and engineers no longer recommend them.

Suitable soil conditions are of basic importance to stabilization pond design, as it is essential that the compacted earth below the maximum water surface be essentially impermeable. Sandy or other granular soils are unsuitable for lagoon construction and require some type of liner. Due to the extensive surface area involved, lining of large stabilization ponds with any material other than clay soils found in upper soil layers or nearby excavation is usually prohibitive in cost. Smaller ponds may be sealed or lined with bentonite or some type of vinyl or asphalt liner.

One of the major drawbacks to utilization of stabilization ponds for final treatment is the development on the lagoon surface of algae growth which escapes with the pond effluent and creates an undesirable appearance, odor and taste in the receiving stream. In areas where effluent would flow into a recreational body of water, discharge is often prohibited entirely, or the BOD and suspended solids must be reduced to 5 mg./liter or less. The ammonia nitrogen must be reduced to less than 3 mg./liter. In such cases, the effluent would be disposed of by irrigation and/or evaporation.

It is generally not necessary to chlorinate the effluent from a stabilization pond, although it may be required whenever effluent standards for pathogenic bacteria are not met. The large surface area required for adequate treatment of meat processing wastes often results in ponds sufficiently large to have significant wave action and accompanying erosion of dikes. Riprap is often placed on those dikes subject to the wave action caused by high winds. Continuous maintenance of the dikes is essential for good operation, as excessive weed growth will lead to septic areas and mosquito breeding, and weakening of dikes caused by erosion or burrowing by rodents can result in potential flooding or surrounding land.

The configuration of stabilization ponds is generally rectangular, with acute angles avoided to prevent dead areas. Inlet and outlet structures are placed to prevent short circuiting of the flow through the lagoon. Two or more ponds may be used in parallel, to avoid the excessive unbroken surface area of one large pond. Oxidation ponds are often constructed in series, to provide succeeding degrees of treatment. Stabilization ponds which follow anaerobic or aerated lagoons will generally have an average efficiency of approximately 80% (in the first stage) and as high as 90% in the summer and 70% or less in the winter months. Efficiency tends to drop off somewhat in successive stages, reaching as low as 50% in a third stage aerobic pond.

Stabilization ponds provide an excellent means of treating meat processing wastes prior to use of the wastewater for irrigation purposes. However, due to increasingly stringent effluent quality standards, the discharge from a stabilization pond may frequently not be satisfactory for discharge into a receiving body of water.

Facultative Ponds

This pond is much deeper, and there will be two layers: an aerobic surface layer and an anaerobic bottom layer. Depth of ponds will vary from 3 to 6 feet and an 80% BOD removal can be expected.

Anaerobic Ponds

These are loaded to such an extent that anaerobic conditions exist throughout. These ponds are usually much deeper so that there is a high volume to surface area ratio, which will help to maintain the temperature of the waste. Anaerobic decomposition requires high temperatures for efficient decomposition of the material. Meat packing waste is especially suited to anaerobic decomposition because it is a very strong waste and comes from the packing house at a temperature of 80°C. The more common practice is to use an anaerobic-aerobic pond system in series using the aerobic pond as a polishing pond.

Anaerobic lagoons are widely used for treatment of meat packing wastes and function extremely well when the wastes have the desired characteristics. Typically, meat packing wastes have an appreciable amount of fats and proteins, high concentrations of nutrients, and an elevated temperature, all of which are essential for good anaerobic biological treatment.

Such lagoons are designed with a low surface to volume ratio in order to conserve heat in the pond. Depths are much deeper than aerobic ponds, ranging from 12 to 17 feet. Loadings range from 12 to 25 pounds BOD/1,000 cubic foot, with 15 to 20 pounds BOD/1,000 cubic foot frequently used in meat processing waste applications. A typical anaerobic lagoon system consists of one or more square or rectangular ponds with a depth of 15 feet and an inlet near the bottom. A layer of sludge on the bottom of the lagoon which contains active microorganisms comes in contact with the incoming waste. Excess grease floats to the surface and forms a scum layer or grease cover, which serves to both retain heat and restrict odors. Recirculation is generally not considered necessary, although it has been used in some installations.

Site conditions which must be evaluated when considering anaerobic lagoons are: (1) proximity to residential or commercial areas where potential odors may cause a nuisance (1/4 mile distance from any single family dwelling is usually considered minimum and at least 1/2 to 1 mile from any residential area, preferably downwind); and (2) soil conditions, i.e., location of the ground water table and nature of the soil with respect to workability and impermeability. It is essential that a natural cover be developed as soon as possible after the lagoon is placed in operation, particularly in northern climates. The cover will minimize odors and assure adequate heat retention. Recently, concern with air pollution has resulted in consideration of artifical covers for odor control.

A natural cover will usually form if enough grease is present in the waste. To accelerate development of a cover, paunch manure or normally recovered grease may be by-passed to the lagoon for a short period. Since high winds may disturb the scum layer and result in heat loss and odor problems, a windbreak, such as a board fence sheltering the lagoon from high prevailing winds, may be advisable to keep the natural cover intact. Low pH may adversely effect formation of a natural cover and the influent may require some pH adjustment.

Styrofoam, polyvinyl chloride, and nylon reinforced hypalon have been used as artificial covers, and other materials are currently being investigated. A major consideration in constructing a cover is providing an adequate gas collection system to trap the methane gases which rise to the surface. Also sunlight and wind action on the cover will affect the life of the cover depending upon the material selected. Properly designed inlet and outlet structures are important to successful functions of the anaerobic lagoon system. Good operation has been achieved with a feed inlet near, but not on, the bottom. The effluent piping should be near the surface and designed to prevent short circuiting and disturbance of the grease cover.

Advantages of an anaerobic lagoon system are low initial cost, ease of operation, ability to accept shock loads while continuing to provide a consistent quality effluent, and ability to handle large amounts of grease. Problems may arise if a sufficient cover cannot be maintained and odor results. Where water used for meat processing is high in sulfates, waste flows cannot be treated in anaerobic lagoons. Oxygen is stripped from sulfates by anaerobic bacteria, and hydrogen sulfide is produced, causing severe odor problems as the gas is released to the atmosphere.

It should also be noted that the effluent from an anaerobic lagoon system generally contains up to 100 mg./liter of ammonia nitrogen. The presence of ammonia nitrogen is toxic to fish in concentrations of 3 to 5 mg./liter, depending upon pH, and water quality standards in most states limit the concentration to 2 to 5 mg./liter.

Consequently, the secondary treatment method selected to follow the anaerobic lagoon system should provide for nitrification of the ammonia nitrogen where water quality standards place this limitation. The anaerobic lagoon system will not produce an effluent suitable for discharge into a stream without further treatment. It is highly efficient as a first-stage treatment unit and is generally followed by some form of aerobic system. However, some states will not permit the use of anaerobic lagoons or are requiring that they be provided with a cover.

ACTIVATED SLUDGE PLANTS

The activated sludge process involves the aeration of screened, presettled wastewater mixed with a small volume of activated sludge which has been collected in a sedimentation basin shortly before it is mixed with the sewage preceding aeration. There are a very few activated sludge plants specially devoted to the treatment of meat packing waste, primarily because of the high capital cost of the system and the necessity to have well-trained personnel supervising the operation of the process. When used, however, it is assumed that a 95% BOD reduction could be obtained.

Probably one of the most efficient and widely used systems of biological treatment of wastewater is the activated sludge process. Aeration of wastewater containing biologically degradable material in the presence of microorganisms produces a mass of settleable solids known as activated sludge. Stabilization occurs as organic matter in the wastewater is used as food by the microorganisms. There are several variations of the activated sludge process, four of which are shown in Figure 8 on the following page.

Conventional Activated Sludge

The conventional activated sludge process is composed of four functional steps: (1) primary sedimentation to remove settleable solids; (2) aeration of a mixture of waste and biologically active sludge; (3) separation of the biologically active sludge from the treated waste by sedimentation; and (4) recycle of this settled biological sludge.

Following sedimentation in a primary clarifier, the wastewater is mixed with recycled sludge in an aeration basin. This insures that adequate numbers of microorganisms are present to carry out the degree of waste stabilization desired. In the aeration basin the mixture of wastewater and recycled sludge is aerated for a specified length of time to provide an aerobic environment for the biological oxidation of the organic matter present. Final sedimentation following this aeration allows the activated sludge to settle producing both a clear effluent, low in organic content, and a biologically active sludge for recycle.

FIGURE 8:   VARIATIONS OF THE ACTIVATED SLUDGE PROCESS

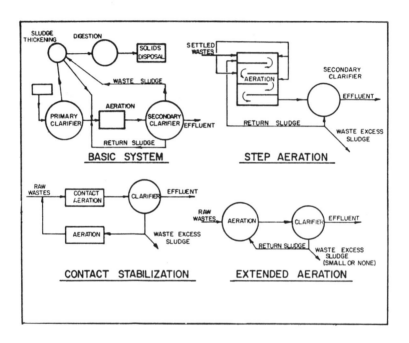

Source: Bell, Galyardt and Wells, EPA Technology Transfer Seminar, Kansas City, Mo. (1973)

The conventional process is capable of achieving BOD reductions of 90 to 95% and can produce a stable effluent with little nitrification.

The conventional activated sludge is adversely affected by the occasional spills or dumps of high organic wastes such as blood. Also the widely varying flows can be troublesome. Due to problems encountered in the basic activated sludge system when dealing with a particular waste or when a higher degree of treatment is desired, a number of modifications exist.

Tapered Aeration and Step Aeration

In the basic activated sludge system, air requirements decrease as flow
proceeds through the aerated basin. Two systems, the tapered aeration system and the step aeration system, have been devised to match the oxygen
supply with the oxygen demand.

The tapered aeration system provides for the introduction of air to the
aerated basin in decreasing amounts in an attempt to match the air applied
with the air requirements of the system. Reducing the air applied in no
way affects the biological process in the basin as long as sufficient amounts
of air are present. It does, however, increase the air application efficiency
as only that air actually required is supplied to the basin.

The step aeration system splits the wastewater flow to the aerated basin
and feeds it separately at different points along the aeration basin. The
return activated sludge is introduced with the first portion of the raw waste
at the head of the basin. Step aeration evens out the air requirements over
the length of the tank, allowing higher BOD loadings, shorter detention
times and more efficient use of applied air.

Contact Stabilization

The BOD in sewage is rapidly adsorbed by microorganisms after initial
contact between waste and organisms. In the conventional activated sludge
system, the time and air necessary to stabilize this adsorbed material is
provided in the same tank where original contact between waste and organisms was made.

The contact stabilization process provides separate tanks for initial microorganisms waste contact and stabilization. The microorganism waste contact part of the process generally requires 15 to 30 minutes. Following the
tank in which initial contact takes place, a clarifier is used to settle out
the microorganisms and the organic material entrapped with them. The
settled sludge is then pumped to a second aerated basin where the time and
air required to stabilize the entrapped organic material is furnished. The
overflow from the clarifier is then chlorinated and discharged directly to a
receiving stream.

The contact stabilization process allows a substantial savings in basin size
over the conventional system. The short detention time in the first basin
and the smaller volumes of sludge recycled to the second basin make this
savings possible. There are not many designed true contact stabilization
systems and none for meat packing wastes.

Completely Mixed Activated Sludge

By providing enough mixing in the aeration tank to completely mix the incoming wastewater with the contents of the tank, it is theoretically possible
to obtain any degree of treatment desired. The rapid mixing produces a
homogeneous mixture of wastewater and activated sludge within the aeration
basin. Any slugs of incoming waste are quickly mixed and distributed evenly
throughout the basin, reducing the chance of system upset commonly associated with conventional systems.

Extended Aeration

A completely mixed activated sludge system designed for long detention
time (24 hours or more) is known as an extended aeration system. Extended
aeration systems operate at the lowest BOD loadings of any activated sludge
system. Due to the smaller amounts of food available to the organisms,
nearly complete oxidation occurs for microorganisms and BOD removals are
high. Removals in excess of 95% are not uncommon.

Provision must still be made, however, for wasting sludge as solids tend to
accumulate within the system. Generally, provision is also made for 50
to 100% sludge recycle to the aeration basin from the final clarifier. Advantages of the extended aeration system include ability to handle shock
loads, low capital investment due to elimination of primary clarifiers and
sludge digestion equipment, as well as the capability to produce a nitri-
fied effluent.

Channel Aeration

This process is really a modification of the activated sludge process or,
more specifically, the extended aeration activated sludge process where
a cage rotor is used as the aerating device. The Pasveer concept is to put
the wastewater in an oval ditch and use the cage rotor to aerate the liquid
and at the same time cause it to flow around the oval. This process was
developed in Holland and is now and has been utilized on a pilot plant
scale at one plant in the United States. The full scale plant will be built
at one of the major packing plants. The simplicity and efficiency of this
system make it a promising addition to the methods of treatment meat packing waste.

Nitrification in Extended Aeration

Long detention times and aerobic conditions found in extended aeration
systems provide an ideal atmosphere for the process of nitrification. Under
aerobic conditions, ammonia is converted to nitrites and nitrates by specific

groups of nitrifying bacteria. A sludge detention time of 8 to 10 days is required for the nitrifying organisms to establish themselves in sufficient numbers to accomplish any appreciable degree of nitrification. Usually, extended aeration systems designed to accomplish nitrification are designed for sludge detention times in excess of 10 days. Although liquid detention times in the system are generally approximately 24 hours, the sludge age may be controlled by regulating the amounts of sludge recycled and wasted each day.

Oxygen (for the oxidation of ammonia) must be supplied in excess of that required for BOD reduction. About 4.33 pounds of oxygen are required to convert 1 pound of ammonia nitrogen to nitrates. This results in a substantial increase in air requirements over those required for BOD reduction alone, necessitating the installation of larger, more expensive aeration equipment.

Extended aeration systems which follow anaerobic lagoons are capable of producing an effluent low in BOD and ammonia nitrogen. Anaerobic lagoons are capable of BOD reductions in excess of 80%; however, under anaerobic conditions the protein in the packing plant wastes are decomposed resulting in the conversion of most nitrogen forms present to ammonia nitrogen and some nitrogen gas. The nitrogen gas escapes to the surrounding atmosphere, but the ammonia nitrogen remains in the anaerobic pond effluent creating an additional oxygen demand if discharged to a receiving stream.

Further, this chemical is toxic to fish at low concentration. The use of an extended aeration system following anaerobic lagoons provides the time and air required to reduce the remaining BOD and convert the ammonia nitrogen to nitrates. Following final sedimentation and chlorination, the effluent may be discharged to a receiving stream with a minimum of impact.

It should be noted that although the nitrogen in the plant effluent does not create a significant oxygen demand upon the receiving stream, it does remain a nutrient source, enhancing the possiblity of undesirable aquatic plant growth and algae blooms.

Activated Sludge Treatment for Meat Processing Wastes

All of the previously mentioned activated sludge systems may be used to treat wastes characteristic of the meat processing industry. The particular system chosen will depend upon the degree of treatment desired and the existing facilities available for use. The conventional, tapered air, step aeration, contact stabilization, completely mixed and extended aeration systems will all produce an effluent capable of meeting effluent standards for BOD reduction. In many cases the particular system chosen will depend to a large extent upon the characteristics of the effluent from existing treatment facilities. For example, many meat processors utilize anaerobic lagoons for reduction of BOD. The effluent from these lagoons is generally still quite high in BOD and contains large amounts of ammonia nitrogen. Extended aeration following anaerobic lagoons, as mentioned earlier, performs quite well in reduction of the remaining BOD and nitrification of ammonia nitrogen. This treatment system functions well, meeting both BOD and ammonia nitrogen effluent standards.

Some of the loading and operational parameters for the activated sludge processes described previously are presented in Table 20 below. BOD loadings to aeration tanks are calculated using the influent wastewater BOD only. Loadings are expressed as pounds applied per day per 1,000 ft.^{3} of aeration tank volume and pounds of BOD per day per pound mixed liquor suspended solids in the aeration basin. Aeration periods, expressed in hours, are calculated using the daily average flow without regard to return sludge flow. The return sludge flow is usually expressed as a percentage of the daily average flow.

TABLE 20:   GENERAL LOADING AND OPERATIONAL PARAMETERS FOR ACTIVATED-SLUDGE PROCESSES

Process	BOD Loading		Aeration Period, hr.	Average Return Sludge Rates %	BOD Efficiency %
	lb. BOD per 1,000 cu. ft.	lb. BOD per lb. MLSS			
High rate (complete mixing)	100 up	0.5 – 1.0	2.5 – 3.5	100	85 – 90
Step aeration	30 – 50	0.2 – 0.5	5.0 – 7.0	50	90 – 95
Conventional (tapered aeration)	30 – 40	0.2 – 0.5	6.0 – 7.5	30	95
Contact stabilization	30 – 50	0.2 – 0.5	6.0 – 9.0	100	85 – 90
Extended aeration	10 – 30	0.05 – 0.2	20 – 30	100	85 – 90

Source: Water Supply and Pollution Control, Clark, Viessman and Hammer, International Textbook Co., 1971, pp. 507.

ANAEROBIC CONTACT

Again it will be mentioned that the anaerobic digestion process is especially suited to meat packing waste because of its relatively high organic content and high temperatures. The high organic content means that relatively large amounts of methane gas will be released which can be utilized as a source of heat. The anaerobic contact process separates seed organisms and recirculates them to the digester. When operating efficiently, the process requires retention periods of 6 to 12 hours. Waste flows into an equalizer tank, from there into a digestor and then through a vacuum degasifier which removes residual gases to facilitate settling, and finally into a settling basin from which the sludge is removed and returned to the digestor as seed. This method of decomposition is usually followed by polishing lagoons or by other secondary treatment methods to achieve further decomposition of the organic material.

The anaerobic contact process consists basically of an anaerobic digester with mixing equipment, a degasification system and a clarifier. Solids from the digester are sent to a degasifier in order to minimize floating material, and are then settled, with sludge from the clarifier being returned to the raw waste line. The separation and recirculation of seed sludge permits short retention periods, ranging from 6 to 12 hours. Solids retention time for a high degree of treatment is approximately 10 days at 90°F. As the operating temperature drops, the solids retention time must be increased.

Control of pH is essential to insure proper operation, and lime or sodium bicarbonate is commonly used to raise the pH of the raw wastes. Inorganic salts in high concentrations may be toxic to the anaerobic organisms. Anaerobic contact digester units are loaded in the range of 0.10 to 0.20 lb. BOD/ft.^{3}/day at approximately 90° to 95°F. Flow equalization is employed in order to maintain a uniform feed rate to the digester. This is necessary because of the short contact time involved in the process. Either draft tube or turbine-type mixers are utilized to provide complete mixing. Digester gas may be used to heat the digester.

The degasification step may be accomplished by vacuum degasification or air-stripping. In vacuum degasification, a vacuum of 20 inches of mercury is maintained in a vessel which has a diameter equal to its length. The influent is elevated to the top of the vessel and cascaded down over slotted trays with removed gases sent to a waste gas burner. The air-stripping process involves passing diffused air through the waste to scrub off the gas. This method is less expensive but has more operational problems than the vacuum process.

The clarifier receiving the sludge should be provided with a well designed recirculation system in order to move the light floc and to avoid a temperature loss. Treatment efficiencies of 85 to 93% removal of BOD can be obtained with the anaerobic contact system, but generally additional aerobic treatment is required. The overall cost of such a system usually lies between that of anaerobic lagoon system and an activated sludge plant.

A modified anaerobic contact system is in use at the Wilson Certified Foods Plant in Albert Lea, Minnesota. This facility consists of a flow equalizing basin, two digesters of approximately 12 hours detention time which are loaded at 0.156 lb. BOD/ft.^{3}/day, two vacuum degasifiers, two sludge separation units (clarifiers), and two oxidation ponds receiving the separation effluent. The separators are designed for a detention time of 1 hour, based on total flow including recirculation. The recirculation rate is approximately 1/3 of the raw waste flow.

In Table 21 below is actual operating data taken from the Wilson & Co. anaerobic contact system. BOD removal is approximately 91% through the anaerobic contact process and 98% in the stabilization ponds. Good removals (80%) were also obtained for suspended solids. Lagoon treatment provided after the contact process is lowering the effluent concentrations to acceptable levels and is an essential segment of the total treatment system.

TABLE 21: ANAEROBIC CONTACT SYSTEM

Average operating data (all killing days in 1960)

	Raw Waste		Anaerobic Process Effluent		Pond Effluent	Loss in Pond
Flow,Gallons	1,410,000		1,410,000		772,000	638,000
	Raw Waste		Anaerobic Process Effluent		Plant Effluent Corrected for Seepage	
	mg/1	Pounds	mg/1	Pounds	mg/1	Pounds
BOD	1381	16220	129	1517	26	304
Suspended Solids	998	11610	198	2325	23	268
Suspended Volatile Solids	822	10370	153	1800	20	232
Total Solids	2100	36500	2080	24450	1076	12500
Total Solids-Water Supply	560	6500	560	6500	560	6500
Total Solids after deducting TS in Water Supply	2540	30000	1520	17950	516	6000
Total Volatile Solids	1700	19980	800	9400	367	4310
Total Volatile Solids in Water Supply	300	3520	300	3520	300	3520
Total Volatile Solids after Deducting TVS in Water Supply	1400	16460	500	5880	67	790

*Wilson Certified Foods, Inc., Albert Lea, Minnesota

Source: "An Industrial Waste Guide to the Meat Packing Industry," U.S. Department of Health, Education and Welfare

A process developed by E.H. Pavia; U.S. Patent 3,520,802; July 21, 1970 involves the treatment of high protein liquid wastes under anaerobic conditions as a digester. Such wastes are distinguished by very high protein content in the form of liquid solubles and insolubles, and a very high BOD, which may range up to 600 to 30,000 ppm. Figure 9 shows a suitable form of apparatus for the conduct of the process.

FIGURE 9:   ANAEROBIC DIGESTER DESIGN

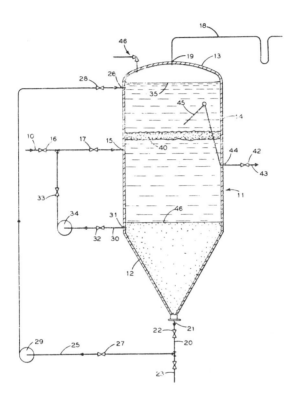

Source: E.H. Pavia; U.S. Patent 3,520,802; July 21, 1970

As shown in the figure, (10) designates a line carrying the raw liquid waste of high protein content, which is to be treated in a sealed chamber generally indicated at (11). Chamber (11) may take the form of a tank having a coni- cal lower portion (12), a domed top portion (13) and an intermediate cylin- drical portion (14). The incoming waste line (10) enters tank portion (14) at inlet (15), with valves (16), (17) in the line. The tank (11) is sealed and therefore the treatment is conducted under anaerobic conditions. A water seal line (18) extends from an outlet (19) in crowned tank portion (13).

A drainage line (20) extends downwardly from the bottom outlet (21) in conical tank portion (12); with valves (22), (23) in the line. Mixing in tank (11) is accomplished by continuous circulation, via line (25) which extends from drainage line (20) at a point between valves (22), (23) therein, to an inlet (26) at the top of tank portion (14), with valves (27), (28) and a pump (29) interposed in line (25).

Selective mixing in tank (11) is also accomplished by continuous circulation via a line (30) extending from an outlet (31) located at a level depending on the characteristics of the waste being treated, to line (10) at a point between valves (16), (17); the line (30) having valves (32), (33) and a pump (34) interposed therein.

In operating the system, with tank (11) empty, all valves except valves (16), (17) are closed and the raw waste is supplied to tank (11) from line (10) until a level (35) therein is reached. Valves (16) and (17) are then closed, while valves (22), (27) and (28) are opened and pump (29) is started. Pump (29) operates at a relatively high rate of speed to provide a very fast mixing of the entire contents of tank (11) and to achieve a proper mixture of liquid and suspended solids at a selected ratio thereof. During this mixing period, some gas is generated which will drive some of the water out of seal (18), a relief chamber, not shown, being provided to receive such water.

When the proper mixed liquor-suspended solids ratio is reached, valves (22), (27) and (28) are closed; pumpage is stopped and valves (32) (33) and (17) are opened. Pump (34) is started and operates at a relatively low rate of speed to continue mixing. This mixing operation is effected to provide a gentle mixing of the contents of tank (11) at the lower portions thereof and the formation of a blanket of colloidal form as at (40) which is slightly above the level of inlet (15).

The speed rate of mixing at both the high and low rate will depend on the characteristics of the waste being treated and the hydraulic characteristics of the tank. In tests, the ratio between the high rate of mixing and the low rate has varied from 2:1 to 6:1 depending on the individual waste treated.

Blanket (40) is effective to prevent solids from rising into the liquid zone lying between level (35) and a level at inlet (15). During the low rate mixing operation, the pH of the recirculated liquid is checked carefully as it drops from an initial value of the order of 3.5 to 6.0 to a value of the order of 2.0 to 3.5. At this time, gas generated is reabsorbed by the liquid waste through oxidation and the reduction in pH causes soluble protein to precipitate out from the liquid. When the pH has been suitably reduced, valves (32), (17) and (33) are closed. A valve (42) in a line (43) connected to a draw off outlet (44) in an upper portion of tank portion (14) is opened. Internally of tank portion (14) is a jointed draw off conduit (45), connected to outlet (44), which is used to draw off the treated liquid to a selected lower level. Draw off conduit (45) may be manipulated by suitable means, not shown.

Valve (42) is then closed and valves (22), (23) are opened to draw the sludge accumulated in the lower portions of tank (11) to a level (46), immediately above outlet (31). This provides seed material for the second mixing phase as described above. The two phase mixing operation described above is then repeated. The high protein content sludge drawn off may be recovered and utilized commercially. A pressure-vacuum relief valve is indicated at (46).

It has been found that the initial mixing phase may extend over a period of from about 5 to about 20 minutes while the second mixing phase has a time period of from about 50 to 70 minutes. Accordingly, the treatment has a total time period not exceeding 55 to 90 minutes. The mixing intervals will vary with the protein content of the waste, the suspended solids of the waste and the temperature maintained in the tank. In tests it has been found that utilizing the same waste, the time for the completed reaction will be decreased approximately 1 minute per each 3°F. increase in temperature maintained.

OPERATION AND MAINTENANCE
OF WASTE TREATMENT PLANTS

The construction of a wastewater treatment facility is only the first step
in the process of achieving successful waste treatment, as pointed out by
Bell, Galyardt and Wells, Architect-Engineers of Rapid City-Omaha, in
an EPA-approved Technology Transfer Seminar at Kansas City, Missouri,
in March 1973. The second and equally important step is the proper operation and maintenance of the physical plant to insure the treatment that the
system was designed to achieve. Responsibility for this program should be
in the hands of well-trained and conscientious personnel.

Industries which utilize complicated treatment facilities and plants which
use relatively simple treatment systems both require someone in charge who
has a thorough knowledge of his job. The plant operator is often called
upon to make adjustments or modifications in the treatment units to obtain
maximum treatment efficiency. The equipment must receive proper care
if the treatment system is to provide the degree of treatment designed into
the system.

A good program of waste flow sampling can help substantially in obtaining
the optimum degree of treatment. In addition to providing the required
data for regulatory agencies, a complete record of treatment factors may
help the operator cope with present inconsistencies and future expansion
in the waste treatment system. Familiarity with the physical appearance
of the raw influent and of the well-treated or under-treated effluent flow
will provide an indication to the operator of an upset or change which will
require more detailed and careful sampling. A reliable and workable
arrangement must be made for the necessary analytical work that is required,
whether it is performed by company personnel or by an outside agency.

The operational problems to be encountered will depend upon the waste characteristics, type of treatment, climate and design. All manufacturers' data should be read, understood and kept as a permanent record along with all shop drawings. A detailed manual relating to proper operation of treatment plants such as published by the Water Pollution Control Federation should be readily available as a reference to all employees associated with the waste treatment facilities. Such manuals contain information on the causes and cures of many operational difficulties encountered in usual types of treatment. Operational practices for anaerobic and aerobic lagoons may be found in numerous textbooks or published articles in wastewater journals. Furthermore, an operation and maintenance manual dealing with the specific waste treatment system should be provided to the industry by the engineer who designs the facility.

In addition to proper operation, the importance of maintaining the physical structures cannot be underestimated. A system of routine inspection and maintenance should be established, based upon the nature and needs of the equipment. All literature from the manufacturer relating to equipment upkeep should be filed away after being read by the operations staff. A supply of spare parts, as recommended by the manufacturer, should be kept on hand at all times.

If possible, daily attention should be given to the operation and maintenance of the system. Simple systems may require little day-to-day care, but should be checked on a regular basis. Care of the treatment site is also important. Mowing should not be neglected, fences and gates should be kept in good repair, and utilities maintained.

The following schedule lists some of the many types of maintenance required on various segments of the complete system. It should serve only to provide a base upon which each individual plant operator may build his own operation and maintenance programs.

Typical Operation and Maintenance Program for Waste Treatment System

Pumping Stations:

1. Hose down wet well to control grease accumulations.
2. Check packing glands for correct tightness (centrifugal pumps).
3. Adjust V-belt drive as necessary.
4. Lubricate pumps according to manufacturers' recommendations, using high grade lubricants.
5. Check bearings for overheating after starting pump.
6. Inspect pump and bearings on shutdown so that necessary maintenance can be performed during shutdown period.

7. Inspect water level controls in wet well to insure functioning.
8. Check electric motor pump drives periodically.
9. Alternate pumps on a weekly basis if automatic alternation is not provided.

Screening Facilities:

1. Check daily to determine if screens require cleaning.
2. Rake screens and dispose of material by burying or other suitable means.

Sedimentation Tanks (Clarifiers):

1. Check tanks and equipment several times daily for proper operation.
2. On a regular basis, clean inlet baffles, effluent weirs, and scum removal mechanisms.
3. Hose down all spills.
4. Keep lubrication records for all equipment and use high grade lubricants.
5. Drain tanks annually and inspect all systems for wear and corrosion. Replace badly worn equipment and adjust all chains.

Trickling Filters:

1. Inspect rotating arm nozzles daily for clogging; clean as required.
2. Check bearings and lubricate in accordance with manufacturer's recommendations.
3. Adjust guy lines to account for seasonal temperature variations thus allowing arms to remain horizontal.
4. Check filter surface daily for contaminants such as leaves or debris.
5. Periodically inspect underdrain system for clogging.
6. Follow recommended courses of action if trouble develops such as ponding, filter flies, odor and icing.

Chlorination Facilities:

1. Check daily for proper functioning of all systems.
2. Check for leaks every 8 hours.
3. Check safety equipment monthly.
4. Check feed rates every 8 hours.

Activated Sludge Systems:

1. Check air compressors for lubrication and overheating.
2. Check air filters daily for cleanliness. Clean monthly.

3. Use rotation schedule for compressors to insure even wear.
4. Check compressor for satisfactory performance.
5. Check air flow in tanks every 8 hours.
6. Check all aeration tanks annually and repair or replace worn equipment.

Sampling:

1. Check raw flow rate weekly, preferably daily.
2. Perform periodic settleable solids tests on influent and effluent flow.
3. Perform daily dissolved oxygen, BOD, suspended solids, and settleable solids tests on activated sludge systems to insure proper operation.
4. Run BOD, suspended solids, DO tests daily or biweekly at trickling filter plants but not less than 2 times a week.
5. Run tests for nitrates, ammonia nitrogen and organic nitrogen, and possibly phosphate on samples collected preceding and following treatment at regular intervals.
6. Perform daily tests for settleable solids, suspended solids, total and volatile solids on samples from sedimentation units. Check sludge for total and volatile solids to provide information required for proper operation of sludge recirculation and drawoff systems.
7. Perform at regular intervals, grease determination on all grease removal systems, for both influent and effluent.
8. Perform all tests (on plant effluents) required by regulatory agencies.

General:

1. Mow grass on ground dikes.
2. Keep in good repair all external construction, such as buildings and sheds.
3. Check for leaks in valves and other appurtenances.
4. Check operability of all valves and gates.

REGULATORY CONSIDERATIONS

Public Law 92-500, amending the Federal Pollution Control Act, was passed by Congress on October 18, 1972, and contains several points of direct interest to industry. In providing grants for new or expanded municipal treatment plants (now amounting to 75% of the construction cost), the Federal government requires that the municipality "has made provision for the payment.... by the industrial user of the treatment works, of that portion of the cost.... allocable to the treatment of such industrial wastes.." for which he is responsible. [Section 204 (b) (1)].

The Law also provided that, by April 16, 1973, the EPA shall "issue guidelines applicable to payment of waste treatment cost by industrial and nonindustrial recipients of waste treatment services which shall establish (A) classes of users of such services, including categories of industrial users; (B) criteria against which to determine the adequacy of charges imposed on classes and categories of users reflecting factors that influence the cost of waste treatment, including strength, volume, and delivery flow rate characteristics (surges and maximum flows) of wastes; and (C) model systems and rates of user charges typical of various treatment works serving municipal-industrial communities." The reader is referred to the Future Trends section at the end of this volume for citation of the 1973 EPA Guidelines.

Thus the EPA will be involved in the rate structure or formula developed for sewage charges for all municipalities (including sanitary districts) where grant funds are allocated, in order to assure repayment of the government's cost in proportion to the cost of the treatment works attributable to the industry's wastewater discharged to the municipal sewer.

The accompanying Table 22 is excerpted from "Federal Guidelines — Equitable Recovery of Industrial Waste Treatment Costs in Municipal Systems" (Oct., 1971).

Pretreatment prior to discharge to "publicly owned" (i.e., municipality, sanitary district, county, etc.) treatment works is also regulated under the Act. Sec. 307 (b) (1) required that the EPA, by April 16, 1973, "publish proposed regulations establishing pretreatment standards for introduction of pollutants into treatment works...., which are publicly owned, for those pollutants which are determined not to be susceptible to treatment by such treatment works or which would interfere with the operation of such treatment works.

Not later than 90 days after such publication, and after opportunity for public hearing, the Administrator shall promulgate such pretreatment standards." The Act allows a maximum of three years for compliance by industry and also provides for revision of these standards as new technology warrants.

TABLE 22: QUANTITY OR QUALITY FORMULAS BASED ON TOTAL COST OR AVERAGE UNIT COSTS

This method of cost allocation or derivation of industrial charge is computed by several forms of the generalized formula:

$$C_i = v_oV_i + b_oB_i + s_oS_i$$

Note: The principle applies equally well with additional terms (e.g., chlorine feed rates) or less terms (e.g., v_oV_i only).

Where C_i = charge to industrial users, \$/yr.

v_o = average unit cost of transport and treatment chargeable to volume, \$/gal.

b_o = average unit cost of treatment, chargeable to BOD, \$/lb.

s_o = average unit cost of treatment (including sludge treatment) chargeable to SS, \$/lb.

V_i = volume of waste water from industrial users, gal./yr.

B_i = weight of BOD from industrial users, lb./yr.

S_i = weight of SS from industrial users, lb./yr.

(continued)

TABLE 22:   (continued)

The terms b_0 and s_0 above may include charges (surcharges) for concentrated wastes above an established minimum based on normal load criteria.

Inasmuch as it is an objective of the Guidelines to encourage the initiation and use of user charges, this general method of allocation is both preferable and acceptable.

Source: A.J. Steffen, EPA Technology Transfer Seminar, Kansas City, Mo. (1973)

The limits may be anticipated to be in two general categories: one, pro-hibited items (such as ashes, hair, whole blood, paunch manure, and sim-ilar materials untreatable in municipal plants), and the second category, maximum concentrations of such items as BOD, suspended solids and other constituents which, in excess, could interfere with the operation of hte municipal plant.

Many municipalities will use such maxima in their structure of charges, figuring a volume cost per 1,000 gallons per month (perhaps on a sliding scale similar to water billing or, more conveniently, a definite multiplier of the municipal water bill). To this volume cost, surcharges are added for BOD, suspended solids, grease, and possibly other pollutional ingre-dients at a determined rate in cents per pound of each such pollutional in-gredient beyond a certain basic concentration, the base being representa-tive of the concentration of domestic sewage.

The following effluent guidelines for discharges in the meat processing in-dustry are based on the application of the best practicable control tech-nology currently available. The following EPA limitations reflect the Agency's best technical judgment of the effluent levels which can be main-tained through the application of the highest levels of pollution control that are currently available and practicable.

Meat Processing	BOD_5*	Suspended Solids
Slaughterhouse	0.17	0.23
Packinghouse	0.26	0.35
Processing plant only	0.26	0.26

*Values expressed in terms of pounds/1,000 pounds of live weight killed.

STATE PROGRAMS

This discussion will be limited to the state's role in in-plant conservation and pretreatment prior to discharge to public sewers. Recycling and reuse of water and any other major in-plant changes should be reviewed with the state meat inspection agency if the plant is under state, rather than federal inspection.

Approval of plans for pretreatment of wastewaters prior to discharge to public sewers may be a requirement under the state regulations for approval of plans for sewage treatment. States differ on this point. In some states, the plant may also be required to have a state-licensed wastewater treatment plant operator for such pretreatment facilities.

Municipal ordinances relating to wastewater are generally reviewed by the state stream pollution control authority. Thus ordinances and regulations regarding industrial wastewater and charges and surcharges will most likely be reviewed by the state before passage. If the city has not passed the legislation required by the EPA for a federal grant for sewage treatment construction, the state (which allocates these funds) may adivse EPA to withhold a portion of the grant until all requirements are met.

When a new plant is planned for connection to a public sewer and such connection will substantially increase the flow or pollutional characteristics of wastewaters reaching the municipal wastewater treatment plant, the agency owning the sewer is required by federal law to advise the state of such change.

Effluent requirements as determined by a state will vary considerably throughout the country, and will also vary within an individual state, depending upon the water quality standards for the receiving stream into which the treated wastewater will be discharged. By December of 1975, all waste treatment facilities must provide a minimum of secondary treatment. However, in some states, tertiary treatment is already required on some streams and lakes.

MUNICIPAL PROGRAMS

Most municipalities have ordinances which place limitations on the characteristics of the wastewater which may be discharged into the municipal sewer system. These limitations are set to prevent operational problems at the municipal waste treatment facility and to prevent the plant from becoming overloaded. Any industry which fails to meet this limiting value must pay a surcharge. Because of the high flows and concentrated wastes discharged from a meat packing plant, it is generally necessary to pretreat these wastes to a degree that will permit the municipality to handle the wastes. Also, further reduction of BOD and suspended solids would be economically advantageous. Screening, grease skimming, and solids removal are perhaps the most important initial types of pretreatment. In some cases, waste flow must also be treated biologically in order to meet BOD limitations.

When a municipality builds or expands its waste treatment facility, the industries are expected to pay their share of the construction and operational costs. This cost can become extremely high, particularly in smaller communities where the industrial flow is a substantial percentage of the total. In these cases, the economics of extensive pretreatment, partial treatment, or completely separate and industry owned waste treatment facilities must be carefully studied.

Municipal ordinances and regulations that are less stringent than those set up under the Federal Act discussed above, will be required to alter them to conform, but if they exceed the federal standards, they need not be reduced, unless the city elects to do so.

Existing municipal ordinances and regulations covering discharge to the public sewers vary widely. A large number of cities use, as a guide, the so-called Model Ordinance published as part of Manual of Practice No. 3 of the Water Pollution Control Federation. Article 5 of the Model Ordinance contains an extensive list of limiting characteristics applicable to meat packing wastewaters discharged to public sewers.

The background material, along with Article 5, are too voluminous to reproduce here. The "Regulation of Sewer Use" (Manual of Practice No. 3) is available at $1.50 ($1.00 to Federation members) from: Water Pollution Control Federation, 3900 Wisconsin Ave., Wash., D.C. 20016. A 15% quantity discount is available in lots of twelve or more copies.

Municipal ordinances generally cover the subject under two headings: Limitations and Surcharges.

Limitations: Prohibition of Objectionable Matter — Various minerals, toxic materials and waste characteristics and materials that are difficult to treat are excluded. The following examples are typical. The Metropolitan Sanitary District of Greater Chicago includes the following exclusions on ingredients that may affect packing plant effluents: Noxious or malodorous liquids, gases or substances which either singly or by interaction with other wastes are sufficient to create a public nuisance or hazard to life or are sufficient to prevent entry into the sewers for their maintenance and

repair. Solid or viscous wastes which cause obstruction to the flow in
sewers or other interference with the proper operation of the sewerage system or sewage treatment works, such as grease, uncomminuted garbage,
animal guts or tissues, paunch manure, bone, hair, hides and fleshings.

Waters or waste containing substances which are not amenable to treatment
or reduction by the sewage treatment process employed or are amenable to
treatment only to such degree that the sewage treatment plant effluent can
not meet the requirements of other agencies having jurisdiction over discharge to the receiving waters.

Excessive Discoloration — Other cities use similar limiting clauses in
their ordinances, often copied from the Manual of Practice No. 3, from
which the above wording was adapted in part.

Concentration of Pollutional Characteristics — (a) The Ordinance of the
Metropolitan Sanitary District of Greater Chicago provides no top limits
for BOD or suspended solids but does include "surcharges" for these items
(see below). It does, however, limit the temperature to a maximum
of 150°F. (65°C.) and fats, oils or greases (hexane solubles) to a maximum
of 100 mg./l. These limits are included in many municipal ordinances.

(b) Other cities may limit BOD to possibly 300 mg./l. and suspended solids
to 350 mg./l., more or less. "Catch-all" clauses are also common, such as
"The Town Board of Trustees is authorized to prohibit the dumping of wastes
into the Town's sewage system which, in its discretion, are deemed harmful
to the operation of the sewage works of said Town."

Surcharges: (1) The Metropolitan Sanitary District of Greater Chicago
charges 2.1 cents per 1,000 gallons, 1.4 cents per pound of BOD and 2.4
cents per pound of suspended solids, after deducting the first 10,000 gallons
per day (and the BOD and suspended solids it would contain). Also deducted
are the sewer district tax (a property type tax) plus 4 mills per day per employee, an allowance for sanitary sewage discharged during the working
day.

(2) Most of the simpler sewage billing systems are based on the water usage,
ranging from about 50% to as high as 125% of the water billing, with maxima for BOD, suspended solids, grease and sometimes other ingredients.
These are basic sewer charges applicable to all users, domestic, commercial and industrial and are not classified as surcharges unless they include
escalation for BOD, suspended solids, grease, etc. and possibly flows, in
excess of a "domestic" base. Thus the surcharge portion of the ordinance
might be similar in structure to the Chicago ordinance, but with a charge
for flow in excess of a base, and a charge per pound of ingredients above

a base represented by discharge from a single residence.

(3) Also note the guidelines under Federal Program (above).

In general, the new Federal Act cited in the Future Trends section at the end of this volume may radically modify existing municipal ordinances and regulations.

It should also be noted that recycle and reuse of used water must be checked by the USDA and any other agency having jurisdiction over product sanitation.

UTILIZATION OF WASTE TREATMENT FACILITIES

Estimates of utilization of waste treatment facilities by type of facilities have been made for the years 1950, 1963, 1967, 1972, and 1977. These estimates are shown in Table 23.

Future estimates will reflect the assumption of increased use of industry-owned treatment facilities. Future estimates indicate shift in the treatment mix, indicating increased use of methods especially suited for the degradation of meat packing wastewater; that is, wastewater with high concentrations of BOD and high temperatures. Future estimates further assume that only those meat packing plants utilizing municipal waste treatment facilities will be allowed to operate no more than "catch basins" or air flotation units.

Questionnaires were sent to all fifty states in order to obtain data on the status of meat processing waste treatments in the United States as part of a study conducted by Bell, Galyardt and Wells, Architect Engineers of Rapid City-Omaha, and reported at an EPA-sponsored Technology Transfer Symposium at Kansas City, Missouri, in March 1973.

Many states did not have data available and fourteen states responded to the questionnaire. Several of the states indicated the existence of few meat processing facilities and in these locations existing plants were usually very small, often not discharging a waste stream into a surface body of water. In such cases, septic tanks were employed or other underground waste disposal schemes practiced. Ponds which had only seepage as effluent were also noted in some localities, notably in the western United States where the climate is arid. These treatment facilities apparently were meeting state standards because of subsurface discharge or no effluent discharge.

91

TABLE 23: UTILIZATION OF WASTE TREATMENT FACILITIES

Type of Waste Treatment Facility	Estimated Percentage of Plants Employing Waste Treatment Process				
	1950	1963	1967	1972	1977
"Catch Basin" Only (Sedimentation and Grease Skimming)	60	50	46	10	10
Air Flotation	0	5	8	20	20
It is assumed that a "catch basin" will precede the following methods of treatment.					
Lagoon Systems	10	15	17	20	14
Trickling Filter	1	3	3	3	2
Activated Sludge	1	2	3	3	1
Anaerobic Contact (followed by Lagoons, Activated Sludge, or Trickling Filter)	0	5	6	20	25
Channel Aeration (Pasveer Process)	0	0	2	5	10
Joint Industrial	0	1	2	10	15
Other (including Chemical Treatment)	8	4	4	8	2
Total (Plants with Some Type of Treatment Facility)	80	85	91	99	99
No Treatment Facilities	20	15	10	1	1
Total	100	100	100	100	100

Source: FWPCA Publ. IWP-8

Questionnaires returned from states where more and larger meat processing operations were located showed that more complex methods of treatment were employed. It is interesting to note, however, that the regulatory agencies from these states felt that only half the treatment facilities under their jurisdiction were effective. Many plants were operating well, but it was indicated that upgrading was needed, and in some cases work was already in progress.

The types of treatment indicated as generally in use are anaerobic lagoons, anaerobic-aerobic lagoons, anaerobic-aerated lagoons, various types of activated sludge systems (mostly extended aeration), aerobic lagoons or oxidation ponds, aerated lagoons and trickling filters. An anaerobic lagoon system followed by aerobic treatment was the most frequently listed type of treatment and was reported as working well in achieving good BOD reduction. Values reported were in excess of 90% BOD removal, generally over

95%. Extended aeration systems also showed high BOD removals, in the range of 90%. There seemed to be a tendency to use extended aeration on smaller plants with the lagoons being employed on large installations, (i.e. greater than 500,000 gpd). Less frequently used systems were aerated lagoons or oxidation ponds. Spray irrigation was used as a means of disposal, particularly in arid climates. Use of trickling filters, based on the limited data, was not widespread. Such installations are in existence, of course, and are capable of providing good treatment if properly loaded and operated.

Table 24 lists the types and number of waste treatment facilities reported by the fourteen states responding to the questionnaire.

TABLE 24: EXISTING WASTE TREATMENT FACILITIES FOR THE MEAT PROCESSING INDUSTRY

Treatment	Number of Installations	Size Range, mgd	BOD Reductions, %
Anaerobic-Aerobic Lagoons	18	0.40-2.50	90-99
Anaerobic-Aerated Lagoons	6	0.66-1.97	98-99
Aerated Lagoons Aerobic Lagoons	8	0.005-0.75	91-98
Lagoons	14	0.005-1.20	87-99
Extended Aeration	13	0.001-0.10	70-97
Activated Sludge	2	0.060	98
Trickling Filters	3	1.0-1.85	92-96
Spray Irrigation	2	-	-
Septic Tanks	30	-	-
Other	9	-	-
None	2	-	-

Source: Based on results of a questionnaire distributed to state water pollution control agencies. Data received from the following states: Alaska, Arizona, Florida, Iowa, Kansas, Kentucky, Louisiana, Maine, Nebraska, New York, Nevada, Ohio, Utah, and Wyoming. Reported by Bell, Galyardt and Wells at EPA Technology Transfer Seminar, Kansas City, Mo. (1973).

Table 24 is general in nature; in many cases the treatment scheme has
been simplified for use in this table. For example, if a system consisted
of grease removal, primary screening, flow equalization, extended aeration and chlorination, the overall system was classified as extended aeration. Flow and performance data was taken from systems on which the
information was provided, some units being reported without data. It is
interesting to note that one of the plants with no treatment slaughtered
1,000 head/day and had a BOD of 2,250 mg./l. However, the report
went on to state that a program is underway to provide treatment.

COSTS OF POLLUTION REDUCTION

SUBPROCESS CHANGE

Capital and operation and maintenance costs have been estimated for three subprocess changes by the Federal Water Pollution Control Administration in their Publication IWP-8. These costs are shown in Table 25.

TABLE 25: COST OF WASTE REDUCTION BY SUBPROCESS CHANGE

Subprocess Change	Small Plant 20 mil.lbs/yr. LWK		Medium Plant 100 mil.lbs/yr. LWK		Large Plant 300 mil.lbs/yr. LWK	
	Cap. Costs $	O. & M. Costs $	Cap. Costs $	O. & M. Costs $	Cap. Costs $	O. & M. Costs $
Add Evaporator to Wet Rendering System[a]	30,000	2,000	70,000	5,000	140,000	10,000
Change To Nonpolluting Rendering System[b]	60,000	-----	120,000	-----	200,000	------
Precede Wet Cleanup With Dry Cleanup[c]	0	8,000	0	40,000	0	100,000

[a]The addition of an evaporator will cut BOD by 50%. The economic life is assumed to be fifteen years.

[b]The complete changing of the rendering system would reduce BOD by 60%. The economic life is assumed to be fifteen years.

[c]Dry cleanup would reduce BOD by 10%. To be effective this subprocess would require constant enforcement.

Source: FWPCA Publ. IWP-8

None of these costs should be interpreted as anything but "ball park" estimates. The salvage value of the "more polluting" rendering system which
is being replaced by a "less polluting" rendering system would constitute
one adjustment of the costs shown in Table 25. The physical layout of the
meat packing plant would influence greatly the installation portion of the
capital costs listed.

Costs shown in Table 25 would require additional adjustment if, for example, there is increased revenue due to higher prices received for animal
feed as a result of its increased protein content because of the addition
of dried and processed evaporated "stick water." Adjustments of the cost
estimates would also be required. The enforcement of "dry cleanup" may
result in lower water use per unit of product and thus lower total water
costs. These are only two examples of possible cost adjustments which
should be included in the analysis of alternatives for a specific plant.
Geographical location affects construction costs and labor costs and re-
finements of this nature would also be necessary.

INDUSTRIAL WASTE TREATMENT

Costs of treatment by type of waste treatment process were developed for
the typical small, medium, and large plant. Plant size in annual liveweight killed and wastewater flow associated with the typical plant in a
size class are indicated at the top of Table 26. The costs of treatment

TABLE 26: COST OF WASTE TREATMENT FACILITIES

Type of Treatment Facility	Small Plant 20 mil.lbs/yr. LWK 33 MGY Wastewater 0.125 MGD Wastewater		Medium Plant 100 mil.lbs/yr. LWK 143 MGY Wastewater 0.54 MGD Wastewater		Large Plant 300 mil.lbs/yr. LWK 444 MGY Wastewater 1.68 MGD Wastewater	
	Cap. Costs $	O. & M. Costs $	Cap. Costs $	O. & M. Costs $	Cap. Costs $	O. & M. Costs $
"Catch Basin" Only	12,000	1,000	35,000	10,000	250,000	18,000
Air Flotation			60,000	13,000	150,000	30,000
It is assumed that a "catch basin" will precede the following methods of treatment.						
Lagoon Systems			215,000	11,000	415,000	21,000
Trickling Filter	70,000	21,000	700,000	30,000	900,000	35,000
Activated Sludge	275,000	65,000			1,900,000	150,000
Anaerobic Contact (Followed by Lagoons, Activated Sludge, or Trickling Filter)			410,000	20,000	630,000	30,000
Channel Aeration (Pasveer Process)			15,000	6,000	350,000	20,000

Source: FWPCA Publ. IWP-8

were based upon the average cost per thousand gallons experienced by
plants in the "sample" with occasional adjustments by engineering cost
estimates. The lagooning cost data from the sample was felt to be especially unreliable since land costs were not consistently included in the
reporting of capital costs.

MUNICIPAL TREATMENT

It is impossible to estimate for a given size of plant the charges which
must be paid to the municipality for its treatment of the industry's wastewater. These charges vary greatly from one city to another. If the meat
packing plants in the questionnaire sample used by the Federal Water
Pollution Control Administration and reported in Publication IWP-8 are
representative of the entire industry, the entire meat packing industry
paid six million dollars in 1967 to municipalities for waste treatment services, for instance.

INDUSTRY INVESTMENT

The estimates of capital and operation and maintenance expenditures on
waste treatment facilities by the meat packing industry shown in Table 27
require explanation. These estimates were based upon questionnaire data
obtained by the Federal Water Pollution Control Administration and reported in Publication IWP-8.

The average capital investment (measured in terms of 1967 replacement
cost) per plant was determined for each size group and then inflated to
reflect the number of plants under federal inspection. The number of
federally inspected plants seems more appropriate than all plants because
of the extremely small size of the nonfederally inspected plants. The use
of plant numbers rather than liveweight killed introduces a source of
error, but since the plants have been grouped by size class, the error
should not be significant.

Since federally inspected plants kill 85% of the liveweight, the estimated
costs for the entire federally inspected sector of the industry were increased by 17.6% to account for the remaining liveweight slaughter in
locally inspected plants. The 1967 replacement value of waste treatment
facilities would then be approximately thirty-five million dollars.

The estimate of industry investment is felt to be an extremely conservative
estimate. Several meat packing companies have arrangements with municipalities whereby the city owns the facility but the packing plant in effect

TABLE 27: CAPITAL AND OPERATING AND MAINTENANCE COSTS OF WASTE TREATMENT FACILITIES BY SIZE CLASSIFICATION (ACTUAL SAMPLE DATA AND DATA PROJECTED FOR ALL FEDERALLY INSPECTED MEAT PACKING PLANTS)

Type of Treatment	Small 0-24.9 Mil. lbs. Annual Kill			Medium 25-199.9 Mil. lbs. Annual Kill			Large 200-Up Mil. lbs. Annual Kill			All Plants		
	No. of Plants	Capital Costs	O. & M. Costs	No. of Plants	Capital Costs	O. & M. Costs	No. of Plants	Capital Costs	O. & M. Costs	No. of Plants	Capital Costs	O. & M. Costs
SKIMMING & CATCH BASINS ONLY												
Sample Plants:Average		4,014	270		15,052	6,436		66,071	10,000		20,482	5,474
Sample Plants:Total	12	48,168	3,240	33	496,716	212,388	18	1,189,278	180,000	63	1,734,162	395,628
Federally Inspected Plants:Total	45	180,630	12,150	107	1,610,564	688,652	29	1,916,059	290,000	181	3,707,253	990,802
TRICKLING FILTER												
Sample Plants:Average		40,000	4,250		250,000	10,000		160,000	70,000		112,500	16,646
Sample Plants:Total	2	80,000	8,500	1	250,000	10,000	1	160,000	70,000	4	490,000	88,500
Federally Inspected Plants:Total	7	280,000	29,750	3	750,000	30,000	2	320,000	140,000	12	1,350,000	199,750
ACTIVATED SLUDGE												
Sample Plants:Average		150,000	35,000		20,000	3,000					85,000	19,000
Sample Plants:Total	2	300,000	70,000	2	40,000	3,000				4	340,000	73,000
Federally Inspected Plants:Total	7	1,050,000	245,000	7	140,000	21,000				14	1,190,000	266,000
LAGOONS-ANAEROBIC AND/OR AEROBIC												
Sample Plants:Average		16,800	878		100,333	6,810		1,000,000	68,000		87,640	5,843
Sample Plants:Total	9	151,200	7,902	14	1,404,662	95,340	1	1,000,000	68,000	24	2,555,862	171,242
Federally Inspected Plants:Total	34	571,200	89,852	46	4,615,318	313,260	2	2,000,000	136,000	82	7,186,518	479,112
ANAEROBIC DIGESTION												
Sample Plants:Average					55,000	3,365		200,000	5,000		71,731	3,571
Sample Plants:Total				7	385,000	23,695	2	400,000	10,000	9	785,000	33,695
Federally Inspected Plants:Total				23	1,265,000	77,855	3	600,000	15,000	26	1,865,000	92,855
CHEMICAL TREATMENT												
Sample Plants:Average		1,000			70,000	8,000					44,909	5,127
Sample Plants:Total	1	1,000	100	2	140,000	16,000				3	141,000	16,100
Federally Inspected Plants:Total	4	4,000	400	7	490,000	56,000				11	494,000	56,400
JOINT INDUSTRY												
Sample Plants:Average					1,750,000	83,000					1,750,000	83,000
Sample Plants:Total				2	3,500,000	166,000				2	3,500,000	166,000
Federally Inspected Plants:Total				7	12,250,000	581,000				7	12,250,000	581,000
AIR FLOTATION												
Sample Plants:Average		23,500	4,250		25,000	6,500		100,000	10,000		31,500	6,341
Sample Plants:Total	2	47,000	8,500	7	175,000	45,500	2	200,000	20,000	11	422,000	74,000
Federally Inspected Plants:Total	7	164,500	29,750	23	575,000	149,500	3	300,000	30,000	33	1,039,500	209,250
OTHER												
Sample Plants:Average		500	1,650		55,000	3,745					26,452	2,648
Sample Plants:Total	3	1,500	4,950	3	165,000	11,235				6	166,500	16,185
Federally Inspected Plants:Total	11	5,500	18,150	10	550,000	37,450				21	555,500	55,600
GRAND TOTAL												
Sample Plants:Average		19,616	3,174		95,476	8,304		131,694	15,667		76,583	7,521
Sample Plants:Total	31	628,868	103,192	71	6,556,378	583,158	24	2,949,278	348,000	126	10,134,524	1,034,350
Federally Inspected Plants:Total	115	2,255,830	365,052	233	22,245,882	1,954,717	39	5,136,059	611,000	387	29,637,771	2,930,769

Source: FWPCA Publ. IWP-8

guarantees to cover the operating and amortization costs. Such facilities are often especially designed units to handle meat packing wastes yet the legal arrangement precludes their inclusion in Table 27.

Operation and maintenance costs for the federally inspected sector were likewise inflated to account for the remaining liveweight. Total operation and maintenance costs for 1966 were $3.5 million.

INDUSTRY EXPENDITURES

Table 28 summarizes all expenditures on waste treatment in 1966. The capital expenditures are expressed as an annual average payment assuming a fifteen year life and interest rate of 6%. Total expenditures then were approximately thirteen million dollars.

TABLE 28:   EXPENDITURES FOR WASTE TREATMENT BY THE MEAT PACKING INDUSTRY, 1966

Replacement Value of Treatment Facilities Millions of Dollars	Annual Equivalent Millions Of Dollars	Annual O & M Costs Millions Of Dollars	Annual Payments To Municipalities Millions Of Dollars	Total Payments For Waste Treatment Millions of Dollars
35	3.5	3.5	6	13

Source: FWPCA Publ. IWP-8

CASE HISTORIES
OF MEAT PACKING POLLUTION CONTROL

AMERICAN BEEF PACKERS, COUNCIL BLUFFS, IOWA

The American Beef Packers plant at Council Bluffs, Iowa, was constructed in 1969. The plant consists of beef slaughtering and processing facilities in a main plant, with hide processing facilities located in an adjacent building. Waste treatment facilities included with the plant construction consisted of an air flotation tank to remove grease from the slaughtering-processing waste stream, followed by an aerated lagoon. Effluent from the flotation tank and the hide processing building were discharged separately to the aerated lagoon prior to disposal in the city sewer system. Four 50-hp., slow-speed, pedestal-supported mechanical aerators, located at the south end of the aerated basin, were used to supply oxygen for BOD reduction.

Anaerobic odors emanating from the aerated basin due to an insufficient amount of aeration, coupled with recently increased sewer surcharge fees established by the City of Council Bluffs for discharge of the plant effluent into the municipal sewer system, made upgrading of the existing treatment facilities necessary and economically advantageous. Modifications to the existing facilities were investigated which would stop the odor nuisance caused by anaerobic conditions in the aerated basin and increase overall BOD removals to comply with standards required for discharge to the city sewer without surcharge.

The system which was designed to upgrade the existing facilities was an extended aeration system based upon the following design data: BOD loading, 18,000 lbs./day; design flow, 1.5 MGD. At a design flow of 1.5 MGD, the existing basin provides a detention time of 3.5 days which is

more than adequate for the extended aeration system. The air being supplied to the basin was considered insufficient for both the necessary mixing
and BOD reductions, as evidenced by the anaerobic conditions existing at
the northern end of the basin.

Consequently, eight 40–hp., high–speed floating aerators were added to
the existing aeration basin to provide the additional air required. As an
integral part of the extended aeration system, a 55–foot diameter concrete
clarifier is being constructed, with provisions for sludge return in an amount
equal to 100% of the design flow. Effluent from the clarifier will be discharged to the existing city sewer system. The schematic flow diagram for
the plant is shown in Figure 10.

FIGURE 10:   FLOW SCHEMATIC — AMERICAN BEEF PACKERS, INC.,
COUNCIL BLUFFS, IOWA

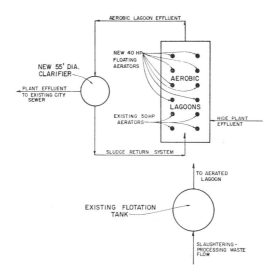

Source: Bell, Galyardt and Wells, EPA Technology Transfer Seminar,
Kansas City, Mo. (1973)

Grease skimming and solids screening are provided for the hide processing
effluent (brine curing) prior to discharge to the aeration basin. The eight
40–hp. aerators were installed in the aerated basin prior to completion of
the clarifier in order to correct the prevailing anaerobic conditions. Following completion of construction, the system will be operated as an

extended aeration system, providing a high degree of secondary treatment.

IOWA BEEF PROCESSORS, INC., DENISON, IOWA

Iowa Beef Processors, Inc., recognized in 1966 the need for secondary waste treatment for their beef slaughtering plant at Denison, Iowa. An anaerobic-aerobic lagoon system was determined to be the best type of treatment facility, and was designed using the following factors:

BOD loading	9,600 lbs./day
Design flow	720,000 gpd
Anaerobic lagoon loading	15 lbs. BOD/1,000 ft.^{3}
Depth of anaerobic lagoon	15 feet
Assumed efficiency	65 percent
1st Stage aerobic lagoon loading	150 lbs. BOD/acre
2nd Stage aerobic lagoon loading	50 lbs. BOD/acre

Figure 11 shows the schematic layout and flow diagram for the system.

FIGURE 11: FLOW SCHEMATIC — IOWA BEEF PACKERS, INC., DENISON, IOWA

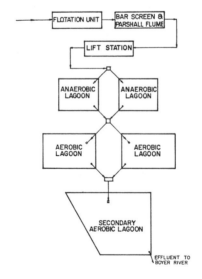

Source: Bell, Galyardt and Wells, EPA Technology Transfer Seminar, Kansas City, Mo. (1973)

Plant waste undergoes pretreatment in an air flotation unit, while pen wastes flow through a settling basin prior to discharge to the lift station. The combined pen and plant wastes flow through a mechanically cleaned bar screen and measuring flume, and are then pumped to the anaerobic lagoons. These two lagoons are operated in parallel with the effluent discharged to two first-stage aerobic ponds, also in parallel. The effluent from the two cells received further treatment to discharge into the Boyer River.

Sampling data obtained by the State of Iowa Hygienic Laboratory indicates that the lagoon system has performed well since its completion in November, 1968. BOD removal efficiencies of over 80% have been consistently achieved in the anaerobic lagoons, and the overall efficiency of the system is approximately 98%.

With an operating anaerobic lagoon treatment efficiency of 80% rather than the assumed design value of 65%, the loading to the first stage aerobic pond was reduced to 85 pounds of BOD per acre, and the final stage is reduced to 30 pounds of BOD per acre.

FARMLAND FOODS, DENISON, IOWA

The wastewater treatment system serving the hog processing plant owned by Farmland Foods, Denison, Iowa, was designed to treat the varied waste flows from the killing floor, holding pens, blood recovery system, rendering, and processing operations and also domestic sewers.

The plant kills 5,000 hogs per day, of which 40% are usually kept for further processing operations, the rest being shipped. The processing operations include cutting and processing into hams, bacon and picnics. Rendering operations are performed on fat and bones, and there is a blood recovery system for the kill floor. The major consideration in designing the waste treatment facility was the small amount of available land.

Construction on the project was initiated in April of 1969. The facility has been in operation for several years. The raw waste criteria employed in the design of this treatment system are given below:

Raw Waste Design Criteria

BOD loading   21,500 lbs. BOD/day
Flows:
   Average   850,000 gpd
   Maximum daily   1,000,000 gpd
   Maximum hourly   1,500,000 gpd

The preceding table is taken from D. Baker and T. White, "Treatment of Meat Packing Waste Using PVC Trickling Filters", National Symposium on Food Processing, Denver, March 23-26, 1971.

The flow diagram for the treatment facilities is shown in Figure 12. The wastes from the kill floor are pumped to an air flotation unit for separation of grease, which is then returned for rendering.

The effluent from the flotation unit is combined with the raw waste from the pens, scald tank and domestic lines and is sent to two parallel anaerobic lagoons. The lagoons provide biological treatment and also serve as flow equalizing basins.

FIGURE 12:   FARMLAND FOODS, DENISON, IOWA

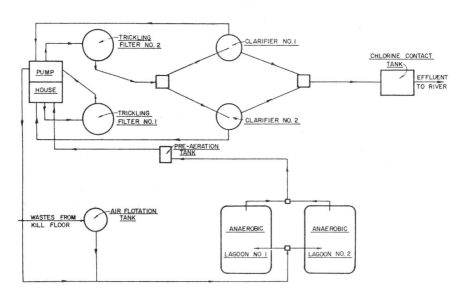

Source: Bell, Galyardt and Wells, EPA Technology Transfer Seminar, Kansas City, Mo. (1973)

After anaerobic treatment, the waste flow is preaerated to satisfy oxygen demand in preparation for discharge to the plastic media trickling filters. These filters are normally used in series, with provisions for parallel operation. The filter effluent is then clarified and disinfected in a chlorine contact basin prior to discharge to the Boyer River. Sludge is wasted back to the anerobic lagoons.

The air flotation unit functions primarily to remove grease and was designed with the following dimensions and performance criteria:

Hydraulic loading	1,500 gpm
BOD removal	40 percent
Grease removal	85 percent
Diameter	22 feet, 6 inches
Depth	12 feet, 0 inches

The anaerobic lagoons were designed to achieve a significant reduction in BOD and to prevent shock loads from upsetting the filters. The basis of their design is as follows:

BOD loading	12,900 pounds/day
Design loading	15 pounds BOD/1,000 ft.^{3}
Depth	14 feet
Surface area	1.97 acres
BOD removal	80 percent

The preaeration basin serves to help reduce odors which may emanate from the anaerobic effluent. Such odors would create serious problems due to the close proximity of a residential area. The design engineers also hoped to begin converting the effluent from the anaerobic lagoons to an aerobic state prior to sending it to the filters. With these factors in mind, the unit was designed with 30 minute detention time and an applied air flow of 100 cfm.

The trickling filters have shown the best results when they have been operated in series. The synthetic filter media is polyvinyl chloride (PVC). This type of media may be loaded at higher rates, is lighter in weight and is more uniform than standard rock media. The media is formed in 2 feet by 4 feet by 2 feet sections which are stacked in layers of 11 cells, resulting in a total depth of 22 feet. Design data for the filters is as follows:

BOD Loading

First stage	101 lbs./1,000 ft.^{3}
Second stage	31 lbs./1,000 ft.^{3}
Hydraulic loading	0.5 gpm/ft.^{2}
BOD removal	91 percent
Diameter	39 feet
Media depth	22 feet

The final clarifiers are considered part of the trickling filter system and are designed to provide adequate settling times for the filter effluent. Two

26-foot diameter clarifiers are utilized at Farmland Foods, each with a surface overflow rate of 800 gpd/ft.^{2}. The chlorine contact chamber was designed for a contact time of 49 minutes and a chlorine dosage rate of 10 mg./l. Table 29 shows the plant efficiencies, both for the total plant and on a unit by unit basis.

TABLE 29:   PLANT EFFICIENCIES IN PERCENT REMOVAL — FARMLAND FOODS, DENISON, IOWA

Unit	BOD	COD	Grease	SS	Coliform
Flotation	33	11	62	32	–
Anaerobic lagoons	82	68	78	59	–
Trickling filters	74	73	69	80	–
Chlorine	–	–	–	–	99+
Total plant removal excluding flotation	97.4	91.5	96.5	93.5	99+

Source: D. Baker and T. White, "Treatment of Meat Packing Waste Using PVC Trickling Filters", National Symposium on Food Processing, Denver, March 23-26, 1971

The operating expenses for the year 1970 are given below. When determined on a daily basis, the cost of operation was approximately $304/day.

Operating Expenses 1970

Salaries	$ 47,893
Utilities	1,443
Maintenance	10,413
Operating debt service	50,900
	$110,649

IOWA BEEF PROCESSORS, INC., DAKOTA CITY, NEBRASKA

The Dakota City, Nebraska, plant of Iowa Beef Processors, Inc., (IBP), lies just outside of the metropolitan Sioux City, Iowa, area. The plant is bounded by Dakota City on the south, South Sioux City on the north, the Missouri River on the east, and a populous surburban area to the west.

The plant has the capacity to slaughter 2,400 head of beef cattle per day, to process 3,000 head per day into institutional cuts, and to bone completely

900 animals per day. Average wastewater flow rates amount to 3 mgd, 33,600 lbs. BOD per day, and 28,000 lbs. SS per day. The average temperature of the waste coming from the combined slaughtering and processing operations ranges between 90° and 105°F. This temperature, combined with the high strength of the waste, is the reason anaerobic lagoons were chosen for the first stage of the new waste treatment facility.

The concept of utilizing rotating biological discs following anaerobic treatment had not been tried prior to development of the IBP Dakota City project. All previous research and operational data had been in the area of domestic wastewater, and it was necessary to establish independent data for the design. As a result, a pilot test program using the anaerobic effluent from one of IBP's existing waste treatment operations, was initiated to evaluate the rotating biological discs.

The pilot plant consisted of three stages of 4-foot rotating discs, each capable of delivering 1,750 gpm, with 50 discs in each stage; followed by a small steel circular clarifier. Composite samples were taken on a regular basis of the influent and effluent from each stage, and the effluent from the final clarifier. Variations were made in speed of rotation of the discs, as well as rate of flow to the units. As a result of the pilot study, design parameters were established for application in the full scale design.

The total waste treatment facility, now nearing completion, consists of a lift station and force main, anaerobic lagoons, rotating biological discs, final clarifiers, and chlorination facilities, as shown in Figure 13. Iowa Beef Processors, Inc., Dakota City, applied for and received a Federal demonstration grant to assist in the construction of the project. The following design criteria were used in the design of the waste treatment facilities:

Design BOD	33,600 lbs./day
Design average flow	3,000,000 gal./day

The lift station consists of three self-priming centrifugal pumps each capable of delivering 1,750 gpm. The pumps are driven by 40 hp.–motors, and deliver the wastewater to the anaerobic lagoons through 6,200 feet of 18-inch force main.

The wastewater is discharged into four anaerobic lagoons operating in parallel. Each lagoon is 15 feet deep with a water surface are of 1.5 acres. The design BOD loading for these lagoons is 12 pounds per 1,000 cubic feet, and BOD removal averages approximately 85%. The wastewater then flows to the rotating biological discs, which are housed in a timber pole building. The design hydraulic loading on the discs is 4.8 gallons per day per square foot, resulting in a total required disc area of 625,000 square feet. This results in a total of 24 shafts of 139 discs each. The discs are 11 feet in diameter and have a surface area of 190 square feet each. The anticipated BOD reduction through the disc system is approximately 70%.

FIGURE 13:   WASTE TREATMENT FACILITIES — IOWA BEEF PROCESSORS, INC., DAKOTA CITY, NEBRASKA

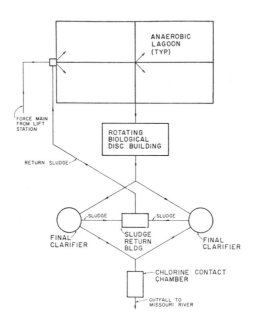

Source: Bell, Galyardt and Wells, EPA Technology Transfer Seminar, Kansas City, Mo. (1973)

Following treatment in the RBS units, the wastewater is discharged to two fifty-five foot diameter clarifiers, each designed for a design average flow of 1.5 mgd. Sludge from the clarifiers is returned to the anaerobic lagoon. The wastewater then flows to the chlorine contact basin, which provides a chlorine contact period of approximately 20 minutes at design average flow. The chlorine facilities include a building and overhead crane for handling ton containers. The effluent from the chlorine contact basin flows 800 feet to the Missouri River through an 18 inch outfall line. The anticipated overall BOD removal through the facility is approximately 90 to 95%.

LYKES BROTHERS, PLANT CITY INDUSTRIAL PARK, FLORIDA

The Lykes Brothers Packing Plant, is located in Florida, a state which does not permit construction of anaerobic lagoons. Moreover, the site available for construction of waste treatment facilities was characterized by high ground water and sandy soil, weighing heavily against any type of large lagoon. The treatment system effluent is discharged into a dry ditch, so a high degree of secondary treatment is required. After consideration of several different treatment schemes, the design engineers concluded that the extended aeration modification of the activated sludge process would best meet the treatment needs of this typically high strength waste.

The packing plant slaughters up to 350 head of cattle per day, and includes beef dressing, smoking and sausage processing in its operation. An extensive program of water conservation and waste flow pretreatment was undertaken prior to commencement of design, in order to minimize the hydraulic and organic loading on the treatment system. The final design criteria, based on 6 pounds of BOD_5 and 900 gallons per head, were as follows: Total daily flow was 315,000 gpd; total BOD_5 was 2,100 lbs./day. The treatment system consists of a grease skimming and sedimentation tank, two extended aeration tanks, final clarifier, polishing lagoon, aerobic disgester and sludge drying beds. The flow diagram is shown in Figure 14.

FIGURE 14: LYKES BROTHERS PACKING PLANT, PLANT CITY, FLORIDA

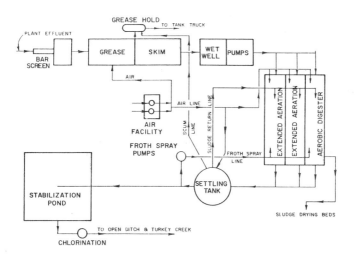

Source: Bell, Galyardt and Wells, EPA Technology Transfer Seminar, Kansas City, Mo. (1973)

The settling-grease skimming basin is sized for 30 minutes detention with a small amount-of air added to aid in water and grease separation. The extended aeration tanks are operated in parallel and are sized on the basis of 20 pounds per day of BOD removed per 1,000 cubic feet of tank volume. The two tanks have a total volume of 105,000 cubic feet, and on the basis of the design flow, provide a retention period of 30 hours. Air is supplied to the aeration tanks at the rate of 1,500 cubic feet per day per pound of applied BOD. Sludge is wasted periodically to the aerobic digester.

The final settling tank is designed for a surface overflow rate of 800 gallons per day per square foot. Settled sludge is returned at a rate of 540 gpm by an air lift pump to the head of the aeration tank or to the aerobic digester. Effluent from the settling tank flows into a five-acre stabilization pond, which serves to provide tertiary treatment prior to chlorination. A 30-minute detention period is provided by a small final pond where chlorine is added at a fixed rate to produce an effluent having a 2 mg./l. minimum chlorine residual.

The aerobic digester has a volume of 37,200 cubic feet. Air is introduced into the digester at the rate of 350 cfm to reduce further the well-oxidized solids developed in the extended aeration process. Periodically, a portion of the digested sludge is wasted to sludge drying beds. Recent sampling data obtained from personnel at Lykes Brothers Packing Plant are given in Table 30 using average values for a recent six month period. This sampling data is based upon an average water usage of 240,000 gallons per day. Concentrations are given in mg./l.

TABLE 30:   WASTEWATER ANALYSIS — LYKES BROTHERS PACKING PLANT

Item	Raw	Effluent from Final Settling Tank	Effluent from Pond
pH	6.9	7.4	7.4
BOD	1,574.0	89.0	15.7
Total solids	5,507	3,621	2,884
Suspended solids	396	180	56
Dissolved oxygen	0.0	0.80	4.40
Chlorides*	1,787	1,700	1,425

*Approximately 1 ton of salt is used every 2 weeks for plant process.

Source: Bell, Galyardt and Wells, EPA Technology Transfer Seminar, Kansas City, Mo. (1973)

Information concerning the design of this facility was obtained from a paper published in the January 1968, Journal of the Water Pollution Control Federation and quoted by Bell, Galyardt and Wells in a paper before an EPA Technology Transfer Seminar at Kansas City, Mo., March 7-8, 1973.

AIR POLLUTION PROBLEMS
AND THEIR CONTROL

RENDERING OPERATIONS

In the processing of various materials including waste in meat packing plants, a very strong stench permeates the atmosphere in the neighborhood of these plants because of the odoriferous materials which escape into the atmosphere as a result of these rendering or cooking operations. While attempts to decrease or avoid this stench have been made, they have been generally unsuccessful in view of the fact that a considerable amount of noncondensible gas emanates from these cookers.

Since the removal of such odors does not involve recovery of any materials from the atmosphere which would have any economic advantage, the purpose of such removal is merely for improving the working conditions of plant employees and the living conditions for persons living in or passing through the neighborhood. Therefore, the expense of such odor removal is not offset in any way by recovery of chemicals, and in order to be attractive for such plants, must be inexpensive as well as efficient.

An investigation of odor control in the rendering industry has been published by D.M. Doty, et al, of the Fish and Proteins Research Foundation Inc. of Des Plaines, Ill. as Report PB 213,386, Washington, D.C., National Technical Information Service (Oct. 1972). Odor controls for rendering plants have been described in a feature article in Environmental Service and Technology 7, (6), 504-510 (June 1973).

As of June 1973, new EPA regulations for stationary source emission covered a number of industrial sources but did not cover rendering plants. As the Wall Street Journal for Wed., June 6, 1973 put it: "Anyone waiting

for Uncle Sam to do something about those smells from the neighborhood
rendering plant had better look instead to state and local air pollution
officials for relief."

A process developed by A.J. Teller; U.S. Patent 3,183,645; May 18,
1965; assigned to Mass Transfer, Inc. involves the deodorization of gases
from rendering vessels or cookers. In this process the odoriferous gas is
passed into a spray chamber and thereafter is passed through a demisting
zone before passage through a bed of adsorbent material such as activated
carbon, the noncondensible gases being pulled through the bed by a
vacuum applied on the opposite side of the adsorbent bed, preferably by
a steam ejector.

The gas from the cookers, etc., enters into the spray chamber in a lower
region and is drawn upward toward the water sprays by a vacuum which is
applied at the gas outlet end of the apparatus which is at a point remote
from the gas inlet. The spray section is located between the gas inlet
and the gas outlet.

Steam and other easily condensible vapors are condensed by the cooling
effect of this spray and the condensate falls to the bottom of the chamber
with the spray water and passes through an outlet having a hydrostatic
leg to insure the reduced pressure conditions. The noncondensed gas is
then passed through a demister which can comprise a finely knit wire mesh
preferably having an open space of about 80 to 90%. This demister removes entrained liquid and solid particles so that they are not deposited
in the bed of adsorbing material through which the gas is next passed.

This adsorbent material is preferably activated carbon, although any other
adsorbent material can be used that will serve as an adsorbent or otherwise effect removal of the odiferous element.

By condensing the condensible vapors from the steam as well as removing
entrained liquid from the steam before the noncondensible gases are ad-
mitted to the bed of adsorbing material, it has been found that the adsorbent is allowed to act more efficiently and in a more concentrated fashion
on the offensive or odiferous material and thereby to effect more efficient
removal of odor from the gas stream.

The separation of the noncondensible gases from the condensible material
is effectively controlled and directed by the application of the vacuum
on the outlet side of the adsorbing bed. This vacuum or decreased pressure
is inexpensively and advantageously effected by a steam ejector or aspirator which has the low pressure side connected to the outlet of the deodor-
izing equipment. The exhaust from the ejector or aspirator can be connected

to the outside atmosphere and the exhaust steam from the ejector together with the deodorized gas can be passed directly into the outside atmosphere.

Figure 15 shows a suitable form of apparatus for the conduct of this process. In the modification shown, the odoriferous gas is fed through inlet (1) into the lower section of chamber (2) in which sprays (3) are located at an intermediate point so that the odoriferous gas must pass through the spray region. In this case, the sprays are supplied with spray water from manifold (4). The spray water and condensate are drained from the bottom of the chamber through outlet (5) which has hydrostatic leg (6) to prevent air from being drawn into the chamber by the vacuum which is maintained therein. Water is supplied to the manifold and sprays through water inlet

FIGURE 15:   VERTICAL SPRAY CHAMBER DEVICE FOR DEODORIZATION OF RENDERING EFFLUENTS

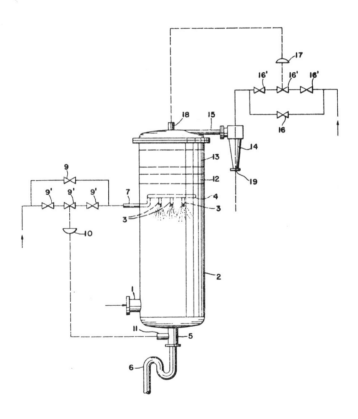

Source: A.J Teller; U.S. Patent 3,183,645; May 18, 1965

(7). Valves (9) and (9') are appropriately adjusted and the water flow is controlled by control (10) which is automatically adjusted in accordance with the temperature of the water in the outlet from the spray chamber. This control is actuated through actuating means (11) which is responsive to the temperature of the outlet water.

After the spray zone, the noncondensible gas is passed through demister (12), which can comprise a series of finely knit wire mesh screens, for the removal of entrained liquid and solid particles. Following this, the gas is passed into an adsorbing bed (13) which can comprise finely divided particles of activated carbon. After passing through the bed of adsorbing material, the gas is completely deodorized and pulled through the top of a chamber by the vacuum effected on the upper region by steam ejector (14) which is connected to outlet means (15) of the chamber.

The rate of steam feed into the ejector is controlled by valves (16) and (16') which are adjusted to give the appropriate conditions and are controlled by steam flow control (17) which reacts to the pressure in the top region of chamber (2) by virtue of pressure sensing means (18) connected at the top of chamber (2). Exhaust steam and deodorized gas pass through outlet (19) of steam ejector (14).

Figure 16 shows a modified form of apparatus for use in this process, in which the spray chamber is arranged in a horizontal position and the apparatus is further modified by the insertion of a cyclone separator through which the gas is passed prior to entry into the spray chamber. The odoriferous gas is passed through tangential inlets (1') which aid in giving a circular motion to the gas as it enters into the chamber (20). Spiral baffle (21) accentuates the centrifugal force applied to the gas, thereby aiding in the precipitation or deposit of entrained fats. The fats thus removed by centrifugation in this cyclone separator section drain out of outlet (22) and then pass into the spraying zone of chamber (2) where spray nozzles (3) are arranged tangentially to aid in the spiral motion for promoting the separation of the condensate from the noncondensible gas stream.

The spray water and condensate are removed through bottom outlet (5'). Water is fed into the spray nozzle through water inlet (7'). This unitary arrangement of equipment rests on supporting legs (22). The noncondensible gas is passed from the spray zone through demister (12), following which it passes through adsorbing bed (13) and then out outlet (15). The vacuum applying means (not shown in this figure) is attached to outlet (15). Hinged cover (23) is designed to permit easy access to the interior of the equipment for cleaning and repair. The cyclone separator section has proved very successful in the recovery of fats entrained in the gas stream coming from cookers. Normally, about 1 to 2% of the fat charged to the cookers is lost

FIGURE 16:   HORIZONTAL SPRAY CHAMBER FOR RENDERING EFFLUENT
DEODORIZATION

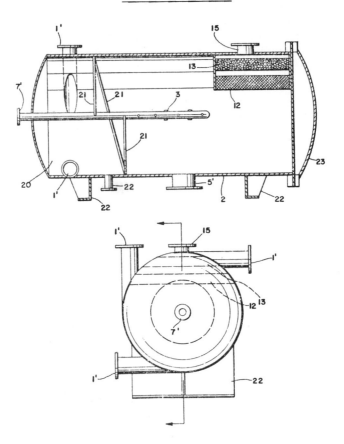

Source: A.J. Teller; U.S. Patent 3,183,645; May 18, 1965

by entrainment in this gas stream. This cyclone separator modification
effects a recovery of at least half of this lost fat. In operating according
to this process, a vacuum of between 0.25 and 14 inches of mercury is
maintained on the exit side of the adsorbing bed. Also, it has been found
that very effective deodorization can be accomplished and various improvements over previous practice can be effected.

As an illustration of the effective operation accomplished, a fully automated unit having a chamber three feet in diameter and eight feet high of
the vertical chamber design shown, utilizing 125 gallons per minute of

water and 50 pounds of steam per hour, was able to completely deodorize the noncondensible gases and to effectively condense the steam from four rendering units and one blood cooker which provided an average of 4,000 pounds per hour of steam together with the noncondensible and odoriferous gases. In addition to the solution of the air pollution problem, the efficiency of the cookers was increased 5 to 10% because of the improved conditions resulting from the process.

In addition, the water consumption was decreased 25% compared with that used in previous operations whereby gas was merely sprayed with water. Moreover, the resultant dried blood product was increased in value because of the improved drying conditions that were effected. Furthermore, because of the lower boiling temperatures resulting from the use of this process, the tallow product recovered from the rendering units had considerably less color than had previously been possible.

A process developed by H.S. Ashley; U.S. Patent 3,499,722; Mar. 10, 1970 involves removing atmosphere polluting odors from systems such as rendering operations by introducing an oxidant and in selected instances a fuel into a combustion chamber located in a low pressure region between a cooker and a condenser.

In the past the gaseous products emitted from the cooker were introduced through a conduit into a condenser, usually a barometric condenser, which produced below atmospheric pressures in the cooker. Then the water from the condenser and the gaseous products were separated and the gaseous products burned in an attempt to remove the odors from the exhaust gases. Such attempts have been unsuccessful, for packing houses continue to emit unusually offensive odors.

Previous attempts to solve the problem of packing house odors failed to prevent the water-soluble gases and substances from going into solution with the condensate water. This system also utilizes a condenser, which is a highly efficient means for producing a vacuum in a cooker, but prevents the pollution of the condensate water with offensive odor-causing water-soluble gases.

The soluble gases from the cooker, when allowed in the past to mix with the condensate water, polluted the water to an extent that some municipalities refuse to permit its reuse. Since 86,431 gallons of water are required to condense 6,000 pounds of steam to produce a vacuum of 24" Hg if the water has a temperature of 80°F., the requirement for using fresh condensing water imposes a burdensome expense on packing house owners. This system will prevent pollution of the condensate water and prevent further contamination of the sewage in municipalities in which condensate water from rendering operations and the like is dumped. The previous systems for eradicating odors from rendering operations that permit the mixing of water-soluble gases and substances with condensate water do not prevent pollution of the atmosphere with offensive odor-causing gases. For once the polluted water is introduced to the atmosphere, as in a cooling tower, some of the soluble gases are liberated from the water and thereby pollute the atmosphere. It is, therefore, the general object of this process to produce an improved system for removing atmosphere polluting odors generally emitting from rendering or other atmosphere polluting operations.

Figure 17 shows a suitable form of apparatus for the conduct of this process. The numeral (11) designates a cooker of the type used in packing houses. It has a gooseneck portion (13) and means (not shown) for introducing residual animal by-products or scraps thereto. This cooker may be of any one of the many suitable forms utilized (usually steam jacketed) in such operations and may have a gas furnace or other suitable form of heating device for raising the temperature of the residual animal products and the broth in which they are cooked to a suitable temperature. This cooker is hermetically and liquid sealed so that a vacuum may be maintained. A conduit (15) extends from a region of the gooseneck portion (13) to a condenser (17). To maximize the efficiency of condensation, the condenser may be of the barometric type so that the condensing water is sprayed directly into the steam. Interposed in conduit (15) is a combustion chamber (19).

FIGURE 17:   INCINERATOR FOR ODOR REMOVAL FROM RENDERING
EFFLUENT VAPORS

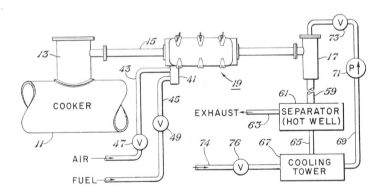

Source: H.S. Ashley; U.S. Patent 3,499,722; March 10, 1970

To further facilitate oxidation of combustible materials emitted from the cooker, a manifold (41) is provided which communicates with a free oxygen-containing gas such as air conduit (43) and a fuel conduit (45), each of the conduits having conventional flow control means such as valves (47), (49).

The substances leaving the combustion chamber are carried through conduit (15) to the condenser (17) and, upon being condensed, flow through another conduit (59) to a separator (61). Here the water condensate, the gases, and the solid products of combustion are separated. In a common type separator (called a hotwell in the meat packing industry) the water is passed through a number of baffles which causes the solid particles to settle to the bottom of the separator and which causes the water-soluble gases as well as the insoluble gases to rise to the top of the separator.

The gases are thereafter introduced to the atmosphere through exhaust (63). These gases are free of offensive odors since all the combustible, odor-causing gaseous substances emitted by the cooker have passed through combustion chamber (53) and have been oxidized. There is, therefore, no contamination of the water condensate. Thus, the odor-free exhaust gases may be dispersed into the atmosphere.

The water condensate may be reused since it has not been contaminated with odor-causing gases or substances. Thus, a conduit (65) extends from separator (61) to a cooling tower (67) and another conduit (69) connects the cooled water in the cooling tower with the condenser (17). A pump (71) may be provided in conduit (69) to cause water flow from the cooling tower to the condenser and a valve (73) provided to regulate the amount of flow. Outside or makeup water may be provided to a collecting pan (not shown) through a conduit (74) and the level of the water controlled by a conventional float valve (76).

A process developed by C.O. Schmidt; U.S. Patent 3,592,614; July 13, 1971; assigned to The Cincinnati Butchers Supply Company is one in which the noncondensable gases from a cooking device are incinerated by the intensely hot high velocity flame of an afterburner which is self-contained and may be associated with any exhaust pipe in which noncondensable gases are present. The flame of the device is produced in an area in which water from the incinerated gases cannot extinguish the flame.

Figure 18 shows such an apparatus, and Figure 19 is a detail of the after-burner. Referring first to Figure 18, there is shown a cooking device (10) for cooking material such as animal offal, bones, or the like. One suitable example of the cooking device (10) is a cooker in which offal, bones, and the like, are cooked to remove most of the water from the waste material. The cooker, which is shown, is steam heated, but any other type of

FIGURE 18:   AFTERBURNER SYSTEM FOR COOKING DEVICE

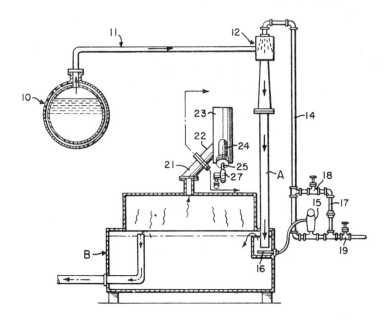

Source: C.O. Schmidt; U.S. Patent 3,592,614; July 13, 1971

suitable heating means may be employed. In cooking the waste material, the vapors escape from the cooking device (10) through a vapor line (11) to a vapor condenser (12). Water is supplied to the vapor condenser (12) through a pipe (14), which is connected to a suitable source of water under pressure, to cause condensation of the condensable vapors, the condensate flowing from the vapor condenser (12) through tail pipe (A) into the hot well (B).

The pipe (14) has flow of water therethrough controlled by a control means (15). The control means (15) is connected to a heat sensing means (16) such as a thermostat, for example, within the hot well (B). Accordingly, the control means (15) allows water to flow to the vapor condenser (12) only when the condensate in the hot well (B) is at a sufficiently high temperature to require additional condensation of the vapors coming from the cooking device (10).

All of the condensable vapors are condensed within the vapor condenser (12). All of the water, which is produced from condensing the condensable vapors, escapes from the vapor condenser (12) through a tail pipe (A) into

FIGURE 19:   AFTERBURNER DETAIL

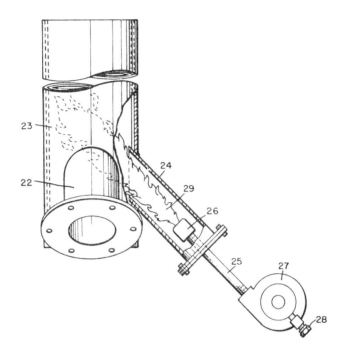

Source: C.O. Schmidt; U.S. Patent 3,592,614; July 13, 1971

the hot well (B). However, the vapor condenser (12) does not remove
the noncondensable noxious gases which are produced by the cooking device (10), since some of the gases from the cooking device (10) are not
condensable. If these noncondensable gases were allowed to pass to the
atmosphere, their noxious property and offensive odors would create pollution of the air and possibly cause the cooking device (10) to have to be
shut down. Accordingly, all of the noncondensable gases pass from the
hot well (B) through a pipe (21). The pipe (21) is connected to and communicates with a pipe (22), which is formed integral with a vertical stack
(23).

The vertical stack (23) has a duct (24) extending therefrom at an angle of
45° (Figure 19) to the longitudinal axis of the stack (23). The duct (24)
is closed at its lower end except for a pipe (25) extending therethrough.
The pipe (25) has a fuel, which is preferably gas, and air flow therethrough
for introduction into the duct (24). The end of the pipe (25) has a nozzle
(26) thereon and within which the ignition of the gas occurs. The initial

combustion of the gas within the nozzle (26) is accomplished by utilizing a match, which is inserted through a small opening (not shown) in the duct (24). The pipe (25) is connected to a high velocity blower (27). The high velocity blower (27) sucks in air from the atmosphere for mixing with gas, which is introduced into the blower (27) through a pipe (28). The pipe (28) is connected to a suitable source of gas under pressure. A valve in the pipe (28) controls the flow of gas therethrough.

Then, as shown in more detail in Figure 19, the ignited gas from the nozzle (26) creates a very hot jet flame (29). This flame has a very high velocity due to the blower (27) so that the flame extends into the vertical stack (23). The velocity of the flame (29) is sufficient to create a sufficient suction in the vertical stack (23) to cause the noncondensable gases to flow or be drawn from the hot well (B) through the pipes (21) and (22) to the vertical stack (23). Furthermore, the flame has a sufficiently high temperature to cause complete incineration of the noncondensable gases within the vertical stack (23). As a result, the oxidable hydrocarbon constituents of the noncondensable vapors are converted to carbon dioxide and water vapor.

The carbon dioxide escapes through the upper end of the vertical stack (23) to the atmosphere. The water vapor is partly condensed into water and flows downwardly to the bottom of the vertical stack (23). The water escapes from the vertical stack (23) through an opening in its lower wall, which closes the bottom of the vertical stack (23).

Since the duct (24) extends into the stack (23) a sufficient distance as shown, the water on the inner surface of the vertical stack (23) is deflected around the duct and cannot flow into the duct (24) but must flow to the bottom of the vertical stack (23). Accordingly, the water within the vertical stack (23) cannot flow into the nozzle (26) to cause the flame (29) to be extinguished. The inner surface of the vertical stack (23) is lined with a refractory material. This is to protect the vertical stack (23) from the intense heat created by the flame (29).

Considering the operation of the afterburner, the cooking device (10) is loaded with waste material. As previously mentioned, the waste material could be offal, bones, and the like, that are to be cooked within the cooking device (10). If the offal, bones, and the like, weighed 10,000 pounds, 5,000 pounds of this total would be water that must be evaporated. Accordingly, this would require approximately 2,000 pounds of water to be condensed each hour by the vapor condenser (12). The gases which have not been condensed in the vapor condenser (12) pass from through the tail pipe (A) into the hot well (B).

When the noncondensable gases escape from the hot well (B) through pipe

(21) and (22) into the vertical stack (23), the intensity of the jet flame
(29) is sufficient to cause all oxidizable hydrocarbon constituents of the
noncondensable gases to be converted into carbon dioxide and water vapor.
The carbon dioxide escapes through the upper end of the vertical stack
(23) while the water vapor is partly condensed and flows through the opening in the lower wall of the vertical stack (23).

A process developed by E.C. Hungate, H.A. Ogletree and G.T. Nickell;
U.S. Patent 3,726,062; April 10, 1973; assigned to Air Conditioning Corp.
involves controlling the emission of odors and particulate matter, for example, from a rendering and meat packing plant. The method comprises
the steps of providing a source of gas, for example air, containing an undesirable level of odor and particulate matter, causing the gas to pass
through a chamber containing a densely sprayed chemical solution which
contacts the gas at a high contact efficiency between the gas and the
liquid to collect and suspend particulate matter in the solution and absorb
odors. This causes the gas again to be placed into forced intimate contact with the solution while simultaneously separating the chemical solution from the cleansed gas.

The method may also include the step of creating a uniform gas velocity
prior to treatment, and in an alternate embodiment, the gas may be subjected to a plurality of spraying treatments with the same or different solutions. The solutions may be acidic, basic, masking, oxidizing, neutralizing, or reacting. Specific solutions disclosed include solutions of water
with sodium bicarbonate, sodium bisulfite, sodium hydroxide, chlorine
dioxide, potassium permanganate, and calcium hypochlorite. Chlorine
gas may also be introduced into the air stream for the same purpose.

SMOKEHOUSE OPERATIONS

A process developed by S.R. Porwancher; U.S. Patent 3,511,224; May 12,
1970; assigned to Michigan Oven Company provides an incinerator for exhausting smoke from a food product smokehouse. The apparatus includes
an insulated vertical cylindrical chamber tapered inwardly at the top, a
deflector for directing smoke from the smokehouse in a turbulent flow into
an intermediate combustion region in the chamber, a burner for burning
the smoke in the combustion region, and means to introduce cooling air
into the base of an exhaust stack extending upwardly from the top of the
chamber.

In cooking and smoking meat and other food products, the product to be
smoked is suspended within a smokehouse. During a part of the cycle of
treatment carried out in the smokehouse, the interior of the smokehouse

is flooded with a heavy dense smoke. This smoke is produced by incomplete combustion of wood chips, carried out in an oxygen-starved atmosphere to produce the desired dense form of smoke.

After the smoking operation is completed, it is necessary to remove the smoke from the smokehouse in order to permit completion of the cooking and other processing and to allow for changing of the smokehouse contents. As might be expected, the exhaust from the smokehouse is extremely dirty and presents substantial problems with respect to air pollution control ordinances and similar regulations. Incinerators have been provided, for use in the smoke exhaust systems of smokehouses, to reduce the undesirable components in the smoke exhaust by burning the smoke. But incinerators employed for this purpose tend to be rather bulky and expensive, particularly because they must handle large volumes of dense smoke within short periods of time in order to permit the smokehouse to be used efficiently.

Furthermore, incinerator systems have presented substantial problems due to the fact that the heavy, dense smoke used in the smokehouse tends to foul any exhaust equipment and incinerator apparatus through which it flows. It is an object of the process, therefore, to provide a new and improved compact smokehouse incinerator that is highly efficient in operation and that will permit the exhaust from a commercial smokehouse to meet antipollution requirements in metropolitan areas.

Figure 20 shows various aspects of the smokehouse exhaust incinerator design. The view at the upper left shows the overall equipment. The view at the upper right is a sectional elevation of the incinerator. The bottom view is a plan view of the incinerator.

The smoke exhaust incinerator system illustrated in the drawings is employed in conjunction with a smokehouse (10) having a roof (11) and side walls (12) and (13). Smokehouse (10) includes two smoke inlet ducts (14), each affording a series of nozzles for introducing a dense, heavy smoke into the interior of the smokehouse. Ducts (14) are connected to a suitable smoke generator (not shown) which may be of conventional construction. In operation, the meat or other food product to be smoked in the smokehouse is suspended on appropriate racks such as the rack (15).

In smokehouse (10), an exhaust duct (16) is located in the center top portion of the house. Duct (16) is provided with a plurality of openings (17) into which smoke, steam, or other components of the smokehouse atmosphere can flow when it is necessary to exhaust the smokehouse as described more fully below.

Duct (16) is connected to an external exhaust duct (18) that leads into a

FIGURE 20:   SMOKEHOUSE EXHAUST INCINERATOR

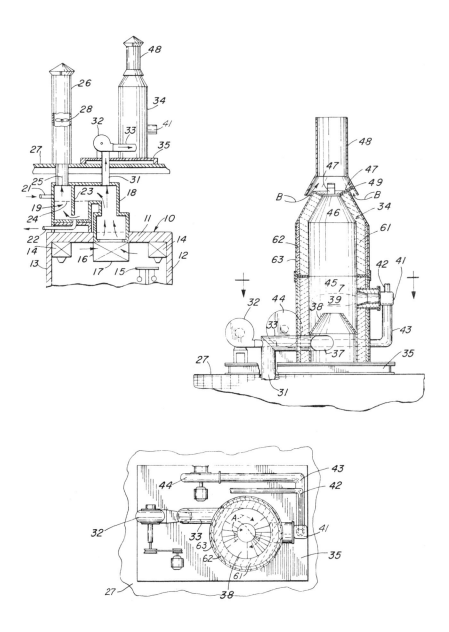

Source: S.R. Porwancher; U.S. Patent 3,511,224; May 12, 1970

water damper (19). Water damper (19) has an inlet (21) through which water may be introduced into the damper, and a drain or outlet (22). There is a central barrier (23) in the water damper. In operation, the water damper can be filled with water to the level indicated by the dashed line (24) to close off the external exhaust duct (18) from a main exhaust outlet (25). Outlet (25) leads to a main exhaust stack (26), through the roof (27) of the building in which the smokehouse (10) is located. The main exhaust stack (26) includes an appropriate main exhaust blower (28).

The external exhaust duct (18) is also provided with a second outlet constituting a smoke exhaust duct (31) that is independent of the main exhaust leading through the water damper (19). Duct (31) is connected to an exhaust blower (32) having an outlet duct (33) that extends into the base of a vertical cylindrical combustion chamber (34). As shown, combustion chamber (34) may be mounted upon an appropriate frame or support (35) mounted on the building roof.

Combustion chamber (34) is a principal element of a smoke exhaust incinerator that is shown in greater detail in the upper right and bottom diagrams. In the preferred construction shown in those figures, blower (32) is an induction blower that forces air under pressure into duct (33) to induce a flow of smoke and air outwardly of the smokehouse from duct (31). This induction exhaust arrangement avoids passing the smoke through blower (32) and thus prevents the substantial solid content of the smoke from fouling the blower.

Duct (33) terminates within the base portion of chamber (34) at one side of the chamber, as indicated by the outlet opening (37). A deflecting means comprising a frusto-conical metal baffle (38) is located within the base of chamber (34) and directs the flow of smoke from the base of the combustion chamber circumferentially upwardly, as indicated by arrows (A), into an intermediate combustion region (39) in the chamber.

The incinerator apparatus comprising combustion chamber (34) further includes a burner (41) for heating and burning the smoke as the smoke traverses the combustion region (39) within the incinerator. Preferably, burner (41) is a gas burner, provided with a gas inlet conduit (42) and an air inlet duct (43), this duct being connected to a blower (44). Burner (41) projects a flame into the intermediate combustion region (39) of the incinerator as generally indicated by the dashed line (45) in the detail at the upper right.

The upper portion of combustion chamber (34) is sloped inwardly toward an outlet opening (46). A series of brackets (47) are mounted around the periphery of the outlet opening (46); these brackets support an exhaust stack (48) that extends upwardly of the combustion chamber outlet and is open to the atmosphere. The lower portion of stack (48) is a flared sleeve (49) that is spaced from the outside wall of combustion chamber (34) to permit the introduction of cooling air into the bottom of the exhaust stack as indicated by the arrows (B).

In operation of the incinerator and exhaust system shown in the drawings, water damper (19) is drained and is empty when steam or other innocuous atmospheric components are exhausted from the interior of smokehouse (10). In this regard it should be noted that for much of the operation of the smokehouse the meat or other food products in the smokehouse are cooked in the absence of smoke, either by steam or dry heat, or both.

When it is desired to evacuate the smokehouse and there is no substantial quantity of smoke present in the house, as when a steam cooking cycle has been completed or when one charge of food product is to be removed and another substituted, the main exhaust stack (26) is employed to the exclusion of the smoke exhaust (31) and incinerator apparatus (34). This makes it possible to exhaust the smokehouse at a high rate and to reduce the cycle time for the smokehouse to a minimum.

Before the beginning of an operating cycle in which smoke is to be exhausted from smokehouse (10), and preferably even before the smokehouse is filled with smoke, water damper (19) is filled with water. This can be accomplished manually or may be effected by automatic controls controlling the operation of the smokehouse. Once the water damper is filled, air or other atmospheric constituents from the smokehouse can no longer escape from the house through main exhaust stack (26).

When it becomes necessary to clear the smokehouse of smoke, blower (44) is started in operation and burner (41) is ignited to heat incinerator chamber (34) in the intermediate region (39). Typically, the incinerator may be heated to a temperature of approximately 1500°F.

With the gas burner (41) in operation, and the incinerator heated, smoke exhaust blower (32) is started in operation. This blower induces a flow of smoke and other gases from smokehouse (10) through exhaust duct (17), external duct (18), smoke exhaust duct (31), and duct (33) into the base of incinerator chamber (34). The smoke swirls around in the lower part of the combustion chamber, as indicated by arrows (A) in the plan view at the base of the figure, and is discharged through the top opening of baffle (38) into the intermediate combustion zone (39) in combustion chamber (34).

The smoke requires a fixed time to pass through the heat portion of the incinerator chamber. Typically, the combustion time for the smoke in chamber (34) may range from 0.3 to 0.5 minute. In a given installation, for use with an eight-cage gas fired smokehouse, the velocity of the smoke at the 1500°F. temperature may be of the order of 500 to 600 feet per minute and the heater (41) may provide a heat input to the incinerator between 500,000 and 800,000 Btu per hour. The foregoing exemplary data are provided on the basis of an assumed requirement of 300 scfm in exhausting the smokehouse.

The incinerator of the process provides effective and rapid burning of the smoke from the smokehouse and makes it possible to exhaust the smokehouse, while meeting air pollution control requirements, in a matter of a few minutes. There is little tendency for the smoke to foul the incinerator apparatus; the smoke never passes through blower (32) and is maintained continuously in movement as it passes through incinerator chamber (34). Virtually all of the smoke is thoroughly and completely burned by the time it escapes from the incinerator through exhaust stack (48).

In the preferred construction illustrated, combustion chamber (34) is provided with a refractory liner (61) and the cylindrical portion of the refractory liner is encompassed by a layer of high temperature insulation (62). The entire combustion chamber is encased in a metal housing (63) which may, in a typical installation, be formed from relatively heavy gauge aluminized steel. The provision of the flared sleeve (49) at the bottom of stack (48) and the mounting of that sleeve in spaced relation to the outer surface of the combustion chamber on the brackets (47), as shown, allows a substantial influx of cooling air to the stack when the incinerator is in operation. This materially reduces the construction cost for the incinerator, because it avoids the necessity of providing a refractory liner, or the use of high temperature alloy steel for stack (48).

PART II.

THE POULTRY PROCESSING INDUSTRY

STRUCTURE OF THE INDUSTRY

As pointed out by R.H. Jones, J.D. Crane and T.A. Bursztynsky of Enviromental Engineering Inc. of Gainesville, Fla. in an EPA Technology Transfer Seminar at Little Rock, Ark. in January 1973, the poultry processing industry is characterized by vertical integration from hatchery through feed mill, processing, and disposal of product on contract basis. The overwhelming mass of production is in broilers, turkeys, and mature chickens.

The rise of poultry production reflects the general growth of the consumptive market with 3.8 billion pounds of broilers and chickens produced in 1950, 6.9 billion pounds in 1960, 9 billion pounds in 1965, and 10.8 billion pounds in 1971 according to the U.S. Department of Agriculture Statistical Reporting Service (January, April 1972). This represents a substantial number of birds at a 1971 average live weight of 3.7 pounds per bird. Turkey production in 1950, 1960, 1965, and 1971 was 0.8 billion pounds, 1.5 billion pounds, 1.9 billion pounds, and 2.3 billion pounds, respectively.

Average turkey live weight may be considered 18.8 pounds per bird. In 1970 the percentages of Federally inspected poultry slaughter by product class were broilers at 77.7%, mature chickens at 6.3%, turkeys at 15.3%, and other poultry at 0.7%. The plants under Federal inspection slaughtered over 90% of the U.S. Poultry production in 1970 according to The Poultry Processing Industry; Marketing Research Report No. 965, Economic Research Service, U.S. Department of Agriculture (June 1972).

The large size and concentration of the poultry processing industry becomes particularly important in view of its waste generation. In poultry processing, feathers, blood, dirt, and viscera are removed from a product that must be made acceptable for human consumption. Large quantities of water are consumed in both washing and cleaning the poultry in processing and also to carry away large amounts of waste to screening and ultimate disposal. The highly organic nature of the waste may cause bacterial blooms, depressed oxygen levels, and severely disrupted biota in receiving streams. Waste discharged to a sewage treatment system provides a substantial loading in terms of population equivalent, escaping grease, feathers, and offal. These constituents hamper treatment processes and are subject to substantial sewer use surcharges by municipalities.

DEFINITION OF POULTRY PROCESSING

Poultry processing is defined for purposes of this section to include all plants engaged in slaughtering, dressing, and packing of poultry. The deletion of small game dressing and egg breaking was necessitated because of the lack of information for these categories, according to the Federal Water Pollution Control Administration in Publication IWP-8.

Two types of plants are considered in this section, the turkey processing plant and the chicken/broiler processing plant. Both plants are engaged in the slaughtering and packaging of their respective products. The two types of plants were considered separately because of the seasonal operation of the turkey processor.

Poultry processing is carried out under government supervision for interstate commerce shipments. The industry is characterized by a large number of small, independent local processors, usually not being government inspected. For this reason average figures had to be used many places in the report because of the lack of adequate information. It should be noted by the reader that this classification as defined above differs from the SIC classification number 2015 used by the Federal Government.

MEASURE OF PLANT AND INDUSTRY SIZE

Poultry processors typically indicate size of plant by referring to the number of birds processed per time period. The literature in the field, therefore, incorporates this measurement of size. The water use and pollution per bird for a broiler processor will differ from that of the turkey processor. Total liveweight, therefore, is used as the common denominator for the calculations in this report.

Since the majority of poultry statistics are in numbers of birds processed, a conversion factor had to be developed for converting numbers of birds to liveweight figures. The conversion factor utilized here is 4.25. When the number of birds is multiplied by 4.25, the result is liveweight in pounds. This factor is accurate only when applied to annual data because of the seasonal effect of turkey processing.

DEFINITION OF RELEVANT TERMS

In the interest of clarity the definitions of terms to be used throughout this report are given below.

Eviscerated poultry — poultry which has had its head, feet, and viscera removed.

Offal — includes head, feet, and viscera.

Viscera — the heart, lungs, liver, and intestines of the bird.

Broiler — a bird grown eight to nine weeks with a liveweight of approximately 3.5 pounds.

Chicken — a catch-all classification of poultry with an average weight of approximately 4.8 pounds.

Turkey — a type of poultry with the average weight of 14.1 pounds. In this report turkeys can weigh from eight to thirty pounds, the heavier birds being less popular than those of lighter weight.

SOURCE OF DATA

Questionnaires were sent to the poultry processors in the course of the Federal Water Pollution Control Administration study reported in Publication IWP-8. A sample was selected from each state and weighted to reflect the position of the state, as compared with total U.S. production. The names and addresses of plants were obtained from the Who's Who in the Egg and Poultry Industries, published by the Watt Publishing Co., Mount Morris, Illinois, 1967 edition. The questionnaire received a 41% response which represented 28% of the total number of birds processed in 1966. This indicates that a large percentage of the large processors did not answer. Nevertheless, it is assumed that the sample obtained was sufficiently large and typical to justify its use as basis for this report.

CHARACTERISTICS OF THE POULTRY PROCESSING INDUSTRY

The poultry processing industry has undergone a process of vertical integration. The integration process has been carried out to ensure the constant

supply of uniformly high quality birds. The process of integration has en-
abled the processor to avail himself of the economies achieved by scheduling production at near optimum capacity.

Vertical integration was preceded by a change in the form of the marketable product. When the "cold pack" or eviscerated bird replaced the
"New York Dressed" bird, it was possible to freeze and store processed
poultry. The change in the dressing process also made it possible for the
processor to locate farther from the market areas. Therefore, it can be
stated that the dressing change helped to speed up the integration process.

An Agricultural Marketing Service study lists the six following points as
contributing factors for the growing integration of the poultry industry:

(1) The opportunity to increase profits by lowering
     costs through more efficient coordination of
     both the production and marketing processes

(2) The need for outside financing and technical
     assistance for many producers

(3) The increasing awareness among retailers of the
     need for uniformly high quality... (poultry)

(4) The increasing size of retail operations which
     give retailers greater power in enforcing their
     demands

(5) The inability of pricing methods to bring forth
     production of uniformly high quality... (broilers)
     and a uniform seasonal distribution of volumes
     and sizes

(6) The inability, in many instances, to obtain the
     benefits from larger sales of feed by developing
     contractual arrangements

The integration process is proceeding at a rapid pace in most regions; however, the large producing regions are showing the greatest amount of change.
Finally, it should be noted that the shift from the "New York Dressed"
poultry, where only blood and feathers are removed, to cold pack or eviscerated poultry in 1955-1957 presented the industry with its first waste disposal problems. Now it is all but impossible to find "New York Dressed"
poultry in the market place. The effect upon the processing industry has
been the development of poultry by-product rendering facilities to handle
the increased amounts of waste material created through the sale of eviscerated poultry.

The industry has undergone a tremendous phase of integration in past years as just noted above. With profit margins decreasing as a result of falling market prices, the poultry processor was forced into cutting costs in order to survive. Because economies of scale existed, costs were reduced by increasing the size of processing plants.

Growth of the processing plant was accompanied by vertical integration within the industry, since large processors required large numbers of high quality, uniformly sized birds delivered on predetermined schedules to meet the demands of faster, mechanized equipment. In order to guarantee the regular delivery of birds, the processor gained control of poultry growing and distribution channels. Thus, the processing industry moved closer to its source of supply, the South Atlantic and Central Atlantic States.

REGIONAL DISTRIBUTION OF THE POULTRY INDUSTRY

Poultry is processed in every state, but nine states produce and process approximately 75% of the nation's broilers and 70% of the nation's chickens. The nine states are Alabama, Arkansas, Delaware, Georgia, Maryland, Mississippi, North Carolina, Texas, and Virginia. Table 31 gives the breakdown of states contained within each poultry region as defined by the USDA. As the industry has grown over the past decade, processing plants have become larger, and the industry in general has become more centralized.

TABLE 31:   STATES IN POULTRY REGIONS

North Atlantic	Western	East North Central
Maine	Idaho	Ohio
New Hampshire	Colorado	Indiana
Vermont	Arizona	Illinois
Massachusetts	Utah	Michigan
Rhode Island	Washington	Wisconsin
Connecticut	Oregon	
New York	California	
New Jersey		
Pennsylvania		

South Atlantic	South Central	West North Central
Delaware	Kentucky	Minnesota
Maryland	Tennessee	Iowa
Virginia	Alabama	Missouri
West Virginia	Mississippi	Nebraska
North Carolina	Arkansas	Kansas
South Carolina	Louisiana	
Georgia	Oklahoma	
Florida	Texas	

Source: FWPCA Publication IWP-8

The industry's low profit margin will exclude the survival of all but the large processor. As noted before, the survival of large processors is due to the tremendous economies of scale experienced in both the growing and processing industry. Thus, it is expected that the South Atlantic, South Central, and Western regions will continue to grow at the expense of other regions.

DEFINITION OF PLANT SIZE

Table 32 which was constructed from data received from questionnaire responses, defines plant sizes. It defines plant sizes in terms of small, medium, or large. The number and total liveweight of birds processed per day, the total liveweight in each size class as a percent of total industry slaughter, and the number of pounds of liveweight killed for a typical plant in each class is presented. The "typical" plant in each size class is the plant size which will be used in estimating costs of pollution reduction later.

TABLE 32:   DEFINITION OF PLANT SIZE IN NUMBER OF BIRDS PROCESSED PER DAY AND POUNDS LIVEWEIGHT

Plant Size	Range in Numbers of Birds per Day	Range in Pounds Liveweight per Day	% of Total Liveweight Killed in Size Class as of 1966	Typical Plant in Size Group Pounds per Day
Small	0 to 25,000	0 to 100,000	39	60,000
Medium	25,000 to 95,000	100,000 to 380,000	52	200,000
Large	95,000 to 240,000	380,000 to 960,000	9	400,000

Source: FWPCA Publication IWP-8

Table 33 shows the size range of plants by technology level and by size groups of small, medium, and large. A detailed definition of "technology level" as it relates to poultry processing plants will be found in the next section of this volume which deals with Poultry Processing Processes and Pollutants (see Table 36).

The median size plant is also given for each size group by level of technology. An interesting characteristic of the median is that it tends to fall at the lower end of the size group in both the medium and large size groups. The reason for this is that processing plants for the most part tend to fall at the lower end of each size group bringing the median down. The few large plants in each size group account for the extremely wide range of the group but had little influence upon the median. For this reason the median, rather than the mean, was decided upon as the measure of central tendency. Notice that in all size groups the median size plant was larger as technology improved.

TABLE 33:   DEFINITION OF PLANT SIZES BY TECHNOLOGY LEVELS*

Plant Size	Old Technology (Range)	Median	Typical Technology (Range)	Median	Advanced Technology (Range)	Median
Small	1 to 3	2	3 to 10	5	10 to 25	130
Medium	25 to 35	30	35 to 45	40	45 to 95	50
Large	95 to 110	100	110 to 125	115	125 to 240	130

*Daily figures in 1,000's of birds

Source: FWPCA Publication IWP-8

PROCESSES AND POLLUTANTS

All poultry processing plants have the same basic processing flow stream. This flow stream has evolved as the best way to proceed in what is a relatively simple procedure of slaughtering and cleaning poultry for marketing. Live poultry is unloaded at the processing plant and taken to a killing station where jugular veins are cut while the poultry is suspended from a conveyor chain. A bleeding area is reserved to confine blood from the carcass.

The bird is then scalded with hot water to loosen its feathers. Feathers are removed mechanically and manually. Residual hairs and feathers are singed off with a flame or by wax stripping, and the bird is surface washed. The washed bird is eviscerated manually and washed internally and again externally. The carcass is then chilled or frozen, packaged, and shipped to a market.

Figure 21 provides a brief flow chart of a poultry processing plant giving the major steps in poultry processing.

Figure 22 shows each processing step and its place in the process. The dotted line encloses those processes with which this report is concerned. As can be seen from Figure 22 these processes involve many steps, the majority of which contain pollution potential. The area enclosed by the dotted lines represents the processing area with the greatest pollution potential.

FIGURE 21:   FLOW CHART OF POULTRY PROCESSING PLANT

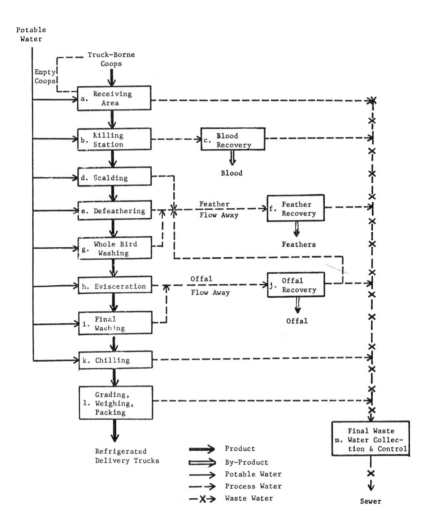

Source: Market Research Report No. 965, Economic Research Service,
USDA (June 1972)

FIGURE 22:   MAJOR STEPS IN POULTRY PROCESSING

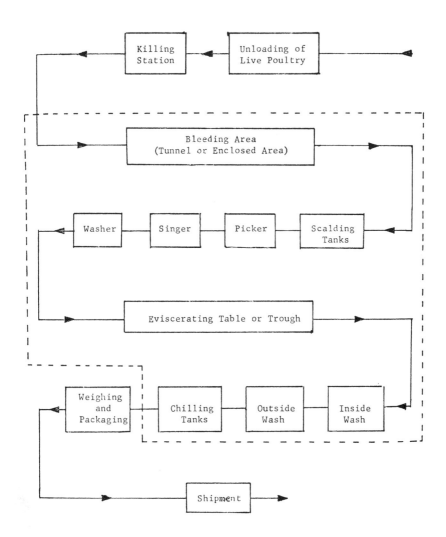

Source: FWPCA Publication IWP-8

RECEIVING LIVE POULTRY

Most processing plants receive their live birds by truck, and the coops containing the birds are moved directly from the truck to the processing line or to storage. In the past it was a common industrial practice to hold the birds in a storage area; storage time varied from a few hours to as long as one week.

The changing face of the industry has proven storage uneconomical as well as unnecessary. Birds are grown under such controlled conditions today that those brought to the processing plant are within a specified weight and age range. The quality of the birds received remains at a constant level because of the controlled environment in which the birds live during their growing life, which is usually a period of eight to nine weeks.

At most poultry dressing establishments truck shipments of poultry are scheduled in a fashion that facilitates the direct movement of poultry from the delivering truck to the processing line. Smaller poultry operations may hold live birds for a few hours to ensure adequate numbers before beginning killing operations. Manure deposits accumulated during the holding period are an additional source of BOD.

The birds are removed from the coops and attached by their feet to shackles suspended from an overhead conveyor line. The conveyor line is moved at a prescribed rate of speed which is governed by the processing operation. Large dressing plants will have more than one conveyor serving the receiving and processing areas of the plant. The birds are moved directly from the receiving dock to the killing area by the conveyor.

KILLING OPERATION

Poultry are slaughtered in several different ways: the two most common ways are debraining and severance of the jugular vein. This operation is not covered by government regulation and is left up to the processor as long as sanitation and health requirements are met. The larger dressing establishments collect the blood which after further processing becomes a salable by-product or is sold raw to a rendering plant.

Some smaller plants flush the blood directly into the sewer, thus increasing the strength of the effluent. Sewage strength at least is doubled if all blood is allowed to enter the plant sewer. From the killing room the birds proceed through a bleeding chamber where blood is collected. Then they proceed to the scalding tanks. Blood collection has the highest amount of pollution potential of any process within the plant. If all blood were allowed to enter the sewer, it would increase the BOD of plant effluent at the rate of forty pounds per thousand birds killed. Blood collection which reaches an efficiency of 90% will reduce the plant BOD by approximately 38%.

The plant sewer system will receive a "shock load" when the blood collection area is cleaned. This amount represents a very small amount of total collectable blood, but the pollution potential of blood is so great that it deserves mention. The entire clean-up operation of a typical plant will give a BOD loading factor of about four pounds per thousand birds.

SCALDING

The purpose of the scalding operation is to remove all dirt and blood from the exterior surface of the carcass and to loosen feathers. The scalding operation can be carried on in either one of two ways:

(1) The birds can be scalded by the use of a spray.
(2) The birds can be scalded by immersion in a tank containing heated water.

The latter operation is the most widely used method. Water temperature can range from approximately 128° to 140°F., depending upon the type of scalding desired by the processor.

Water in the scalding tank is maintained at the desired temperature by the continuous addition of hot water; the rate of addition is approximately one-quarter to one-half gallon per bird. Excess water overflows into the sewer along with the tank drainings at the end of the processing period. The drain water will contain significant amounts of dirt and blood which add to sewage strength.

Scalding Tanks: Scalding tanks present a "shock load" waste problem. Immersion of the birds will result in a buildup of dirt and gum deposits in the tank bottom. These deposits have a high BOD and solids content. The dumping of the tank represents a shock load to the treatment facilities. When the tank water is drained at the end of the processing period, the plant effluent experiences a rise in strength which is incorporated into the clean-up period BOD figures in Table 34.

Spray Scalding: Spray scalding allows the same amount of dirt and gum to enter the plant effluent, but this amount is spread throughout the processing day.

TABLE 34:   WASTE PRODUCTION BY PROCESS

Technology Levels	Wasteload lbs. BOD/day	Wastewater (mgd)
"Typical Technology" (125,000 birds per day) Recovery of blood and		
flow-away system	2,581	0.93 - 1.0
Wet cleanup	1,385	1.0 - 1.6
Total	3,966	
"Old Technology" (25,000 birds per day) No blood recovery and		
nonflow-away system	575	0.065 - 0.11
Dry cleanup followed by		
wet cleanup	80	0.032
Total	655	0.065 - 0.14
"Advanced Technology" (150,000 birds per day) Recovery of blood and		
flow-away system	3,322	0.9 - 1.2
Recirculation of water	-	0.02
Wet cleanup	585	0.27
Total	3,907	0.9 - 1.3

Source: FWPCA Publication IWP-8

DEFEATHERING

Feathers are mechanically removed from the birds immediately following the scalding operation. The feather removal process is carried out in several different fashions.

Batch Removal of Feathers: This is accomplished by removing the birds from the overhead conveyor, by hand, and placing them in a rotating cylindrical machine which removes the feathers. The cleaned birds are then gathered up by hand and resuspended from the moving overhead conveyor. This is not the usual method used because of the excessive amount of hand labor necessary to keep a continuous, even-flowing operation. The batch method is the most commonly used in small slaughtering operations.

Line Defeathering: This is the more popular method, since the bird remains suspended from the conveyor and is passed in front of rotating drums
containing rubber fingers which beat the feathers off the bird.   Continuous
streams of water wash feathers from the carcass to a flume and then from
the picking area to a central gathering location.   A screening operation is
then conducted to separate feathers and water.   This operation will be discussed later.   Nonflow-away operations remove the feathers from the picking area by hand or by machine and deposit them in containers.   Both operations require a washdown of the picking area at the end of the processing period.

After the picking operation has been completed, pin feathers are removed
by hand or by wax stripping.   Wax stripping increases the pollution problem
in that some wax inadvertently escapes into the sewer.   After stripping, the
bird passes through an arc-gas flame to singe fine hair and remaining pin
feathers.   The bird is then passed through an "outside washer, " a continuous
spray of water that washes the exterior surface of the carcass.

The defeathering process has a pollution potential of great magnitude because of the volume of feathers involved.   One thousand birds will yield
approximately seventy pounds of feathers.   If no attempt is made to collect
feathers, the sewage disposal problem becomes overwhelming for a plant
killing twenty-five thousand birds per day.   Such a plant would yield close
to two thousand pounds of feathers per day.

The batch removal processes of defeathering involves the use of water to
wash the feathers from the drum-like machine during the processing period.
In the line defeathering method, water is used to wash feathers from the
carcasses.   There is no substantial pollution difference in these two methods
of removing feathers.   Processing plants use screens to separate the feathers from the water, which emerges from the plant as wastewater.   If the
screens become plugged, the resulting overflow of the screens will carry
feathers into the sewer.

An alternative to the above process is the use of line defeathering with
mechanical conveying of feathers from the picking area to a truck.   The
few feathers which cling to the carcass are washed off with water.   An advantage of this method over the process of flow-away with screening is that
this method eliminate the chance of feather overflow into the sewer due to
plugged screens.

EVISCERATION

The evisceration area of the processing plant is enclosed and separated from

the other portions of the plant to ensure sanitary operation and avoid contamination. The first step of evisceration is the removal of the lower leg
portion. The birds are then suspended from the conveyor in a fashion which
facilitates removal of viscera. Subsequent operations remove inner organs
and separate the edibles (heart, liver, and gizzard) from the inedibles.
Flow-away systems are employed by the great majority of processors because of the convenience offered in handling evisceration wastes. The
only drawback of this system is the large amount of water required to accomplish the physical movement of the viscera.

When evisceration is completed the carcass is thoroughly washed by an
"inside washer" which spray-washes the interior of the bird. The bird is
then inspected by the U.S. Department of Agriculture to ensure that the
final product meets all necessary health specifications. If further processing is desired, the carcasses may be cut up and processed for special pack-
ages such as wings, breasts, legs, etc. This operation may entail packaging
and replacing of neck, heart, liver, and gizzard into the carcass.

PACKING

The cleaned and processed poultry are either chilled or frozen before ship-
ment. The removal of animal heat is very important in the processing operation. At this point flavor and marketing life can be greatly reduced by
improper handling of the chilling or freezing operation.

Federal rules and regulations excerpted below, govern chilling and freezing
operations. Large poultry processors use two or three mechanical chill tanks
in series for carcasses and a series of smaller tanks for giblets. Iced or refrigerated water is added to the first chill tank at a rate to reduce the carcass temperature to around 65°F.

> With respect to chilling systems using continuous chillers,
> the amount of water intake necessary to provide an over-
> flow that will be sufficient to accomplish a sanitary op-
> eration shall not be less than one-half gallon per frying
> chicken in the first section of the chilling unit.

The second and third chill tanks continue to lower the carcass heat to 34°F.,
a process which is accomplished in about 30 minutes. The USDA allows recirculation of the water from the second and third tank to the first tank;
however,

> Sufficient water or ice or ice and water shall be added
> to subsequent sections of the chilling system (tanks two

and three) so that the chilling media in all sections is
maintained reasonably clear and there shall be a continuous overflow from each section.

Older plants generally do not have mechanical equipment for quick chilling, and they generally place birds in portable tubs containing ice and
water. This operation is referred to as slow chilling.

After the birds and giblets are chilled, they are placed on a conveyor line
to allow outer water to drain. The birds are then sized by weight, graded,
and packed. Birds to be frozen are generally wrapped in appropriate containers. The great majority of birds are packed in crates containing ice
and then shipped in refrigerated trucks.

The percent of plants employing the various processing and subprocessing
methods can be seen in Tables 35 and 36. Table 35 presents the percent
of plants employing each subprocess method with projections to 1977. Table
36 gives the percent of plants employing each technology level in 1967 as
ascertained from the questionnaire data.

TABLE 35: PERCENTAGE OF PLANTS USING VARIOUS PROCESSES

Production Process and Significant Subprocesses	Percentage of Plants Employing Process				
	1950	1963	1967	1972	1977
RECEIVING					
(1) Direct placement of birds on conveyor	50	80	90	92	93
(2) Birds retained in storage battery	50	20	10	8	7
KILLING AND BLEEDING					
(1) Recovery of all blood	30	40	60	80	80
(2) Recovery of no blood	70	60	40	20	20
FEATHER REMOVAL					
(A) Scalding					
(1) Immersion in scald tank	80	70	60	70	70
(2) Spray scalding	20	30	40	30	30
(B) Defeathering					
(1) Line defeathering with continuous spray of water	50	65	80	82	85
(2) Batch defeathering in cyclic type machines	50	35	20	18	15
(C) Pin Feather Removal					
(1) By hand	98	95	93	90	89
(2) Wax stripping	2	5	7	10	11
OFFAL REMOVAL					
(1) Dry dumping of offal (nonflow-away)	70	45	27	19	9
(2) Wet dumping of offal (flow-away)	20	50	71	80	90
(3) Dumping offal into sewer (possible side result of either non or flow-away system)	10	5	2	1	1

(continued)

TABLE 35:   (continued)

Production Process and Significant Subprocesses	Percentage of Plants Employing Process				
	1950	1963	1967	1972	1977
REUSE OF CHILL TANK OVERFLOW					
(1) No reuse	80	70	54	45	25
(2) Reuse--to supplement water flow-away system	20	30	46	55	75
CLEANUP					
(1) Dry cleanup followed by wet cleanup	80	50	29	20	10
(2) Wet cleanup	20	50	71	80	90

Source: FWPCA Publication IWP-8

FIGURE 36:   PERCENTAGE OF PLANTS USING EACH TECHNOLOGY LEVEL

Technology Levels and the Associated Typical Subprocesses	Estimated % of Plants by Type of Technology	Proportion of Plants of This Type by Size as of 1967			Size Range of Plants by Type of Technology Million Birds per Day
		Small	Medium	Large	
TYPICAL TECHNOLOGY	56	0.26	0.66	0.08	3 - 240
(1) Direct placement of birds on conveyor from receiving truck					
(2) Recovery of all blood due to immobilization of birds					
(3) Flow-away system for removal of feathers and offal from the processing area					
(4) Shipment of processed poultry in ice					
(5) Wet cleanup of plant					
OLD TECHNOLOGY	41	0.40	0.55	0.05	1 - 50
(1) Holding of live poultry in storage batteries					
(2) Recovery of no blood					
(3) Nonflow-away system for removal of feathers and offal from processing area					
(4) Removal of carcass body heat by submersion in portable vat containing ice and water					
(5) Shipment of processed poultry in ice					
(6) Dry cleanup followed by wet cleanup					
ADVANCED TECHNOLOGY	3	0.05	0.17	0.77	20 - 300
(1) Direct placement of birds on conveyor from receiving truck					
(2) Recovery of all blood due to immobilization of birds					
(3) Flow-away system for removal of feathers and offal from the processing area					
(4) Removal of carcass body heat by submersion into mechanical chilling tanks containing refrigerated water					
(5) Shipment of processed poultry frozen					
(6) Wet cleanup of plant					

Source: FWPCA Publication IWP-8

POULTRY PROCESSING WASTELOADS
AND CHARACTERISTICS

As described by Gurnham & Associates, pollution control consultants of Chicago, Ill. in an EPA-sponsored seminar on upgrading poultry processing facilities to reduce pollution at Little Rock, Arkansas in January 1973, the waterborne wastes from the poultry industry may be summarized as shown in Table 37.

TABLE 37:   TYPES OF WATERBORNE WASTES FROM THE POULTRY
INDUSTRY

Process Wastes:
  Manure
  Blood
  Feathers
  Offal
  Viscera
  Heads, necks, lungs, bones
  Fats and greases
  Decomposed residues of the above

Ancillary Wastes:
  Clean-up wastes
  Sanitary sewage from plant and office personnel
  Water treatment wastes
  Boiler blowdown wastes
  Spent cooling waters
  Kitchen and cafeteria wastes
  Laundry wastes
  Stormwater and runoff:
     From live bird storage areas
     From parking and trucking areas
     From roofs and other areas

Source: Gurnham & Assoc., EPA Technology Transfer Seminar,
          Little Rock, Ark. (Jan. 1973)

From the previous table, which is essentially a definition of wastes in
industry terms, one progresses to an expression of wastes in the standard
parameters of pollution control technology such as are used in waste control regulations. Table 38 gives such a listing in pollution control terminology.

TABLE 38:   MAJOR POLLUTANTS FROM THE POULTRY INDUSTRY

Most significant parameters:
    *Total suspended matter
    Biochemical oxygen demand (BOD)
    Grease

Other Significant Parameters:
    Temperature
    Color
    Odor
    pH value
    Acidity and alkalinity
    Turbidity
    *Settleable matter
    *Dissolved matter
    *Total residue on evaporation
    Chemical oxygen demand (COD)
    Total organic carbon (TOC)
    Ammonia nitrogen
    Total Kjeldahl nitrogen
    Phosphate
    Total coliform
    Fecal coliform

*The items starred may be further classified as Volatile or Fixed.

Source: Gurnham & Assoc., EPA Technology Transfer Seminar,
          Little Rock, Ark. (Jan. 1973)

WASTE CHARACTERISTICS

Some details of the definition, significance, sources, typical values,
limitations and analytical determination of the three major pollutant categories are given in Tables 39, 40 and 41.

TABLE 39:   TOTAL SUSPENDED MATTER

Alternately Called: Nonfiltrable residue, or suspended solids (SS).

Includes: Materials removed by laboratory filtration. However, should
   not include coarse or floating matter (e.g., bones and heads),
   because of the impossibility of obtaining a proper sample.

Significance: A measure of visible pollution. Also a measure of material
   that may settle in quiet parts of natural streams or sewers, causing
   clogging, unsightly deposits or sludge banks, and similar problems.

Sources: Almost all water-using areas in plant, such as holding pens,
   eviscerating and processing. Also all clean-up operations.

Raw Waste Loading: No "typical" value. A recent study of 8 broiler
   plants showed a range from 2.4 to 97 pounds per 1,000 birds;
   average 27. At 8 gallons per bird, this average corresponds to
   a concentration of 400 mg./l.

Limitations: Both waterway and sewer standards usually ban sludges and
   floating debris. Otherwise, some areas have no regulation, and in
   others it may be as low as 35 mg./l. for waterways, 200 for sewers.
   Surcharge ordinances often charge only for excess above 200 mg./l.

Analysis: Filter on glass fiber disc; wash; dry at 103°C.; weigh.

Source: **Gurnham & Assoc., EPA Technology Transfer Seminar,
   Little Rock, Ark. (Jan. 1973)**

TABLE 40:   BIOCHEMICAL OXYGEN DEMAND (BOD)

Significance: An indirect measure of the biodegradable organic pollutant. More specifically, a measure of the oxygen consumed by
   aerobic decomposition of the waste, under carefully specified conditions. It can be related to depletion of oxygen in a natural stream,
   or to the oxygen requirements for waste treatment by aerobic biological processing (secondary treatment).

Sources: All organic materials that enter the waste stream, including
   manure, blood, particles of flesh, fats, and waste products.

Raw Waste Loading: Widely variable. A recent study of 18 broiler
   plants showed a range from 14 to 70 pounds per 1,000 birds; average
   37. At 8 gallons per bird, this average corresponds to a concentration of 550 mg./l.

Limitations: In streams, the BOD concentration should not be high enough
   to reduce the dissolved oxygen (DO) level too far; e.g., not below
   about 4 mg./l. DO for most fish life. This is not a simple relationship, as the BOD reaction is slow, and DO is simultaneously replenished
   by natural means. Many states restrict the BOD of effluents to 20 or
   30 mg./l.; or to lower values if the stream is small in comparison to
   the flow of effluent. For discharge to a municipal sewer, a limitation
   of 200 to 300 mg./l. is often applied, and surcharge rates often apply
   above 200.

Analysis: Incubate a sample at 20°C. for 5 days, after mixing with oxygen-
   saturated water, biological seed, and chemical nutrients. Measure
   DO before and after incubation, and calculate the loss of DO as the
   BOD. All conditions must be carefully controlled, and procedures
   followed exactly (see analytical texts).

Source: **Gurnham & Assoc., EPA Technology Transfer Seminar,
   Little Rock, Ark. (Jan. 1973)**

TABLE 41:   GREASE

Alternately Called: Oil and Grease; Hexane-solubles; Petroleum-ether-
solubles.

Significance: Oily materials form unsightly films, interfere with aquatic
life, clog sewers, disturb the biological process in sewage treatment
plants, and may be a fire hazard.

Sources: Primarily from evisceration, but also significant in other areas
and in clean-up.

Raw Waste Loading: Widely variable. Three broiler plants studied recently
varied from 3 to 11 pounds per 1,000 birds; average 6. At 8 gallons
per bird, this average corresponds to a concentration of 90 mg./l.

Limitations: In waterways, grease is limited in that it must not be visible;
a proposed limitation is 15 mg./l. In sewers, a typical limitation is
100 mg./l.; some cities are more severe.

Analysis: Acidify; filter; dry; extract with hexane or equivalent;
evaporate solvent; dry; weigh. Directions must be followed exactly
(see analytical texts).

Source: Gurnham & Assoc., EPA Technology Transfer Seminar,
Little Rock, Ark. (Jan. 1973)

Some details of the significance, sources, limitations and determination
of the other significant parameters in Table 38 are shown in the tabulation
in the text which follows.

Temperature: In streams, high temperature (thermal pollution) decreases
the solubility of oxygen, is detrimental to aquatic life, and accelerates
the development of septicity. In sewers it accelerates corrosion and
septicity and interferes with settling at the treatment plant. Thermal
pollution is primarily from cooking wastes, also from the use of steam and
hot solutions during cleaning. Temperature rise in streams is usually limited to a few degrees above ambient, with a maximum temperature of 85°
to 95°F. Sewer limitation is commonly 140° to 150°F.

Color: Primarily esthetics; may be troublesome for certain industrial uses,
as in the food, paper, and textile industries. It comes mostly from blood.
Drinking water is limited to 15 color units; food processing water limits
range from 5 to 20 units. Analysis is performed by comparing visually or
photoelectrically, with standards made from chloroplatinic acid compounds.

Odor: Esthetically objectionable; may indicate other types of pollution,
often resulting from septicity (anaerobic conditions). There are many
sources; most important are manure, offal, and blood. It is usually restricted, but by qualitative indication only. Analysis is performed as
follows: prepare sample in a series of dilutions, and determine "threshold"

or barely detectable value. A panel of several experienced judges should be used. Taste is somewhat analogous to odor in significance, sources, and methods of determination. Taste is not commonly measured or estimated in wastewaters; but may nevertheless be significant in the receiving water.

pH Value: pH is a measure of the ionic concentration of hydrogen ion, and thus of the strength of acid or alkali. pH is the base-10 logarithm of the reciprocal of the hydrogen-ion concentration in gram-mols per liter. It is generally considered to range from 0 to 14, 7 being neutral, lower values acidic, higher values alkaline. Either high or low pH values may cause corrosion of metals, concrete, and other materials. Either is harmful to aquatic life.

Problems arise almost entirely from cleaning operations. Soaps and detergents are generally of high pH; boiler blowdown is usually highly alkaline. Strong acids (low pH) are sometimes used for scale removal and other difficult cleaning jobs, and the development of septic conditions in organic wastes may also cause a low pH.

Discharges are usually restricted within the 5.5 to 10 range; frequently to only a portion of this range, such as 6 to 8.5. Analysis is by colorimetry (indicator solutions or test papers). More accurate analysis is by electrometric instrument.

Acidity and Alkalinity: This is a measure of the total quantity of acid (or alkali) present, measured below (or above) the neutral point of pH 7 or some other arbitrary point. Note that pH is a measure of the strength; acidity and alkalinity are measures of total quantity. Thus a small amount of strong acid (e.g., sulfuric) may produce a very low pH, while a large concentration of weak acid (e.g., acetic) may not produce a pH below 3 or 4; however, the latter would require a larger amount of alkaline neutralizing agent to restore a neutral condition.

It is not as significant as pH as a measure of pollutional effects; but indicates quantity of chemicals required for treatment. Sources of problems and discharge restrictions are similar to those described under pH.

Analysis is as follows. Measure the quantity of a standard alkali (or acid) required to bring the pH to the desired point. This point may be neutrality (pH 7) or one of the common colorimetric indicators: methyl orange, 4.5 or phenolphthalein, 8.3. The specific acid or alkali is not significant; values are reported in terms of calcium carbonate ($CaCO_3$) equivalent.

Turbidity: Turbidity has esthetic significance. Also, by interfering with light penetration in streams, it affects aquatic life and retards oxygen regeneration by photosynthesis. It is detrimental to some industrial water uses. Any source of finely suspended or colloidal matter, either solid or liquid, causes turbidity. It comes from practically every operation in the plant, including clean-up.

The limitations are usually 5 to 10 units (JTU, or Jackson turbidity units) for domestic water supplies; 10 to 100 units for critical industrial uses. Analysis is as follows. Measure, visually or photoelectrically, the transmission of light through a sample. This may be by use of standards, or by threshold visibility, or by direct optical measurement.

Settleable Matter: This is also called settleable solids. It is the settleable portion of total suspended matter. The sources are described in Table 39 (page 149). Limitations are usually based on total suspended matter. When limits on settleable matter are stated, they may be very low, e.g., 0.1 ml./l.

Analysis is as follows. Allow the sample to remain undisturbed in a glass Imhoff cone for one hour or other suitable period; record the volume of sediment accumulated, in milliliters per liter. Alternately, measure the total suspended solids in a sample both before and after settling, and report the difference in mg./l.

Dissolved Matter: This is also called filtrable residue, dissolved solids, or total dissolved solids (TDS). It has very little significance except in high concentrations of the order of 5,000 mg./l. (0.5%). It is harmful to humans and other animal life at high strength and troublesome for certain industrial uses. It comes from salt from animal tissues and preservatives; cleaning chemicals; boiler blow-down. Limitations in drinking water are 500 mg./l.

Analysis is as follows. Calculate as the difference between total residue on evaporation and total suspended matter. Alternately, filter, evaporate to dryness and weigh. Ionic dissolved matter (inorganic salts) can be estimated by specific conductance measurement, reported in micromhos per centimeter.

Total Residue on Evaporation: This is also called Total Solids (TS). It has no significance of itself. For its sources and limitations see Table 39 (page 149) and the discussion on dissolved matter. Analysis is as follows. Evaporate to dryness and weigh. Alternatively, add together the values for total suspended matter and dissolved matter.

Chemical Oxygen Demand (COD):   COD is an indirect measure of total organic pollution. It is more rapid than the 5-day BOD test, but not the same in significance. It measures the amount of material oxidized by dichromate-sulfuric acid reagent, under carefully specified conditions. It includes some inorganic substances, and is not identical with the BOD test in what it includes and what it fails to include.

For sources of COD see Table 40 (page 149). COD is not commonly used as a regulatory parameter. It is useful in in-plant studies to compare organic wastes (BOD test is often too slow); sometimes an approximate BOD:COD ratio can be discovered.

For analysis treat the sample with a standard amount of oxidant; hold at boiling temperature for 2 hours; measure the amount of remaining oxidant; and report amount consumed as oxygen equivalent.

Total Organic Carbon (TOC): TOC is similar to COD. The organic matter is oxidized and the resulting carbon dioxide is measured. Corrections are possible for inorganic carbon sources, such as carbonates and bicarbonates. For sources see Table 40 (page 149). For limitations see discussion on COD. For analysis, proprietary equipment (expensive) is required.

Ammonia Nitrogen: Nitrogen may exist in wastewaters in any of several forms, starting (usually) with protein (organic nitrogen), through various products of decomposition to ammonia, then by oxidation to nitrite and nitrate. A chemically intermediate form, elemental nitrogen, is inert and harmless.

In low concentrations nitrogen is a necessary nutrient for aquatic plant life, but too much may encourage eutrophication. Free ammonia is harmful to fish, and corrosive to copper and copper alloys. Nitrogen is present in and develops from protein materials, such as most poultry fractions. It is also present in ammonia leaks from refrigeration systems. It is limited to 0.05 or 0.1 mg./l. in drinking water. A rather severe effluent limit is 5 mg./l. For analysis, add alkali; steam-distill into a standard acid solution; and titrate to determine acid neutralized. Report as N.

Total Kjeldahl Nitrogen: This is a measure of the ammonia and organic nitrogen. It is used in conjunction with the ammonia nitrogen test to determine (by difference) the organic nitrogen. In waterways and sewers it decomposes to form ammonia nitrogen. The sources are similar to those for ammonia nitrogen. It is not a common parameter for regulation. For analysis digest with nitric and sulfuric acid to destroy organic matter and convert to ammonia nitrogen; then determine as such.

Phosphate: Phosphate is commonly reported as P; sometimes as PO_4. One part P equals approximately three parts PO_4. Phosphate is a necessary nutrient for aquatic plant life; thus it is sometimes a cause of eutrophication when present in excess. Phosphates come primarily from detergents; they are also present in bones and other parts. Recent regulations are limiting discharge to streams to 1 mg./l. as P. Analysis is performed colorimetrically by special reagents. It is sometimes desirable to distinguish dissolved and suspended phosphate.

Coliform Counts: Total coliform count and fecal coliform count are used as indicators of bacterial pollution. It is not feasible to determine pathogenic organisms directly as a routine test, so these "indicator organisms" are used instead. Limitations are variable among different areas. A "typical" limitation is 20,000 total coliforms or 1,000 fecal coliforms per 100 ml. The sources of coliforms are manure and sanitary wastes. To analyze, incubate in special plates or culture media. Coliforms are sometimes expressed as MPN (most probable number) and sometimes by direct count. The common unit is number per 100 ml.

WASTEWATER CHARACTERISTICS CONSIDERED BY FWPCA

Because of the short time available for data collection and data analysis in the course of preparation of FWPCA Publication IWP-8, it was decided to use "organic load" as the measure of wastewater strength. Organic load was measured in terms of biochemical oxygen demand (BOD). To be more specific, the organic load was measured in 5-day, 20°C. BOD. The 5-day designation refers to the usual incubation period and the 20°C. to the temperature maintained during incubation. This particular form of the BOD test, as well as the BOD test itself, was chosen because it is the one most generally used.

The reliance upon one measure of wastewater strength (BOD) does not imply that this indicator is the only one or even the best one. In many instances total solids may be an equally important measure of meat packing waste. BOD was chosen in this case because it is one of the most important and most commonly used measures of wastewater strength. Additional studies of poultry processing wastewater should include at least total solids and suspended solids.

The BOD test is a time consuming, expensive, and delicate test of wastewater strength. These characteristics of the test may be one explanation of the lack of information concerning the strength of industrial wastewater.

The poultry processing industry has one unique waste problem, that is, feathers. A large volume of feathers are accumulated during processing, and these feathers must be disposed of by means other than biological sewage treatment. The problem of feather disposal is handled separately from the problem of wastewater disposal as BOD loads do not include feathers. It is assumed that feathers will be removed by a screening process along with other solid materials such as heads and feet.

EFFECT OF PLANT SIZE UPON WASTE PRODUCED

The size of the plant is directly related to the volume of wastewater produced. The chicken and broiler processing plants of typical and advanced technology use approximately nine gallons of water per bird processed. The nine gallons include processing, cooling, and clean-up water. About 8.75 gallons of the process water emerges from the plant as wastewater. The remaining 0.25 gallons is absorbed by the bird and/or evaporated during processing.

The size of a poultry processing plant is defined in terms of the number of birds processed by the plant during a one year period. Therefore, the volume of wastewater emerging from a processing plant is directly related to the plant size. Effluent volumes from turkey processing plants are estimated to be approximately four times larger than broiler processing plants handling the same number of birds per year. The factor of four is due to the large size of the turkey compared with that of a chicken or broiler. Size in this instance constitutes both inches and weight. Plants with "old technology" in general use about two-thirds as much water as more advanced processing plants.

EFFECT OF LEVEL OF TECHNOLOGY ON WASTE PRODUCED

Technology affects both the wasteload volume and wastewater per unit of product. The wasteload, measured in BOD per unit of product, depends upon the technology level of the processing plant. Old technology plants are characterized by low water use and no collection of blood. Low water use results from the absence of a flow-away system for feather and offal removal. The absence of blood collection increases the BOD strength of the wastewater by more than 50%.

Typical and advanced technology plants are characterized by the presence of a flow-away system for feather and offal removal and of blood collection methods. The blood collection process alone can reduce BOD loads by 38%, but the percent of reduction achieved will depend upon the efficiency of the blood collection method employed. It was stated previously that the technology level affected in an indirect manner the volume of wastewater effluent. The old technology plant has low volume effluents because of the absence of the flow-away system. Plants of typical technology use the most water per unit of product while plants of the advanced technology use a slightly smaller amount per unit of product. The reason for the reduced water use in advanced plants is that water is reused within the processing operation.

The United States Department of Agriculture regulations pertaining to the poultry processing industry also affect wastewater volumes. The USDA regulations prescribe the minimum amount of chill tank overflow for each bird entering the tank. This regulation is generally considered excessive by most processors. Therefore, nonfederally inspected plants usually have a lower volume of wastewater.

Plants employing the older level of technology tend to have the highest wasteload per unit of product because of the lack of blood collection. Advanced technology plants tend to have wasteloads whose BOD per bird is reduced by the continuous rescreening of wastewater that is required to permit the reuse of water within the plant. Thus the resulting wasteload is somewhat lower than that of plants with typical technology.

From the questionnaire data a wasteload and wastewater volumes per unit of product were developed for each of the three levels of technology. These per unit values are shown in Table 42. The immense increase in wastewater per unit of product between old and typical technology was caused by the introduction of the flow-away system. The drop in water use per unit of product between typical and advanced was due to recirculation of water in advanced technology plants. In other words, process water was used more than once in the processing operation.

Old technology and typical technology differ in amount of wasteload because of their differences in terms of blood collection. The fact that blood is collected in typical technology and not in old technology constitutes the difference in wasteload reduction of these two technology levels. The slight decrease in wasteload between typical and advanced technology is the result of the continuous screening which is required by in-plant reuse of water which is assumed in advanced technology plants.

Table 42 also contains the per unit wasteload and wastewater in index form. Old technology was used as the base of 100. The index is presented to facilitate comparisons among technology levels.

TABLE 42:   WASTE INDEX BY TECHNOLOGY*

| | Waste Characteristics per 1,000 Birds Killed | | | |
Type of Technology	BOD in Pounds	Wastewater in Gallons	Index of Waste BOD	Index of Wastewater
Old Technology	31.7	4,000	100	100
Typical Technology	26.2	10,400	83	260
Advanced Technology	26.0	7,300	82	190

*As of 1966.

Source: FWPCA Publ. IWP-8

GROSS WASTELOADS 1963–1977

Table 43 presents annual poultry slaughter statistics and future slaughter projections. The slaughter projections were determined by the use of multiple linear regression techniques based on 15 years of past slaughter statistics provided by the Department of Agriculture. The BOD wasteload projections were functions of the total slaughter and the per unit wasteload, which in turn was based upon an assumed distribution of technology.

Wastewater projections were done in the same manner. From 1970 to 1971 both production and gross wasteloads are shown to increase, while total wastewater volume decreases slightly. This decrease occurs because it was assumed that by 1971 all processing plants of major significance were using advanced technology. It will be remembered that advanced technology plants have lower wastewater volume per unit of product than typical technology plants have.

TABLE 43:   ANNUAL POULTRY SLAUGHTER — WASTELOADS AND WASTEWATER

Year	Millions of Birds Slaughtered	BOD Millions of lbs./yr.	Total Wastewater MG/yr.
1963	2,419	105	18,206
1966	2,668	125	19,350
1968	2,941	135	23,524
1969	3,051	141	24,411
1970	3,262	147	26,098
1971	3,274	153	24,557
1972	3,385	159	25,388
1977 (est.)	3,976	189	29,817

Source: FWPCA Publ. IWP-8

TABLE 44:   COEFFICIENTS USED IN ESTIMATING BY-PRODUCTS,
WATER USE AND WASTELOADS OF POULTRY
SLAUGHTERING PLANTS

Variable	Unit	Value per 1,000 pounds 1/
By-products:		
Blood		
Young chickens.............	Pounds	70
Mature chickens............	do.	70
Turkeys....................	do.	70
Other poultry..............	do.	70
Offal		
Young chickens.............	do.	175
Mature chickens............	do.	170
Turkeys....................	do.	125
Other poultry..............	do.	140
Feathers		
Young chickens.............	do.	70
Mature chickens............	do.	70
Turkeys....................	do.	70
Water Use:		
Young chickens.............	Gallons	2,198
Mature chickens............	do.	2,173
Turkeys....................	do.	1,700
Other poultry..............	do.	2,100
Cut-up.....................	do.	500
Further processing.........	do.	500
Wasteloads:		
BOD--		
Young chickens.............	Pounds	8.2
Mature chickens............	do.	8.7
Turkeys....................	do.	8.0
Other poultry..............	do.	8.0
Suspended solids--		
Young chickens.............	do.	6.3
Mature chickens............	do.	5.4
Turkeys....................	do.	5.0
Other poultry..............	do.	5.0
Time span of operation 2/:		
Young chicken, mature chicken, and other poultry plants...	Days	234
Turkey plants..............	do.	130

1/ Live weight except for cut-up and further processed coefficients which
are ready-to-cook weight.
2/ These coefficients are based on a maximum of 260 operating days per year.
We assumed that the chicken and other poultry plants operated at 90 percent
capacity--0.90 x 260 = 234. Turkey plants were assumed to operate at 50
percent capacity--0.50 x 260 = 130.

Source: Environmental Protection Agency, Industrial Waste Study of the
Meat Products Industry, 1971; U.S. Department of Agriculture,
Processing Poultry By-Products in Poultry Slaughtering Plants,
Marketing Research Report No. 181, 1957; and industry contacts.

A report released by the Statistical Reporting Service, USDA, in 1972 estimated total BOD and suspended solids production for poultry processing plants based on production figures and various sources for pollutant loads. The various sources resulted in Table 44 which lists a collection of co-efficients for by-products, water use, and wasteloads, to be applied to production figures. It must be noted that Table 44 may be reasonably accurate on quantities of by-product, but the numerous variables of processing, such as poultry type, water usage, spray nozzle design, cleaning practices, and screening efficiencies, make predictions on water use and wasteloads a gross estimate at best.

Based on the values in Table 44, however, it was estimated that a typical poultry processing plant releases wastewater with a BOD of 448 mg./l. and suspended solids of 344 mg./l. This is in agreement with experience which indicates BODs of 450 to 600 mg./l. and suspended solids of 300 to 400 mg./l.

SEASONAL VARIATIONS

Seasonal variations in gross wasteload is due mainly to the turkey processing industry. The growth rate of this industry is directly correlated with population growth rates. Therefore, it is safe to assume that the wasteload of the turkey processors will always be a percent of the total wasteload in any given year.

The turkey processor experiences significant seasonal variations. Major processors are active only about 100 days a year, during the months of October, November, and December. Their contributions to total wasteloads, thus, will be of significance during these 3 months. Seasonal variations in the turkey industry are expected to decline little, since the seasonal nature of turkey production stems from consumer demand.

Seasonal variations in the rest of the industry have been reduced to a point where they are no longer of importance. In the past, pre-1950, seasonal variations in the industry plus variations from year to year were common. Technological advances in the growing industry have caused these variations to all but disappear.

IN-PLANT POULTRY PROCESSING
WASTE TREATMENT

POLLUTION REDUCTION BY SUBPROCESS CHANGE

Poultry processing wasteloads can be reduced by practicing good house-keeping methods. Some processing methods in themselves reduce waste-loads. When budget conditions permit, modifications of processing operations should be undertaken. It is more economical to reduce the wastes as much as possible at the source than to treat the gross wastes.

Wastewater from poultry processing plants is screened to remove solids from the effluent. The screening process is an essential part of the flow-away system especially when recirculation of water is practiced, but the practice has also been found useful in nonflow-away plants, especially during cleanup operations.

In the receiving area, there is an accumulation of dirt and manure on their floors during the handling period of live birds. The reduction in holding time for live birds has reduced the wasteload from this sector of the plant by as much as 4%. Drycleaning of the receiving room floors in the typical plant could reduce BOD by 125 pounds per year. If a plant recovers all blood and exercises care in the cleanup of the bleeding area, BOD waste-load of the plant can be reduced by 38%.

Wasteloads from the evisceration and picking area are controlled primarily by screening. The screens must be kept clear to prevent overflows, which result in the dumping of feathers, offal, heads, and feet into the sewer system. In an "older" technology, nonflow-away system, care must be taken to ensure proper use of containers where viscera and feathers are collected. Containers must be emptied often enough to guard against

overflows. Care must be taken to ensure that flow-away systems carry
sufficient quantities of water to effectively carry viscera and feathers from
the processing area.

The utilization of by-products has proven economical to processors. The
sale of blood, viscera, and feathers to rendering firms or farmers has proven
profitable to many poultry processors. In those areas where there are no
rendering firms, the by-products are at least removed from the gross pollution load of the plant if they are given free in exchange for hauling them
away. Table 44 below shows the percentage reduction in BOD which
should accompany the specified change in subprocess according to estimates
made by the Federal Water Pollution Control Administration and published
in Publication IWP-8.

TABLE 44:   CHANGES IN SUBPROCESS AND THEIR EFFECT UPON
WASTELOAD AND WASTEWATER VOLUME

Subprocess Change	Per Cent Wasteload Reduction Associated With Indicated Change of Subprocess
I. Typical Technology	
A. Change subprocess from holding of birds in storage area to direct placement of birds on conveyor	4
B. Change subprocess from recovery of no blood to recovery of all blood	38
II. New Technology	
A. Change subprocess from holding of birds in storage area to direct placement of birds on conveyor	4
B. Change subprocess from recovery of no blood to recovery of all blood	38
C. Change subprocess from no reuse of water to reuse of water	1

Source: FWPCA Publication IWP-8

SPECIFIC SUBPROCESS CONTROLS

A comprehensive discussion of in-plant water management to permit poultry
processing facilities to meet new environmental requirements has been presented by the staff of Environmental Engineering, Inc. of Gainesville,
Florida in the EPA-sponsored Design Seminar for Industrial Pollution Control

at Little Rock, Arkansas in January, 1973. Water management techniques promise to provide the greatest reduction in wastewater flows. The operators of poultry processing plants often do not know how much water they are using, where they are using it, when they are using it, and, in some cases, why they are using it. Water, traditionally a resource of great convenience and minor cost, has not occupied the attention of either managers or workers. As a result, wasteful water use practices have been common throughout the industry. It will not be possible at this time to demonstrate a cure-all technique that will eliminate water use problems, rather it will be shown where water misuse can be prevented or corrected.

Reduction of flows need not be completely at odds with the trend of industry toward modernization and improved processing using flowaway systems. It will remain for the industry to assess the costs of process changes to either "dry" or recirculating systems and compare them against legitimate wastewater treatment charges. In the event of borderline decisions, a processor should be aware that wastewater quality restrictions imposed by states and municipalities will become more stringent in the future and the most economical method to meet those restrictions is often by in-plant process modifications and water management.

The USDA is very strict in its observance of process water quality standards. Great variations in water use and reuse are generally not permitted at this time. Therefore, discussion will be presented on water reuse methods that are permitted by the USDA, methods that are not presently permitted but which with further study may some day be allowed, and also methods that may never be allowed.

The poor quality processing plant in terms of water management must be distinguished from the poor quality plant as measured in terms of product. The best, most modern processing plant turning out an excellent poultry product may be the worst plant from a pollution standpoint. In a typical poor water management situation, hoses are kept running when not in use, excessive amounts of water are used, and poorly designed water supply systems permit little if any control over pressures and rates of flow. In general water is used indiscriminately and the basic philosophy seems to be that the more water used the better the job.

A reduced usage concept can nevertheless be applied to almost every area of almost every plant. Some of the more general reduction techniques are discussed below for the main subprocesses in a poultry plant.

Receiving Area

Live storage of chickens in a battery room may become a temporary necessity in even the most modern processing plant. Studies of the production in this room of wastes from manure and feathers have indicated BOD values exceeding 30 lbs./1,000 birds per day. As a comparison, chicken manure production on farms is normally on the order of 240 lbs./1,000 chickens per day. Water quantities resulting from a daily wet wash of the receiving area will vary greatly among different plants and even in the same plant on different days. The wet wash may contain detergents and cleaning agents in addition to the poultry waste. Drycleaning of the battery room with shovels, scrapers, or brooms can remove most of the deposits to a dry disposal container.

A final wash of the battery room will then require less water and will contain significantly less pollutants. One study measured the reduction of BOD by drycleaning operations to 5 lbs./1,000 chickens per day. This figure may be even further reduced by a rapid turnover of birds in the holding area, accomplished by scheduling staggered deliveries of poultry to coincide with processing line demands. Cleaning techniques using high pressure sprays, as opposed to low pressure-high volume flows, will significantly reduce cleaning water demands. There is at this time doubt as to whether the use of cleaning detergents provides more or less pollution than the manure and feather contents of the waste.

Killing and Bleeding

Blood drained from freshly killed carcasses constitutes an extremely high potential and, as a result, in exceedingly fewer plants is it allowed to wash to the sewer directly. Chicken blood has an approximate BOD of 92,000 mg./liter and 1,000 chickens may drain 17.4 lbs. of BOD in recoverable blood. In a poorly operated plant the blood will wash to the sewer and during post processing cleanup will be contained in the wash water.

Collection of blood may reduce the processing plants sewage strength by 35 to 50%. This is roughly equivalent to 17 to 18 pounds of BOD per 1,000 chickens. Since poultry is bled while it hangs from a moving conveyor, the blood may be collected in a tunnel or a walled area. In a high walled tunnel, for example, the blood may be almost completely recovered and drained into receptacles spaced at regular intervals. A section of the killing room enclosed by a wall high enough to catch most of the spurting blood would provide a contained collection area. In most cases such an area would be cleaned of blood at periodic intervals after the blood has partially congealed to a slurry and can be shoveled or scooped. In this case, final cleanup of the floors and walls of the bleeding area would require more water than for an enclosed tunnel of limited dimensions. Body movement of the slaughtered poultry may splatter blood on the conveyor out of the bleeding area, and onto the feathers of adjoining birds where it can be washed off in the scalders. This is lost blood and increased wasteload. Stunning of the birds at slaughter will reduce such movement, allow greater blood recovery, and reduce wastewater BOD load. Recovered blood may in some cases be sold to a local rendering plant and the profit used to offset pollution control costs. In other instances it may be necessary to give even pay for its removal. In any event, efficient blood recovery practices provide the single most effective step of wasteload reduction.

Scalding

The scalding operation which loosens poultry body feathers also provides a first wash to the carcass. The spent scalding water will contain blood, dirt, feathers, manure, and dissolved fats and greases. The scalding tank is continuously replenished with fresh water at the rate of 1/4 gallon of water per bird. The BOD of scalder water has been measured as high as 1,182 mg. per liter, with suspended solids of 682 mg. per liter, and a grease content of 350 mg. per liter.

Scalding of the poultry prior to defeathering provides an opportune process for conservation of water. Scald water temperatures between 128° and 145°F. inhibit the growth of common bacteria and the water is applied as an initial wash to the dirty poultry. For these reasons scald water need not be fresh water; however, the USDA requires an overflow of 1/4 gallon per chicken processed. Screened chiller overflow water which has been applied to a relatively clean, washed carcass, has twice the overflow rate of the scald water.

Chiller water has fewer pollutants than spent scald water and would, therefore, appear to be an ideal makeup water for the scald tanks. Chiller overflow water from the first contact tank has been substantially warmed by residual body heat from the carcasses and will not differ greatly in temperature from cold water supply lines. The use of a simple heat exchanger between chiller feed to the heating tanks and scalder water overflow can reduce the fuel needed to heat the scalder feed water.

Defeathering

Defeathering under poor water management techniques is performed mechanically with continuous streams of water washing away the feathers and washing the carcass. While this is performed in many new and modern plants for expediency of cleaning, it represents a step backward in pollution technology due to the high volume of water involved in the feather flushing. Defeathering water will contain blood and dirt which exert a BOD while the feathers themselves, although they are somewhat resistant to the standard

BOD analysis, may create a BOD in the feather flume of nearly 600 mg. per liter. Furthermore, feathers in the wastewater stream have a considerable nuisance value by clogging the mechanical recovery screens treating the wastewater flow.

The fresh water supply for mechanical feather removal has been measured to be 1.4 gallons per bird, inclusive of the final outside body wash and periodic area cleanup. This water use was 11% of the total water supply to the plant. Additional in-plant water reuse for the feather flowaway flume raised the total water usage for the defeathering process to 2.8 gallons per bird, which was also the waste discharge for the defeathering process.

Defeathering operations have been shown to carry a pollution potential in wash and flume water. Feathers may be removed by screening operations of the wash water, but they have a high tendency to foul screens and cause polluted water overflow. Screened water from defeathering operations may be reused in the feather flume trough since there is no direct contact with the final poultry product. Reuse of feather flume water in the feather flume instead of another location would prevent mixing of stray feathers with other types of possibly recoverable products. Chiller water has been used in the feather flume at the Gold Kist facility in Durham, North Carolina.

Evisceration

The evisceration process consumes large quantities of fresh water in cleaning of the carcass, in viscera flowaway flumes, and in worker cleanup supplies. Wastewater from evisceration will contain high BOD's, suspended solids and grit, greases, blood, and bacteria from the intestinal tracts. Large volumes of water used to flush the offal would tend to dilute the BOD concentration, but the total pounds of BOD produced would remain unchanged. A typical example of eviscerating flume water has a flow of 3.1 gallons of water per bird and a demand of 24% of the fresh water supply.

Gizzard cleaning is a distinct subprocess of evisceration and presently requires potable water according to USDA regulations as does evisceration water. Gizzard cleaning water is discharged to the viscera flowaway flume for a combined water use of 6.1 gallons per bird and a BOD of 230 mg. per liter. While the BOD appears low due to the high volumes of flushing water in this process, it is still equivalent to 12.2 lbs./1,000 broilers.

Evisceration adds a large quantity of wastewater with a substantial amount of BOD to the plant effluent. During evisceration, workers hands are in contact with recoverable viscera, offal, and bacterial pollutants. Constant supplies of fresh water are used to wash workers hands and recoverable viscera, and to transport waste heads, feet, and offal down a flume to a screening operation. The nature of the waste and its high bacterial content make it inadvisable to reuse offal flume water in any process in which it can contact poultry products; however, in noncontact processes such as feather fluming it may be possible to reuse even this water. Gizzard cleaning water is similar in nature to the eviscerating trough water and should be treated similarly. Lung vacuum pump effluent is low in quantity and usually may be incorporated with the offal flowaway.

Wastewater from the final bird wash after evisceration will contain grease, blood, and scraps of meat. This has been measured at 0.8 gallons of water per chicken and 440 mg./liter of BOD, but it will vary depending on the type of mechanical spray head used.

Final bird wash water, used to wash both the inside and the outside of the carcass, should normally be the freshest water possible and must be conducted with potable water according to USDA. This wash water may possibly be reused in another subprocess within the plant. All bird washing processes may be improved by the use of special water spray nozzles that minimize water use.

Chilling

Other than general plant cleanup, chilling of processed poultry is the final step associated with wastewater. Chillers are often separate for giblets and carcasses. BOD concentrations of giblet chill water have been measured as high as 2,357 mg./liter, while the BOD concentrations of the two stages in a body chiller have been measured to be 442 mg./liter and 320 mg./liter. The overall water demand for chillers is approximately 3/4 of a gallon per chicken. USDA requirements are 1/2 gallon of water usage per chicken. BOD production in a body chiller is on the order of 7.4 lbs./1,000 birds.

Chiller water requirements are established by the USDA and little can be done to reduce them. However, screened chiller water overflow has a great potential for reuse elsewhere in the plant. Also, measurement of water in the slush ice added to chillers should be credited against minimum chiller requirements.

Dry Cleanup

The basic processes presented above have been constrained by the limitation of using a flowaway system. Drycleaning of feathers and dry removal of waste offal have a large potential for reducing wastewater flows and concentrations and were the processes in general use before industry conversion to "modern" flowaway systems. It is understood that flowaway systems have

provided quicker and more economical automatic processing in an age of
rising labor and food costs, yet new regulations on wastewater qualities may
force processors to compare wastewater abatement costs with the return to
more labor intensive, in-house dry cleanup systems.

Dry cleanup of feathers from defeathering operations may be performed
manually or automatically, brushing feathers to a dry collection point
where there is a limited storage before removal by a renderer. Vacuum
removal of feathers may be automated and similarly provide for a central
dry storage. Residual feathers clinging to the carcasses and to equipment
may be washed away with greatly reduced quantities of water and substantially reduced feather screening facilities. The area of dry mechanical
feather collection has great potential for an enterprising equipment manufacturer.

Dry removal of evisceration wastes will reduce wastewater constituent concentrations and some water flowaway requirements. Studies have shown that
if waste solids from evisceration are put directly into containers at the table,
effluent from evisceration would contain 6 to 8 lbs. BOD/1,000 chickens.
This compares to a total evisceration- and gizzard-flowaway BOD of 12.2
pounds. Finally, heads may be pulled and dropped directly into containers
with no waste use whatsoever.

By-Product Recovery

Dry or wet recovered feathers may often be sold to rendering facilities for
processing as proteinaceous animal feed. New agricultural farm products for
field application use poultry feathers as a raw material. The products
control insects, temperature, weeds, and humidity on the field. Offal
collection may also be economically attractive with a rendering plant located in the area. Rendering plants and some farmers will convert offal
to animal feed or return it to the soil.

Recovered blood can at times be sold to rendering plants and rendering plant
delivery trucks can be equipped with blood holding tanks to make pickup
of the blood more economical and attractive to the renderer. In 1972,
blood, feathers, and offal were sold to renderers in Florida at the rate of
nine to ten dollars per 1,000 broilers processed.

In the 1970 survey performed by the USDA, it was found that 0.6% of
processing plants did not salvage offal, 70.8% of the plants sold offal to
renderers, 1% gave offal to renderers, 26.6% rendered offal "in-house",
and 1% dumped or burned collected offal. The same study revealed that
blood was not salvaged by 14.2% of the plants, sold to renderers by 54.6%,
given away by 7%, rendered in-house by 22.4%, and dry disposed by 1.8%.

Feathers were wasted by 0.4% of the plants, sold by 71.6%, given away by 0.8%, rendered in-house by 25.9%, and burned or dumped by 1.3%.

HOUSEKEEPING

In-plant cleaning of equipment and housing is an important source of pollutants. When scald tanks are emptied at the end of a processing period, for example, they contribute a heavy slug load of dirt, feathers, blood, and grease. Little can be done to reduce the waste flow from this cleaning. In other areas, floors and tables should be swept prior to washing to remove gross solids in dry form to storage containers where the contents could be used for rendering. Floor drains and outlets should be accessible to wastes only during final cleanup after sweeping.

Screens placed on the drains of nonflowaway plants will prevent gross organic solids from reaching the sewer system. Organic solids in flowaway plants may be processed through the offal and feather recovery screens. Floor washing and general sanitation is imperative, but there is no reason to provide large quantities of water to wash bulky solids through drain lines.

Employee awareness of the cost of water use will result in improved housekeeping procedures. Letting water hoses run freely on the floor between uses is wasteful and employees should be encouraged to make the effort to turn off the water. Placing control nozzles on the hoses will facilitate this and will also help reduce water usage to the minimum necessary to do a good job.

WATER SUPPLY AND TREATMENT EQUIPMENT

Improved spray nozzle designs at the Gold Kist facility were able to reduce fresh water usage in final bird washers by 60%, in hand washers at evisceration from 285 gpm to 100 gpm, and in whole bird washers from 45 gpm to 30 gpm. Mechanical improvements in the replacement of old free running hoses by a high pressure cleaning system using foam cleansers reduced daily cleanup water from 112,000 gpd to 46,000 gpd. Even plants not contemplating process changes or internal reuse of water can noticeably reduce fresh water usage and wastewater flow by the installation of the best available spray heads and cleaning equipment. Varying line pressures and water demands in different parts of the plant can make automatic or timed spray equipment nonfunctional. Pressure control valves placed at strategic locations in the plant can prevent such difficulties.

Screening is a vital process in the reuse of waste streams and general reduction of poultry plant waste. Rotary drum screens along with stationary flat screens have long been used for by-product recovery. The trends are toward vibrating screens which operate at higher efficiencies and are not as subject to clogging and overflows. But in any case, screening of feathers and offal should be done in separate channels by separate screens to facilitate water reuse without cross-contamination.

GUIDE TO FUTURE EFFORTS

The changes that may be made in each plant to reduce water usage will depend upon the particular circumstances at that plant. A general list of steps for improved water management, which may be used as a framework by each poultry processor for their own actions is presented.

(1) Choose a person specifically responsible for water management. This person should have reasonable powers to make and enforce changes.

(2) Determine where water is used and in what quantities.

(3) Install flow meters and pressure gauges in major flow areas.

(4) Install water pressure regulators to prevent gross line pressure variations. This will help prevent occasional oversupply at unit points in the process.

(5) Tackle each unit process to determine possible water use reductions.

(6) In receiving area, dry sweep wastes to receptacles before washing floors.

(7) In receiving area, replace open garden type hoses with nozzles that given high velocity spray, reduced water flow, and that may be turned off at point of application.

(8) Cleaning with detergents and cleansers may further reduce water usage and will certainly produce a more hygienic area.

(9) Stun carcasses electrically at slaughter to prevent body movement and splattering of blood.

(10) Confine bleeding to a tunnel or enclosed area where blood for collection may easily be accomplished. Recover the blood for rendering or farmland disposal and do not let it into waste stream.

(11) Use the minimum approved USDA quantities of water that will maintain your temperature.

(12) Reuse screened chiller water as scalder feed water. Consider simple heat exchange between scalder overflow water and scalder boiler feed water.

    (13) Pay attention to new developments in vacuum removal of feathers in defeathering. Consider an application of such a system when practical.

    (14) Screen feather flume water and reuse in the feather flume.

    (15) Install spray nozzles on bird wash that will get the job done with a minimum amount of water.

    (16) Place nozzles on hand washers and evisceration meat washers that will clean adequately with minimum water use. Body or foot control valves can supply water only when it is needed for hand washers. Timed sprays can wash evisceration solids away with no wasteful water use between bursts.

    (17) Measure the ice-slush added to chiller water and credit it against chiller water overflow requirements.

    (18) Keep all screens in perfect working order. A clogged and overflowing screen costs the processor money.

    (19) Use dry cleanup in plant prior to "wet rinse" to reduce water use. Collect dry solids in container for disposal or rendering.

    (20) Consider institution of dry removal of wastes, such as on-site containers for heads.

    (21) Recover all possible by-products to improve the economy of in-plant water management.

    (22) Stimulate employee awareness of the expense and undesirability of poor water management. Encourage employees to be careful of their water use.

The methods for reducing water usage as discussed in this section are but a part of what can be accomplished toward recycling of water and reducing fresh water demand. The ultimate goal for industries, as envisioned by some people, is total reuse of water or zero pollutant discharge. Such an ideal goal may never be realized, but pressure will be brought to bear to approach it. Wastewater treatment will become more expensive in the future and incentives for in-house flow reductions will substantially increase.

Several water reuse schemes have been considered. These include total reuse of screened offal water in the evisceration flume, use of screened whole bird wash water in the scalder on the premise that the bird will contact water of that quality anyway, reuse of screened final bird wash. These schemes have not been approved by the USDA. They do, however, have the potential of reducing water usage by 18% over that in an uncontrolled plant. In time, a detailed study will need to be conducted on these methods not only to verify their technical and economic practicality but also to safeguard the public health.

PRETREATMENT
FOR DISCHARGE TO MUNICIPAL SYSTEMS

The pretreatment of poultry processing wastes for discharge to a municipal system has been considered in some detail by A.J. Steffen, Consulting Environmental Engineer of W. Lafayette, Indiana in a presentation before an EPA-sponsored technology transfer seminar at Little Rock, Arkansas in January 1973.

Pretreatment does not include treatment of sanitary wastes (normally discharged directly to the city sewer), storm water, cooling water, or condenser water. Disposal of the recovered screenings, floatables and settled solids is beyond the scope of this section, but concentration of the floatables and settled solids by screening to reduce liquid content is included.

Most poultry plants are now using flow-away systems, thus the subject matter relates largely to this type of waste handling system. The customary screens used in flow-away systems to remove offal and feathers are intended to improve the wastewater for reuse in the processing plant and for recovery of by-products and are thus not considered (herein) as part of pretreatment for discharge to a municipal system. However, it is recognized that effluent may often be improved by improvements in flow-away screening.

A survey in 1970 of Federally inspected slaughtering operations indicated that 29% of the plants had some degree of private waste treatment, 65% had final municipal waste treatment, and 6% had no waste treatment whatsoever. The reduction of water usage in the poultry processing operations and the water reaching the final effluent will thus be a benefit to processors, municipal waste treatment facilities and the general public whose environment is affected.

Many communities are faced with having to provide advanced waste treatment to comply with Federal and State regulations. Individual industrial plants discharging directly to a water course are also coming under more stringent controls. The EPA has indicated that all poultry processors will eventually come under direct or indirect pressure to reduce their wastewater flows and strengths. Either wastewater characteristics will be directly regulated or those processors using municipal facilities will experience substantial sewer surcharges.

While a considerable number of plants are being charged minimal rates for their waste treatment at the present time, there is a rapidly growing trend among municipalities to make industry pay for its share of waste treatment. As regulations force municipal plants to improve their wastewater effluent qualities at greater treatment costs, the costs will be passed on to those industries discharging a significant amount of waste to the system.

Normal sewer charges to industry are based on flow rate and allow up to 250 mg./l. of BOD and suspended solids in the waste stream. Additional concentrations of BOD and suspended solids have been charged at rates of $25 to $80 per thousand pounds of each. The result of these factors is an increased incentive for wastewater reduction.

Based on a sewer charge of 25 cents per 1,000 gallons, typical water use and waste discharges, and a wastewater flow of 18.4 billion gallons, USDA has predicted a cost of municipal waste treatment to poultry processors at $4.6 million. The live weight slaughter at the plants surveyed by the USDA was 8.4 billion pounds with a calculated sewer charge of 5.5 cents per 100 pounds of live poultry. Inefficient plants losing excessive solids to wastewater streams stand to have increased sewer surcharges and concomitantly increased processing costs.

Total treatment costs were estimated for anaerobic-aerobic lagoon systems and extended aeration systems. Private waste treatment by lagooning could cost the processor from 2.2 cents to 0.8 cents per 100 pounds live weight for poorly to properly controlled plants, respectively. Extended aeration plants, which provide a higher degree of treatment with less land area, would require investment, operating, and maintenance costs of 11.0 cents to 4.0 cents per 100 pounds live weight for hydraulically unmanaged and managed plants, respectively.

Careful and diligent in-plant water use reduction by the poultry processor may save him substantial quantities of money by allowing smaller waste treatment systems than those calculated here for "typical" poultry processing plants in 1970. At a normal sewer charge of $0.25 per 1,000 gallons of waste, a water use charge of $0.25 per 1,000 gallons of water supplied, and a sewer surcharge of $50 per 1,000 pounds of BOD discharged over 300 mg./l. in concentration, a typical 100,000 broilers per day, seven days per week, poultry processor with poor water and waste management may pay a monthly bill of over $20,000. With proper water management this bill can be reduced by approximately 50%.

WHY PRETREATMENT?

This section is concerned with the treatment of poultry wastes after the customary screening in flow-away systems and prior to discharge to a municipal sewer. The term "pretreatment" is used to cover all physical, chemical or biological treatment provided for this purpose.

The majority of poultry plants discharge to municipal sewers. In a 1971 USDA survey of 386 poultry plants, almost two-thirds were connected to some type of public sewer system. The survey did not show how many had pretreatment. Whether or not pretreatment is required at a poultry plant depends most frequently upon municipal regulations regarding some of the ingredients in the poultry wastes.

Ingredients such as feathers may be prohibited because they cannot be efficiently removed and disposed of in conventional municipal sewage treatment plants, while other ingredients, such as solids may be subject to special charges to defray the expense of their removal and disposal in the municipal system.

Federal regulations covering grants-in-aid to municipalities touch on pretreatment of industrial wastes. The EPA has set up rules relating to industrial wastes discharged to such municipal systems, as noted in the following excerpt from the Federal Register of July 2, 1970:

"Where project (for which a Federal grant is requested) is to treat industrial wastes, it must be included in a waste treatment system treating the wastes of an entire community. A waste treatment system means one or more treatment plants which provides integrated, but not necessarily interconnected waste disposal for a community, metropolitan area or region. In such a system, industry must provide pretreatment if waste would otherwise be detrimental to the system. Where industrial wastes are to be treated in the proposed project, the Commissioner must be assured that the applicant (municipality requesting a Federal grant) will have an equitable system of cost recovery".

Thus, if the municipality receives a Federal grant, the poultry plant may be required to provide pretreatment if the waste would be detrimental to the system of municipal treatment. Note also that the cost of treating the poultry wastes must be recovered in "an equitable system of cost recovery". In some cases, municipal treatment requirements can be reduced by pretreatment at the poultry plant. This may produce overall savings to the poultry plant operator, if a cost recovery charge is to be levied.

There are many other instances where pretreatment may become an economic advantage. Suppose, for example, that the municipal plant is overloaded and a plant expansion is contemplated. A study shows that pretreatment at the poultry plant will eliminate the overload. The decision whether to pretreat or go along with the municipal plant expansion program depends upon the relative annual cost (of the two alternatives) to the poultry plant operator.

As another example, suppose that excessive discharges of grease, feathers or suspended matter are causing special problems in operating primary clarifiers and anaerobic sludge digestion at the municipal plant. The first step for correction of such problems is waste conservation at the poultry plant and attention to the flow-away system (check for escape of solids in the flow-away screen and offal area). If these elements are all in order and good waste conservation is being practiced in the plant, pretreatment may be the next step.

As a further example, suppose the poultry plant management is considering an increase in poultry production or some additional processing. The added sewage treatment load resulting from such changes can be calculated, to compare the sewage service charges for municipal plant expansion (made necessary by the added load), with the cost of pretreatment to produce the same results.

WHEN PRETREATMENT?

Prohibitory and restrictive limits may make pretreatment necessary. The discharge of some ingredients such as feathers, entrails, and the like into the municipal system may be completely prohibited. If the best in-plant conservation practices and careful operation of efficient flow-away equipment does not eliminate these materials to the municipality's satisfaction, some form of pretreatment will be necessary.

On the other hand, restrictive limits (that is, limits of concentration of, say, BOD, solids and grease in milligrams per liter) may vary with the type of municipal treatment. For example, emulsified fats from poultry cooking operations are amenable to activated sludge treatment, whereas they may be troublesome in a trickling filter type plant. A municipality with activated sludge treatment could then recognize that emulsified fats would be paid for under BOD charges, with grease restrictions applying only to floatable grease.

Pretreatment may reduce a poultry processor's overall waste treatment cost when a municipal surcharge system is contemplated. Surcharge systems vary, and no one can predict whether pretreatment can be economically justified until costs are evaluated. A surcharge system should be based upon an evaluation, by the city's consulting engineer, of the cost of the elements of the municipal treatment plant necessary to accommodate the flow, remove the suspended matter and treat the other ingredients of the industrial wastewater to the required levels, all on a unit basis (cost per pound of ingredient).

Many surcharge systems start with a flow base rate, and apply multipliers for concentrations of such ingredients as BOD, suspended solids, and grease (any or all of these). As an example, the flow base rate, charged to all sewer users, may be, say, 50% of the water bill (flow from private water supplies would be included). Then, taking BOD as an example, assume that 250 mg./l. has been established as a bottom base for surcharges. Then a multiplier might be applied for BOD between, say, 250 and 500 mg./l., and a higher one between, say, 500 and 1,000 mg./l.

Another set of multipliers might be applied for suspended solids, another for grease, etc. These multipliers are then added together to establish a single multiplier which is then applied to the flow base charge to arrive at the total bill. In other surcharge systems, charges for the pounds per month, above a base quantity, of BOD, suspended solids and other ingredients are added to the flow charges based on gallons.

Except for compulsory action to remove materials prohibited from entering the city sewers, the degree of pretreatment is generally an economic decision. However, since plants differ and surcharges differ, no simple set of parameters can be established. Each case must be evaluated individually not only to establish present practices but also to prepare for the future.

HOW TO PRETREAT

Pretreatment can cover a broad range of wastewater processing elements, including screening, gravity separation of solids and floatables, pressurized air flotation, chemical treatment as an adjunct to gravity separation or flotation, and biological treatment such as aerated or unaerated lagoons or some other form of aerobic treatment. Before any pretreatment is considered, an adequate survey should be made, including flow measurement, composite sampling and chemical analysis to determine the extent of the problem and the possibilities for pretreatment. Analyses may include BOD, suspended solids, suspended volatile solids, settleable solids, pH, temperature, and oils and grease. A permanent flow measuring and composite sampling arrangement is warranted if sampling is done regularly to determine municipal surcharges.

Most commonly, pretreatment will consist of separation of floatables and settleable matter. In some instances lime and alum, or ferric chloride, or a polymer may be added to enhance separation. Paddle flocculation may follow alum and lime or ferric chloride additions to assist in coagulation of the suspended solids. Separation may be by gravity process or by air flotation process. A screening process may precede the separation process, and also may be used to concentrate the separated floatables and settled solids.

Removal of floatables and suspended matter will also accomplish some reduction in BOD. Frequently this degree of treatment will satisfy municipal requirements. If additional BOD removal is required, a study of biological processes for pretreatment may be instituted, possibly in pilot scale. Several biological treatment systems have been successfully adapted to the treatment of poultry wastes, such as lagoon treatment.

Other BOD removal systems may be suitable. The so-called "Dutch Ditch", which utilizes an aeration device in an oval shaped shallow "race-track" ditch to recycle the flow, has been applied to meat waste treatment and may be suited to poultry wastes as well. High-rate aeration, with clarification and sludge return (activated sludge) is available in many configurations.

A rotating biological contactor is treating the effluent from an air flotation tank in a pretreatment system at a poultry plant in Illinois. In the contactor, wastewater flows through a tank in which a series of half-submerged discs, about 12 feet in diameter, rotate slowly on a horizontal shaft. As the shaft turns, a film of biological growth forms on the rotating surfaces.

Rotation of the discs alternately passes the bio-mass through the wastewater where the bio-mass absorbs organic matter, then through the air where it obtains oxygen for biological metabolism. Excess bio-mass sloughs off and is separated in a clarification step.

The plant in Illinois treats 130,000 gallons per day and is reported to remove 90% of the BOD in the wastewater leaving the flotation tank (influent at 2,000 mg./l., effluent at 200 mg./l.). Such a device is shown in Figure 23.

FIGURE 23:   ROTATING DISC CONTACTOR

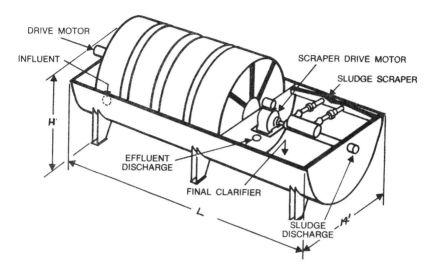

Source: A.J. Steffen before EPA Technology Transfer Seminar, Little
Rock, Arkansas (January 1973)

COSTS OF PRETREATMENT

Costs of pretreatment depend on many factors, such as size of poultry plant,
type of processing, space available for pretreatment, quality of in-house
waste conservation, pumping requirements, municipal requirements regarding quality of effluent, local labor costs, construction costs and federal
and state tax incentives for industrial waste treatment.

However, approximate costs of equipment are given wherever possible, as
well as approximate costs of any chemicals required. Installation costs of
prefabricated systems may be generally estimated at about 30 to 40% of
equipment cost. Processors often prefer prefabricated units for convenience
in installation.

Variations in loading due to changes in processing should not be overlooked
in making rough approximations for sizing pretreatment. For example, cut-
up and packaging can produce 15% greater BOD than processing to eviscerating only, and fowl can increase grease content from the usual 1.0 to 1.5
pounds per 1,000 birds to 1.5 to 2.0 pounds.

In spite of the wide divergence of costs, some examples of costs of plants, as built, may be useful. In one recent instance in Arkansas, in a plant processing 5,000 broilers an hour, with partial cut-up and packaging and some deep fat frying, a 20 x 20 mesh vibrating secondary screen (4' x 10') cost $20,000 installed, including a 200 gpm pump. Dual pumps are, however, advisable and would be expected to add about $1,000 to $2,000 to this figure.

Another plant in Arkansas, killing, eviscerating, and preparing frozen dinners, installed pretreatment in 1969, treating 1,250,000 gallons of wastewater daily. Secondary screening cost $19,500, a vacuator for grease removal cost $45,000 and buildings, flumes, piping and controls cost $259,000 (total $323,500).

A pretreatment plant under design for a Georgia processor will cost $80,000 to $100,000. This will include pumping, and pretreatment to produce an effluent of 300 mg./l. BOD and suspended solids and 100 mg./l. fats and grease. The plant processes 6,000 birds per hour and includes eviscerating, cut-up and packaging. A screen plus a gravity grease separator, in Canada, treating 330,000 gallons per day from a killing and eviscerating plant, cost $85,500, installed, without the building.

A pretreatment facility in South Carolina which handles offal and blood in addition to 2,800,000 gallons of daily flow for a plant killing, eviscerating and preparing frozen dinners cost $278,000 for screening and a vacuator (1965 costs). The building cost an additional $125,000. The plant in Illinois, described in an earlier paragraph, with air flotation and revolving disc contactor system cost $80,000. The contactor alone cost $22,000. To assist in arriving at rough approximations, Table 45 is included, showing raw wastelands.

TABLE 45:   TYPICAL POULTRY PLANT EFFLUENT (UNTREATED)*

Broiler Processing

	SRWL/1,000 Birds	Daily Discharge from Typical Plant Killing 125,000 Birds/day	Population Equivalents**
Flow	8,000 gal.	1,000,000 gal.	7,700
BOD***	30 lbs.		
(450 mg./l.)		3,750 lbs.	18,800
Suspended solids	23 lbs.		
(345 mg./l.)		2,870 lbs.	14,400

(continued)

TABLE 45:   (continued)

Fowl and Duck Processing

	SRWL/1,000 Birds	Daily Discharge from Typical Plant Killing 125,000 Birds/day	Population Equivalents**
Flow	-	-	-
BOD***	40 lbs.	5,000 lbs.	25,000
Suspended solids	25 lbs.	3,130 lbs.	15,700

Turkey Processing

	SWRL/1,000 lbs. Live Weight Kill	Daily Discharge from Typical Plant Killing 1 million lbs./day	Population Equivalents**
Flow	1,700 gal.	1,700,000 gal.	13,000
BOD***	8 lbs.		
(565 mg./l.)		8,000 lbs.	40,000
Suspended solids	5 lbs.		
(410 mg./l.)		5,000 lbs.	25,000

*Based on Standard Raw Waste Levels (SRWL) from EPA Guide Lines for Poultry Processing Plants, assuming good in-plant waste conservation, flow-away systems with customary flow-away screening, but no pretreatment.

**Population Equivalents based on: Flow: 130 gallon capacity per day; BOD: 0.2 pounds capacity per day; Suspended solids: 0.2 pounds capacity per day

***BOD - 5-day BOD

Source: A.J. Steffen before EPA Technology Transfer Seminar, Little Rock, Arkansas (January 1973)

SUMMARY

The following outline suggests procedures in developing a decision matrix for pretreatment:

(1) Select a project manager. He may be a company engineer or a consulting engineer, depending upon the extent to which the study is to progress and the capability of company personnel to produce the necessary information.

(2) Measure flow and collect and analyze composite samples over a period of days sufficient to develop maximum as well as average data.

(3) Make an in-plant waste conservation survey. The annual cost for each possible change should include:

    (a) Amortized cost of improvements, installed.

    (b) Power costs (heating, cooling, pumping).

    (c) Chemical costs (if any).

    (d) Labor cost (maintenance and operation).

(4) Make a study of possible pretreatment systems, with annual costs developed as in item (3) above.

(5) Determine the annual cost of municipal surcharges and compare with costs of (3) and (4).

(6) Select the elements of (3) and (4) that are economically justified.

(7) Design necessary improvements considering:

    (a) Portability of system.

    (b) Flexibility, for alteration and expansion.

    (c) Operating skills required.

    (d) Cost of disposal of residual solids and grease.

MUNICIPAL POULTRY PROCESSING
WASTE TREATMENT

Table 46 shows the amount of wastewater treated by municipal treatment facilities by type of technology and by size of plant. The largest amount of wastewater comes from typical technology plants of medium size. Very little wastewater comes, for example, from "advanced" technology plants of small size because there are few such plants.

TABLE 46:   POULTRY PROCESSING WASTEWATER HANDLED BY
MUNICIPAL TREATMENT FACILITIES

Type of Technology	Small	Medium	Large	Total
Old	1,254	2,318	228	3,800
Typical	2,193	5,230	1,012	8,435
Advanced	70	873	803	1,746
Total	3,517	8,421	2,043	13,981

*Millions of gallons (as of 1966)

Source: FWPCA Publication IWP-8

Table 47 shows the percent of processing plant effluent which enters municipal treatment facilities in selected years. Note the large increase experienced from the years 1950 to 1963. This change can be explained by the shift in industry location mentioned earlier.

TABLE 47:   PERCENT OF POULTRY WASTEWATER DISCHARGED TO
MUNICIPAL TREATMENT FACILITIES

Year	Percent
1950	50
1963	70
1967	72
1972	76
1977	80

Source: FWPCA Publication IWP-8

PLANNING, DESIGN AND CONSTRUCTION OF POULTRY WASTEWATER TREATMENT FACILITIES

As described by Giffels Associates, Inc., Architects-Engineers-Planners of Detroit, Michigan in the EPA Technology Transfer Seminar at Little Rock, Arkansas in January, 1973, the quality of wastewater discharged from process operations in a poultry plant may range from 5 to 10 gallons per bird with 7 gallons a typical value. Poultry processing wastewater is typically organic in character, higher than domestic sewage in biochemical oxygen demand, high in suspended solids and floating material such as scum and grease. Table 46 shows some characteristics of wastewater from a poultry plant.

TABLE 46

Analysis	Unit	Range	Average
pH	---	6.3 - 7.4	6.9
DO	ppm	0 - 2.0	0.5
BOD	ppm	370 - 620	473
Suspended solids	ppm	120 - 296	196
Total solids	ppm	---	650
Volatile solids	ppm	---	486
Fixed solids	ppm	---	164
Settleable solids	ml./liter	15 - 20	17.5
Grease	ppm	170 - 230	201

Source: Giffels Associates before EPA Technology Transfer Seminar, Little Rock, Arkansas (January, 1973)

Such wastewater from poultry processing plants is typically organic and responds well to treatment by biological methods. In biological waste treatment systems, microorganisms utilize the polluting constituents of the wastewater as food to provide energy for survival and growth. The primary microorganisms encountered in wastewater treatment are bacteria, fungi, algae, protozoa, rotifers and crustaceans. Bacteria can only assimilate soluble food and may or may not require oxygen depending on whether the bacteria are aerobic or anaerobic. Fungi must also have soluble food but are strict aerobes; that is, they must have oxygen to survive.

Algae utilizes primarily inorganic compounds and sunlight for energy and growth with oxygen given off as a by-product. Protozoa are single celled animals and utilize bacteria and algae as their primary source of energy. Rotifers are multicellular animals which use bacteria and algae as a major source of food. Crustaceans are complex multicelled animals which possess hard shells. The microscopic forms of crustaceans utilize the higher forms of microorganisms as a source of food. Protozoa, rotifers and crustaceans grow only in an aerobic environment.

Microorganisms find their place in the carbon cycle existing at the elemental levels of conversion of residual organic carbon to carbon dioxide. Briefly, the carbon cycle consists of green plants utilizing inorganic carbon in the form of carbon dioxide and converting it to organic carbon using sunlight for energy for photosynthesis. Animals consume the resulting plant tissue and convert part of it to animal tissue and carbon dioxide. Plant and animal tissue and other residual organic carbon compounds are then oxidized back to inorganic carbon dioxide by microorganisms.

Aerobic degradation of wastewater constituents is a biochemical reaction in which living cells assimilate food for energy and growth in the presence of dissolved oxygen. About 1/3 of the organics are oxidized providing the energy to synthesize the remaining into additional living cells. The end products of these biochemical reactions are carbon dioxide and water. When oxygen is absent from the reaction, the degradation is anaerobic and the end products are organic acids, aldehydes, ketones and alcohols.

Special bacteria called methane formers metabolize about 80% of the organic matter to form methane and carbon dioxide with the remaining 20% utilized to form additional living cells. These above biochemical principals are utilized in wastewater treatment systems to render wastewater streams from poultry processing facilities suitable for discharge to a stream. Wastewater treatment systems in the poultry processing industry usually include primary and secondary treatment and may or may not include tertiary treatment. Primary treatment consists of screening, comminutor and primary sedimentation or flotation for removal of solid and particulate matter.

Primary treatment is discussed in more detail in another portion of this text dealing with pretreatment of poultry processing wastewater.

PLANT WASTEWATER SURVEYS

Planning a wastewater treatment facility for a poultry plant begins with a survey of the wastewater sources within the plant. An industrial wastewater survey in an existing poultry processing facility would consist of determining the volume and characteristics of the composite wastewater discharge. The survey may be as simple as measuring flow and taking a composite sample at a single point or may be as complex as measuring flows and sampling each source of wastewater discharged. The latter has the advantage that each point within the plant may be studied to determine the the possibilities available for reducing the volume of wastewater and pollution at the source.

For a poultry processing facility where wastewater flow streams do not exist, the wastewater for the proposed plant must be synthesized based on experience at similar existing processing plants. Using this method for determining wastewater quantity and character requires great care to insure that all waste constituents are included in the synthetic wastewater sample and that the constituents are included in proportions that will be truly representative of the waste from the proposed facility. It is suggested that an experienced engineer be retained to prepare a study which will determine the properties of the design influent.

The volume of wastewater, in general, will vary with the bird production; increasing with increased bird production and decreasing with low production. Some of the characteristics of wastewater that should be determined include suspended solids, biochemical oxygen demand (BOD_5), toxic substances, grease and fats, dissolved solids, solid matter, temperature, pH, color and septicity.

Another discussion of plant wastewater surveys has been presented by Gurnham and Associates, Pollution Control Consultants of Chicago, Illinois at the EPA-sponsored Technology Transfer Seminar at Little Rock, Arkansas in January 1973.

Table 47 outlines the purposes of such a survey. Table 48 summarizes the points of responsibility for such a survey. Table 49 outlines the factors in planning a survey. Table 50 outlines considerations involved in measurement of flows in a plant wastewater survey. Table 51 outlines the factors in direct monitoring, and Table 52 the factors in sampling.

TABLE 47:   PURPOSES OF THE SURVEY

To determine compliance with regulations
          Or lack of compliance
          Local
          State
          Federal

To prevent public embarrassment
          Or, if too late, to counteract it
          Prevent nuisance suits

To provide data
          For a water management program
          For detection of material wastage and losses
          For water conservation and recycling
          For design of a treatment system
          For a discharge permit application
               Local, State, Federal
          For calculation of surcharge rate
          For use in private lawsuits by neighbors

Source: Gurnham & Associates before EPA Technology Transfer Seminar
          Little Rock, Arkansas (January 1973)

TABLE 48:   RESPONSIBILITY FOR THE SURVEY

Corporate management
Company or plant management
Plant technical staff
          Engineering department
          Plant engineer
Plant laboratory
Consultant
          Should be familiar with:
               Waste treatment processes and design
               Regulatory limits and procedures
               The poultry industry and its operations

Source: Gurnham & Associates before EPA Technology Transfer Seminar
          Little Rock, Arkansas (January 1973)

TABLE 49: PLANNING THE SURVEY

Define and understand the purposes and goals
Study the regulations that must be met
List the data expected from the survey
Obtain and verify maps and plans
    Surrounding area
    Plant area
      Building and department boundaries
      All waste sources
      Detailed sewer maps
Obtain basic information on plant operations
    Shifts and hours
    Cleanup schedules
    Production data
    Water sources and usage
Plan flow measurement and sampling program
    Points to be studied
    Flow measurement methods
    Sampling and analysis program
Train the survey crew

Source: Gurnham & Associates before EPA Technology Transfer Seminar
Little Rock, Arkansas (January 1973)

TABLE 50: MEASUREMENT OF FLOWS

Locations:
    Water intake to plant
    Water effluent from plant
    Intermediate flows
      Individual process streams

Methods:
    Direct meter
    Bucket and stopwatch
      Sump or vessel filling
    Weir
      Sharp-crested rectangular, right-angled V-notch, and other
    Parshall flume
    Cross-section/velocity measurements
    Dilution method

Other considerations:
    Temporary vs. permanent installation
    Indicating vs. recording meters
      Integrating meters
      Signal to automatic sampler

Source: Gurnham & Associates before EPA Technology Transfer Seminar
Little Rock, Arkansas (January 1973)

TABLE 51:   DIRECT MONITORING

Locations
    Plant effluent
    Possibly other locations

Permanence
    Fixed vs. movable

Parameters
    Temperature
    pH
    Turbidity
    Color
    Dissolved oxygen
    Conductance

Source: Gurnham & Associates before EPA Technology Transfer Seminar
          Little Rock, Arkansas (January 1973)

TABLE 52:   SAMPLING

Selection of sampling sites
Selection of sampling period
        Usually 24 hours; other periods may be better
Frequency of sampling
Type of sample
        Grab vs. composite
          At least, a representative composite for each 24 hour period
        Automatic samplers
Sample preservation
Sampling difficulties
        Stratified waste streams
        Coarse solids
        Cleaning and maintenance

Source: Gurnham & Associates before EPA Technology Transfer Seminar
          Little Rock, Arkansas (January 1973)

Table 53 summarizes some considerations in the analyses involved and Table 54 some of the factors in evaluation of such a survey.

TABLE 53: ANALYSIS

Field vs. laboratory tests
References:
  Standard Methods for the Examination of Water and Wastewater
    13th ed., 1970. American Public Health Association, New York
  FWPCA Methods for Chemical Analysis of Water and Wastes.
    1969. U.S. Department of the Interior
  1971 Book of ASTM Standards, With Related Material; Part 23,
    Water, Atmospheric Analysis. American Society for Testing
    and Materials, Philadelphia
Treatability studies
  Settleability
  pH titration curve
  Toxicity (bio-assay)
  Biodegradability

Source: Gurnham & Associates before EPA Technology Transfer Seminar
          Little Rock, Arkansas (January 1973)

TABLE 54: EVALUATION OF THE SURVEY

First survey day is usually only a trial run

Look for inconsistencies, inadequate data, etc.
    e.g., individual waste total vs. effluent flow and analysis
    Some error is inevitable

Preparation of material balances
    On water
    On individual pollutants

Calculation of loadings
    Per day
    Per unit of production
    Variability during the day

Comparison with other plants in the industry

Recommendations
    Based on original (or modified) purpose

Source: Gurnham & Associates before EPA Technology Transfer Seminar
          Little Rock, Arkansas (January 1973)

INITIAL PLANNING FOR A WASTEWATER TREATMENT SYSTEM

Criteria for the design of the treatment plant is available from the authority having jurisdiction for control of discharge to the receiving stream and must be evaluated by an engineer experienced in the design and engineering of wastewater treatment plants for poultry processing facilities. The selection of type of treatment and type, number and size of components may be performed when the required treatment efficiency in terms of removal of contaminants has been established.

Costs, both capital costs and operating costs, must be determined in the preliminary planning phase of the project. The preliminary planning phase of the project should result in a report describing the location of the waste treatment plant, the nature of the wastes, description of all components of the proposed wastewater treatment system, provisions proposed for future expansion, anticipated removal efficiency and character of effluent and an estimate of both capital and operating costs.

The preliminary report performs three primary functions. Firstly, the report may be used in discussions with the authorities early in the project; secondly, it provides the cost data essential to an economic feasibility of the project; and thirdly, it serves as a basis for the preparation of working drawings and construction contract documents.

TYPES OF WASTEWATER TREATMENT FACILITIES

Table 55 gives the breakdown of the types of treatment being used by poultry processors who have their own waste treatment facilities according to the survey made by the Federal Water Pollution Control Administration and reported in Publication IWP-8. It should be noted from the table that a general level of improvement is being experienced. To a large extent this is accounted for by the locational shift which has occurred within the industry.

Treatment facilities were constructed along with the erection of processing plants. It should be remembered that only 95 plants provided the basis for the distribution shown. The implicit assumption is, therefore, that these plants are representative of the entire poultry industry.

TABLE 55:   UTILIZATION OF WASTE TREATMENT FACILITIES

Type of Waste Treatment Facility	Estimated Percentage of Plants Using Process				
	1950	1963	1967	1972	1977
Catch basin only (Grease and solids removal)	49	30	9	5	1
Lagoon systems	30	40	49	50	57
Trickling filter	20	25	34	--	34
Irrigation	1	3	8	--	9

Source: FWPCA Publication IWP-8

Secondary treatment required for discharge to a stream may be in the form of an activated sludge system, a trickling filter system, a system of lagoons or an irrigation system. Each of these methods of biological treatment has been tried with varying degrees of success. Activated sludge systems that may be applied to poultry plant wastes include conventional activated sludge, activated sludge using step aeration, high rate activated sludge, extended aeration activated sludge and the contact stabilization process. Anaerobic lagoons, aerobic lagoons and a combination of an anaerobic lagoon followed by an aerobic lagoon may be used for secondary treatment of poultry wastes. All poultry wastewater effluents should be chlorinated before discharge to the receiving stream.

All of the above processes are described in the text which follows and represent the commonly used waste treatment processes. The use of other systems such as microfiltration, certain chemical processes, etc., while possible, are generally not used due to high first and operating costs.

The secondary treatment processes commonly utilized in the biological treatment of poultry wastes are: (1) various forms of the activated sludge process, (2) standard and high rate trickling filters, and (3) aerobic and anaerobic lagoons. In the past, aerobic and anaerobic lagoons have been employed in the majority of private installations with activated sludge plants as a second choice. Trickling filters have seen their main usage in joint treatment plants treating both municipal and poultry wastes. With the exception of anaerobic lagoons, all of the processes provide complete treatment and achieve upwards of 70 to 90% reduction in the influent BOD and 80 to 95% removal of suspended solids.

Each of the systems to be discussed have their advantages and disadvantages, and in general, the treatment requirements will dictate, to some degree, the particular system selected. The main differences between the systems are construction and land costs. The major costs for activated sludge and trickling filter plants are construction and operating costs, whereas, the major expense for lagoons is land utilization costs. The following discussion will limit itself to the unit operations and treatment plant equipment associated with each process.

ACTIVATED SLUDGE PROCESS

There are four general types of activated sludge processes: (1) conventional, (2) high rate, (3) extended, and (4) contact stabilization. All of the above general processes utilize the activated sludge theory, whereby aerobic bacteria assimilate the organic matter present in the waste stream for cellular growth and in that way provide for the waste stream purification. The

common elements of all activated sludge processes are: (1) an activated
sludge floc, (2) a mixing and aeration chamber, and (3) a clarification or
separation tank.

Conventional Activated Sludge

FIGURE 24:   CONVENTIONAL ACTIVATED SLUDGE PROCESS

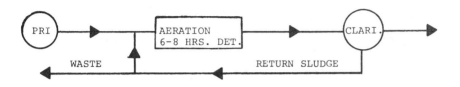

Source: Giffels Assoc. before EPA Technology Transfer Seminar, Little
           Rock, Arkansas (January 1973)

In the conventional activated sludge process as shown in Figure 24, the
waste stream, following primary treatment, is mixed with a proportional
amount of the returned settled sludge from the final clarifier and enters
the head of the aeration basin.

In general, the aeration basin is designed to provide a detention time of
6 to 8 hours. Mixing and aeration are uniform along the tank and are provided for by mechanical mixers and/or pressurized air diffusers. Following
aeration, the mixed liquor is settled in a clarifier, the clear supernatant
being discharged to the receiving water and the concentrated sludge being
proportionately returned and wasted.

One modification of the conventional process is step aeration, where the
waste stream and/or return sludge enters through a number of inlets along
the aeration basin rather than at a common inlet. A second modification
is tapered aeration, where aeration along the tank is varied. The advantages of the conventional activated sludge process are (1) lower capital
costs than equivalent trickling filter plants, (2) low hydraulic head losses,
and (3) a high quality effluent is attainable.

The disadvantages are: (1) higher mechanical operating costs than equivalent trickling filter plants, (2) requires skilled operators, (3) does not re-
spond well to shock loads, (4) generates a large volume of sludge to be
disposed of, and (5) problems in sludge settling are sometimes encountered.

High Rate Activated Sludge

FIGURE 25:   HIGH RATE ACTIVATED SLUDGE PROCESS

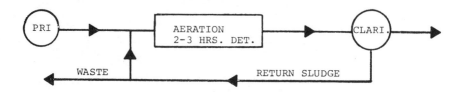

Source: Giffels Assoc. before EPA Technology Transfer Seminar, Little
           Rock, Arkansas (January 1973)

The main differences between the high rate process shown in Figure 25 and
the conventional process are the smaller detention period in the aeration
basin and a smaller return sludge rate. The advantages of this system are:
(1) lower capital costs than the conventional process, (2) the sludge generated is much denser resulting in a less voluminous sludge to be dispensed
with, and (3) because of the shorter detention time, operating costs are
less. The main disadvantage is the lower quality of the effluent.

Extended Aeration

FIGURE 26:   EXTENDED AERATION PROCESS

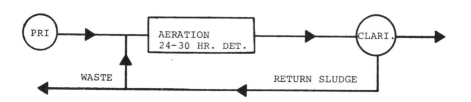

Source: Giffels Assoc. before EPA Technology Transfer Seminar, Little
           Rock, Arkansas (January 1973)

In the extended aeration process as shown schematically in Figure 26, the
aeration basin provides for 24 to 30 hours detention time. The advantages
of this process are: (1) the very high quality of effluent, (2) less manpower

time required to operate the process, and (3) smaller volumes of sludge are
generated. The main disadvantages of this process are the high capital investment required and the possibility of sludge settling problems.

Contact-Stabilization

FIGURE 27:   CONTACT-STABILIZATION PROCESS

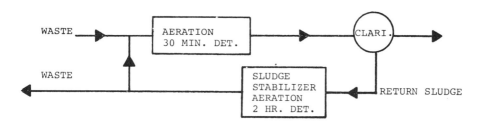

Source: Giffels Assoc. before EPA Technology Transfer Seminar, Little
          Rock, Arkansas (January 1973)

In the contact-stabilization process as shown in Figure 27, the waste stream
does not undergo primary clarification but is mixed with the return sludge
and enters the aeration basin directly. Since the mode of treatment is by
adsorption and absorption, a detention period of only 30 minutes is provided. After settling, the concentrated sludge is stabilized by separate
aeration before being proportionately returned to the waste stream. The
main advantages of this process are: (1) low capital investment, (2) low
operating costs, and (3) ability to handle shock loads and variations in flow.
BOD reductions of 90% and suspended solids removals of 90% have been
reported.

TRICKLING FILTERS

As mentioned previously, the biological mechanism involved in treating
wastewater by percolation through trickling filters is by assimilation of
organic matter into cellular growth by aerobic bacteria. Unlike the activated sludge process, where the biological process takes place in a "fluid
bed", the biological activity in a trickling filter is conducted on the filter
medium in the form of a surface fauna. Portions of the bacterial fauna are
continually sloughing off into the wastewater stream and are removed in
the final clarifier. Trickling filters can achieve upwards of 90% in both
reduction of BOD and removal of suspended solids.

There are two types of trickling filters: (1) standard rate and (2) high rate.
The number of filters in series determines the "stage" of the filter system.
The primary elements of a trickling filter are the covered or uncovered containing structure, the filter medium, the waste flow distribution system,
and the subdrain collection system. Typical mediums utilized are rocks,
slag, and recently honey-combed cellular modules of synthetic construction.
Distribution systems are spray nozzles attached to fixed or rotating manifolds.
The subdrainage system may consist of tile, concrete, or synthetic drainage
tile.

Standard Rate Trickling Filters

FIGURE 28:   STANDARD RATE TRICKLING FILTER

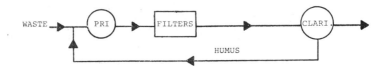

Source: Giffels Assoc. before EPA Technology Transfer Seminar, Little
          Rock, Arkansas (January 1973)

The main distinction of the standard rate trickling filter as shown in the
diagram in Figure 28 is the low BOD loading rate. The main advantages
are: (1) high quality effluent, (2) low operating costs, (3) operating personnel need not be highly skilled, (4) they are resistant to shock loadings
and variations in flow. The main disadvantages are high capital costs and
considerable land space is required. Flies and insects are sometimes a
problem but are usually controllable.

High Rate Trickling Filters

FIGURE 29:   HIGH RATE TRICKLING FILTER

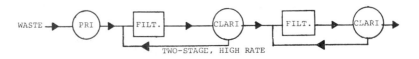

Source: Giffels Assoc. before EPA Technology Transfer Seminar, Little
          Rock, Arkansas (January 1973)

The main distinction of high rate trickling filters as shown in Figure 29 is
the high BOD loadings. These loadings may be as much as twice that of
a standard rate filter. Although for a single pass, BOD reductions are only
60 to 70%, recirculation provides for increasing the total reduction.
The advantages are: (1) versatility of treating high strength wastes, (2) resistance to shock loads and variations in flow, (3) highly trained personnel
are not required, (4) the area required is considerably reduced, and (5)
problems with flies and insects are usually eliminated. The main disadvantage is the high power requirements caused by recirculation.

LAGOONS

As was mentioned previously, lagoons are presently the most common method
of treating poultry waste at private waste treatment installations. This is
primarily a result of the availability of low cost land, when most of the
poultry processing facilities were constructed. Both aerobic and anaerobic
lagoons require very large allocations of land. Successful operation of
these lagoons depends to a high degree on local climatic conditions; generally favoring warm, clear and sunny conditions.

Depending on the geological site conditions, the lagoon may require lining
of the bottom. In general, the waste stream is pretreated by mechanical
screens to remove offal and feathers. The biological mechanisms responsible
for the purification process have been discussed previously. Mechanical
aerators and diffused air systems are used in the aerobic lagoons. A properly
designed aerobic lagoon can be expected to achieve 90% reduction in
BOD and suspended solids removal.

When anaerobic lagoons are used, expected removals are only 70 to 80%.
Odor problems are frequently associated with anaerobic lagoons, although
chemical additives can usually control the problem. In the past, flies, insects and excessive growth of bordering vegetation have been a problem.
Figure 30 shows some common flow schematics of lagoon systems.

As an example of the variety of schemes which may be incorporated into
the design of poultry waste treatment systems, one such plant has combined,
as a single treatment system, the extended aeration and aerobic lagoon concepts to effect a considerable costs savings plus a reduction in land requirements. This system, which could appropriately be called an "aerated lagoon" has been on stream for about 6 years and reportedly achieves upwards
of 90% reduction in influent BOD and suspended solids removal of better
than 80%. Since the waste treatment system has been such a success and
water shortage is also a problem at this plant, the EPA has supported a pilot
plant investigation to determine the feasibility of recycling the treatment

plant effluent for use as process water.

FIGURE 30:   FLOW SCHEMATIC OF VARIOUS LAGOON SYSTEMS

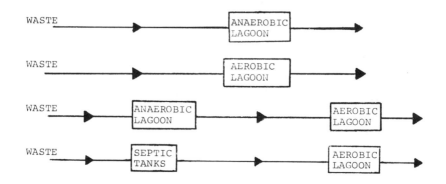

Source: Giffels Assoc. before EPA Technology Transfer Seminar, Little
              Rock, Arkansas (January 1973)

Upgrading Existing Lagoons

As discussed previously, the problems associated with the operation of
lagoon systems depend heavily on the local climatic conditions. Odors
are a common problem; always present in anaerobic systems and occurring
whenever anaerobic conditions develop in aerobic lagoons. Since there
is no control of the biomass, suspended solids removal and the maintaining
of minimum dissolved oxygen levels are frequently troublesome. A major
constituent of the suspended solids present in lagoon effluents is algae.

In the absence of sunlight, algae require molecular oxygen for endogenous
respiration. During periods which are characterized by low intensity sunlight radiation, the algae may deplete the dissolved oxygen below the minimum requirements resulting in algae degradation and thus the algae exert-
ing a biochemical oxygen demand. Anticipated stricter effluent criteria,
perhaps on a total pounds or maximum concentration basis rather than a
percentage removal of influent loading, will ultimately force the abandon-
ment of conventional lagoon systems to other alternatives or the upgrading
of the existing lagoons.

To effect any substantial improvement in the effluent quality, any steps to
upgrade a lagoon system must be oriented towards control of the biomass.
Recent attempts to remove the suspended solids from lagoon effluents have

not met with appreciable success. Because algae do not form dense flocs, clarification, either alone or combined with chemical flocculation, has not been successful. Chemical flocculation followed by air flotation has had limited success but the application of this method to the entire effluent stream would be economically prohibitive.

Conversion of an existing lagoon system to one of the various forms of activated sludge systems previously discussed, is both advantageous and economically feasible. In the activated sludge process, nutrients present in the waste stream, are utilized in the synthesis of the biomass. Since the biomass is ultimately separated and removed from the waste stream, the degree of algae synthesis in the effluent stream is limited.

In order to provide sufficient control of the biomass in converting to an activated sludge system, air supply and solids removal equipment must be provided. Generally, these will require the installation of blowers, air distribution systems, floating aerators, clarifiers, concentrators, strainers, etc. As in all of the biological systems, some solids will have to be disposed of and considerable attention should be given to reclaiming the solids as feed meal or fertilizer. Maximum effort should be made to utilize the existing lagoons as much as possible.

In some cases, portions of the lagoons can be converted to serve as multipurpose units such as clarifiers or aerobic digesters, as well as, aeration basins. Lagoons can also be utilized as "polishing" ponds capable of supporting fish life and providing the capability for recycling the treated wastewater.

Generally, once poultry processing operations have commenced, there is more reliable information available such as flows, loadings, temperatures, waste characteristics, etc., to establish good design criteria for the upgrading of lagoon systems. Likewise, it is often found that changes in existing process procedures can result in reduced flows and loadings, thereby reducing the required sizing of equipment.

Construction for the upgrading of lagoon systems is best accomplished by a "staged" sequence. Construction should be scheduled when plant production and the wastewater flow is at a minimum. In this way, the staged concept may allow for plant personnel to perform much of the required construction. Likewise, present effluent criteria can be satisfied while a future water use and waste treatment program is established.

Staged construction allows for distributing the capital costs for treatment facilities over a period of time resulting in minimization of upgrading costs. Staged construction could consist of initial installation of improved aeration

systems then later installation of a clarification device followed by final
installation of a system for recirculation of process water from a polishing pond.

The costs for upgrading existing lagoon systems are often significantly less
than that which would be required for equivalent new wastewater treatment
systems. In short, to minimize both present and future treatment costs, the
design for upgrading an existing lagoon system should incorporate, where-
ever possible, the existing facilities, process water conservation, and the
flexibility for present or future solids reclamation and treated wastewater
recycling. Figures 31, 32 and 33 are some typical flow schematics showing
various methods of upgrading existing lagoons.

FIGURE 31:   UPGRADING COMBINED AEROBIC AND ANAEROBIC
LAGOONS

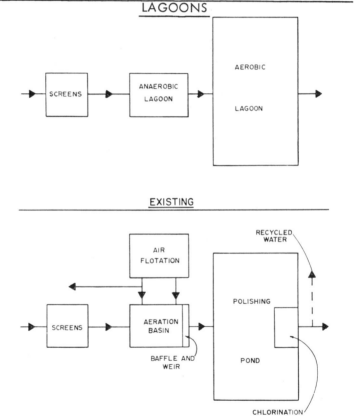

Source: Giffels Assoc. before EPA Technology Transfer Seminar, Little
Rock, Arkansas (January 1973)

FIGURE 32:   UPGRADING AN ANAEROBIC LAGOON

EXISTING

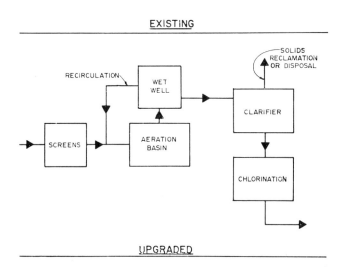

UPGRADED

Source: Giffels Assoc. before EPA Technology Transfer Seminar, Little
Rock, Arkansas (January 1973)

FIGURE 33:   UPGRADING AN AEROBIC LAGOON

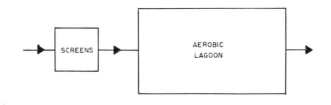

EXISTING

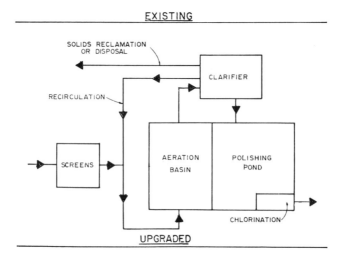

UPGRADED

Source: Giffels Assoc. before EPA Technology Transfer Seminar, Little Rock, Arkansas (January 1973)

NET POLLUTION QUANTITIES AFTER TREATMENT

The gross pollution load of the poultry processing industry is shown in Table 56 by source: blood collection and processing operations.

Pollution reduction of gross wasteload in the base year was the result of blood collection and private waste treatment of poultry processing plant wastewater. Blood collection removed approximately twenty-four million pounds of BOD while private waste treatment removed only about sixteen million pounds. Twelve of the sixteen million pound reduction was probably due to solids removal by screening. The remaining four million pounds BOD reduction would be due to some form of biological waste treatment.

The poultry processing industry is different from the meat packing industry in that the former relies primarily upon municipal treatment facilities to reduce wasteloads.

Table 57 gives gross and net pollution figures for selected years between 1963 and 1977. The gross pollution estimates assume that all processing plants of major blood collection is therefore the primary source of pollution reduction by subprocess change.

It should be noted that the trend of poultry processors to rely upon municipal facilities is expected to continue. Private waste treatment tends to be too costly for this low profit margin industry.

TABLE 56: NET POLLUTANT QUANTITIES*

Source of Waste	Gross Pollution BOD in Millions of Pounds	Pollution Load After By-Product Recovery BOD in Millions of Pounds	Reduction of Pollution by Private Treatment BOD in Millions of Pounds**	Reduction of Pollution by Municipal Treatment BOD in Millions of Pounds	Wasteload Reaching Water Courses Net BOD in Millions of Pounds
Blood	40.0	16.4	3.68	8.7	4.02
Processing	65.4	65.4	11.99	30.32	22.09
TOTALS	105.4	81.8	15.67	39.02	26.11

* The BOD figures used in this table were derived from the article "Wastes From Poultry Processing Plants" by John M. Bolton as the article appeared in the 13th Industrial Waste Conference at Purdue University, 1958. Mr. Bolton's figures were weighted by plant size then applied to the 1963 total slaughter figure. The six plants studied by Bolton were broken down into three groups representing old, typical and advanced technology. The resulting weighted BOD figure then was applied to the appropriate portion of industry which was using the technology in 1963.

** Private treatment is considered to be a screening process of varying degrees of sophistication.

Source: FWPCA Publication IWP–8

TABLE 57: SUMMARY OF BASE YEAR AND NET PROJECTED WASTELOADS*

Year	Gross Pollutant **	Per Cent Removal by Process Changes	Net Pollutant After Process Changes **	Per Cent Removal by By-Product Recovery	Net Pollutant After Process Changes and By-Product Recovery	Per Cent Removal by Private Treatment ***	Net Pollutant After Process Changes, By-Product Recovery and Private Treatment	Per Cent Removal by Municipal Treatment	Net Pollutant to water courses
1963	105.4	0	105.4	22.4	81.8	4.5	78.12	78	17.19
1968	134.5	0	134.5	25.0	100.9	5.0	95.9	79	20.14
1969	140.6	0	140.6	29.0	99.8	5.0	81.4	79	19.90
1970	146.6	0	146.6	34.0	96.8	7.0	90.0	81	17.1
1971	152.7	0	152.7	38.0	94.7	7.5	87.6	81	16.64
1972	158.7	0	158.7	39.0	96.8	8.0	89.1	85	13.37
1977	189.0	0	189.0	40.0	113.4	10.0	102.1	90	10.21

*   BOD per 1,000 birds is that shown in table

**   Gross and net pollutants measured in millions of pounds of BOD per year

*** Private treatment is considered to be a screening process of varying degrees of sophistication

Source: FWPCA Publication IWP-8

COSTS OF POLLUTION REDUCTION

As discussed by Giffels Associates, Inc. of Detroit, Michigan in an EPA-sponsored Technology Transfer Seminar at Little Rock, Arkansas in January 1973, the costs for waste treatment are difficult to project due, in large part, to their dependency upon local conditions. These local conditions consist of local design codes, climatic and geological consideration, etc.

Table 58 is included to provide a rough approximation of the costs of waste treatment as applied to the poultry processing industry. The table was constructed by adjusting average costs of similar municipal waste treatment facilities to fit poultry processing requirements.

The treatment costs presented do not reflect land acquisition costs. The values tabulated are 1967 prices and are based on the present value method of calculating costs. The selected interest rate is 5% and the expected life of the structure is 25 years.

Considering that the actual useful life of the facility will be more like 40 to 50 years and the fact that the costs are based on equivalent municipal facilities, this approach can be considered conservative and the resultant values considered "high". Municipal plants often are required to have parallel facilities and expensive sludge disposal equipment.

Parallel facilities sometimes increase the costs as much as (100 to 300%) and sludge disposal equipment such as sludge digesters, vacuum filters, and/or sludge incinerators can amount to (30 to 50%) of the capital costs. For these reasons, the capital costs shown in Table 58 can be reduced as much as 50% or more for poultry processing waste treatment. The table, therefore, only truly indicates relative costs for the various processes.

206

TABLE 58: POULTRY PROCESSING WASTE TREATMENT COSTS*

TYPE OF TREATMENT	CAPITAL COSTS (THOUS.$)	LEVEL OF TREATMENT (% B.O.D. REDUCTION)	OPERATION & MAINTENANCE COST (¢/1000 GAL.)	LAND REQUIREMENTS (ACRES)	TOTAL TREATMENT COSTS (¢/1000 GAL.)	TOTAL TREATMENT COST (¢/BIRD)
Conventional Activated Sludge	825	90+	10.63	3.0	15	0.15
High-Rate Activated Sludge	660	80+	6.81	2.0	11	0.11
Extended Aeration	1,569	95+	13.61	3.0	25	0.25
Contact Stabilization	473	90+	7.44	2.5	9.4	0.094
Standard Rate Trickling Filter	750	90+	6.00	8.5	12	0.12
High Rate Trickling Filter	555	90+	12.27	5.5	13	0.13
Aerobic Lagoons	740	90+	NEG.	74	8	0.08
Anaerobic Lagoons	300	70-80+	NEG	15	3.3	0.033
Anaerobic/Aerobic Lagoons	450	90+	NEG.	30	4.9	0.049

* Based on a flow of 1.0 MGD having a BOD load of 450 ppm. Values given are calculated by the present worth method based on an interest rate of 5% and an expected facility life of 25 years. Total treatment costs do not reflect land costs.

Source: Giffels Associates, Inc. before EPA Technology Transfer Seminar, Little Rock, Arkansas (January 1973)

For example, the "Gold Kist" waste treatment plant was constructed for a much lower cost than that shown in the table. This reduction in capital costs were the result of: (1) climatic conditions not requiring a facility to house air supply equipment; (2) minimization of sludge disposal costs because of available land and the recycling of by-products; (3) the retaining lagoon permitting a considerable reduction in clarifier sizing, and (4) parallel facilities not being required.

COST OF POLLUTION REDUCTION BY SUBPROCESS CHANGE

The operation and maintenance costs of subprocess changes which should reduce wasteloads are presented in Table 59.

TABLE 59:   COST AND ECONOMIC LIFE OF SUBPROCESSING METHODS*

Waste Reduction Techniques	Reduction of Wasteload, %	Capital Cost, Dollars	Economic Life, Years	Operation and Maintenance**
Dry cleaning of the receiving area	4	0	N/A	5,000
Blood collection	38	—	20	10,000

*Based on a medium sized plant using a typical
level of technology
**Cost in dollars per year

Source: FWPCA Publication IWP-8

Blood Recovery

Blood recovery is the most significant subprocess for reducing total plant wasteloads and will be used here to illustrate the weakness of estimates. The physical space necessary for blood recovery will depend on the speed at which the processing line is moving. The bird should remain in the bleeding area from 1 to 2 minutes. A bleeding cycle of longer duration will cause feather removal to be more difficult.

The type of bleeding area will also affect cost; if a bleeding room is used, the capital cost will be low but labor cost will be high, since blood will have to be coagulated on the bleeding room floor and shoveled by hand into containers. Blood remaining on the floor will be washed into the sewer during the cleanup period. If a bleeding tunnel is used, the initial capital costs will be high but labor costs would be reduced. This process puts the birds through a tunnel type arrangement where several openings are located along the tunnel bottom for the collection of blood.

At the end of the processing period the tunnel is washed and cleaned. The advantage of tunnel bleeding is that more blood is collected with the result that less blood reaches the sewer. Collection containers have to be emptied often enough to guard against contaminating overflows.

When bleeding areas of the type described are used, there are the factors of associated conveyor, time lost, and labor costs which must be considered in any estimation of costs involved in the operation. What must be guarded against is duplication of costs in the estimate. It is necessary for all plants to conduct the bleeding operation; therefore, plant space and processing time has to be set aside in any poultry slaughtering operation for the carrying out of this process.

The difference between the plant which collects blood and the plant which does not, is whether or not the blood enters the sewer. The noncollection plant discharges the blood into the sewer while the collection plant disposes of blood in some other manner. Both types of plants will discharge blood into the sewer during cleanup operations in approximately the same amounts.

In conclusion, the estimates which are presented in Table 59 are based primarily on labor costs, with economic life representing the life of the physical plant. The actual cost to a plant which collects blood is low because the collected blood may be sold to a rendering firm. Rendering of poultry by-products is a complete business in itself, with different pollution potentials than the processing industry. Since about half of a bird's total liveweight is lost during the processing, the amount of material available for rendering is considerable, consisting of feathers, offal, and blood.

COST OF POLLUTION REDUCTION BY INDUSTRIAL WASTE TREATMENT

According to "questionnaire data" the average cost of a secondary sewage treatment plant was $60,000. An average cost of $60,000 and an estimated number of plants with their own waste treatment facilities (ninety-six plants) means an estimated industry investment in waste treatment facilities of almost six million dollars in 1966. Operation and maintenance costs were estimated by the same method to be approximately one million dollars for the ninety-six plants (see Table 60).

The operation and maintenance are a higher percentage of the capital costs for poultry than for meat packing primarily because of the added expense of feather removal.

TABLE 60:   COST AND ECONOMIC LIFE OF TREATMENT FACILITIES*

Waste Treatment Method	Reduction of Wasteload	Capital Cost, Dollars	Economic Life, Years	Operation and Maintenance Cost in Dollars
Screening	95% removal of solids	10,000	8	5,000
Secondary sewage treatment	85% removal of BOD	60,000	15	8 - 10,000

*Based on a medium sized plant using a typical level of technology

Source: FWPCA Publication IWP-8

COST OF MUNICIPAL TREATMENT OF POULTRY PROCESSING WASTE-WATER

Poultry processors are different from meat packers in that they tend to either treat waste themselves or to use municipal treatment facilities but not both. Less than 5% of the plants responding to the questionnaire used a method of joint treatment. This is partly explained by the shifting location of the industry in the past decade. In order for cities to attract poultry processing plants, the cities often agreed to provide treatment facilities for the processing plants' waste. This was one of the criteria processors specified when relocating.

The average annual amount paid to the municipality by a plant of a certain size was obtained in the following manner: The questionnaire asked each processor to report waste treatment charges paid to municipalities. Respondents were classified into three size groups and the average annual payment by plants in each group was determined.

The average charge was then assumed to apply to all processors in the appropriate size group. Table 61 shows the average payment by a poultry processing plant, by size of plant and the total payment by the industry for the year 1966. In 1966 it was estimated that processors paid about

$4.6 million to municipalities to obtain waste treatment.

TABLE 61:   WASTE TREATMENT CHARGES PAID TO MUNICIPALITIES
IN 1966

Size Group	Number of Plants in Size Group	Average Annual Payment by Processors in the Size Group	Total Annual Payments by all Plants in Size Group in Thousands of Dollars
Small	140	$ 8,828	$1,042
Medium	239	12,544	2,998
Large	44	13,108	578
Total	401		4,618

Source: FWPCA Publication IWP-8

CHOICE OF OPTIMUM FINANCIAL STRATEGY

The choice of the optimum financial strategy for pollution control in poultry processing facilities has been reviewed by U.M. Patankar and C.R.
Marshall of J.A. Commins and Associates Inc., Fort Washington, Pa. in
a paper before the EPA-sponsored Technology Transfer Seminar at Little
Rock, Arkansas in January 1973.

As the 1970's proceed, these authors point out that enviroment-related
management decisions will be more complex and frequent. The impact on
businesses of nonproductive enviromental expenditures can be significant
where by-product recovery is limited or nonexistent. It is clear from the
provisions of the Water Pollution Control Act coupled with the existing
Clean Air Act, that industry must commit sizable capital to meet the enviromental standards the nation has set.

Many governmental institutions have shown a form of compassion for these
necessary expenditures by providing means of reducing or softening the financial expenditures for pollution control. There exists a mild governmental practice of spreading some of industries' pollution control costs over
the general public in place of just the company, and, to some degree, its
customers.

This is accomplished by excusing pollution control devices from certain
sales, use and property taxes, by allowing tax-exempt financing by the

company of the expenditures, or through adjustment in company income taxes by the addition of special depreciation alternatives. All of these programs involve a company paying lower taxes than they normally would have to pay if that equipment was for some other manufacturing or service purpose.

To put these incentives or cost reduction practices into perspective, it should be pointed out that these incentives do not pay for the pollution control investment nor do they overwhelmingly reduce the cost. They can, however, have a pronounced effect on cash flow and profit positions depending on what alternatives are selected. Because procurement of control equipment is a relative unique business occurrence, and because of a considerable body of new and involved tax and financing regulations for such purposes, it is likely that company financial managers are not as familiar with the many possibilities as they would be with the more common business operations.

The J.A. Commins and Associates report cited above demonstrates that it is well worth spending time in analyzing the unique added methods of financing pollution expenditures and their equally unique tax treatment. It will alert decision makers as to the availability of, and qualifications for some of the financing incentives that federal, state and local governments have made available.

Obtaining the optimum financial and tax incentives for a company could save tens of thousands of dollars over the life of the equipment. For example, a Business Week article (July 29, 1972 pp. 50-51) demonstrated the cost savings that tax exempt pollution control revenue bonds can provide. "Over the life of a 20 year $10 million issue, the typical interest saving is about $3.6 million."

Some revenue bond issues allow for deferred repayments of principal and permit the largest payments at the end of a 20-30 year issue. Meanwhile, the company can take depreciations and use investment tax credits which lower taxes. Thus, it can build up a cash flow which is used in other areas of the business. On that cash flow, earnings are generated which help to repay the bond principal at the later time.

The emphasis of this discussion thus far has centered on equipment purchases. Poultry processors with their own waste treatment facilities, and any processor-renderer with air pollution control equipment, will find the equipment emphasis appropriate. Those poultry processors whose waste becomes part of the municipal system will find the equipment analysis pertinent only if pretreatment of wastes requires capital expenditures. The municipal treatment users, who already pay charges, are expected to face increased user charges under the 1972 Federal Water Pollution Control Act, where federal funds are used for construction of the municipal treatment facility.

Now that the EPA has published its guidelines for effluents as quoted in the final section of this volume on "Future Trends", poultry processors and others will then be able to analyze whether it would be financially preferable to make a capital equipment investment for their own private treatment facilities, or whether being hooked into municipal treatments system is better. There may be regulations, however, that might preclude the exercise of the results of such a decision.

Presently, there is little that can be said quantitatively with respect to the preference of a user charge versus private treatment decision because of the anticipated changes in rates. This discussion will indicate, however, how to proceed with an analysis once the permissibility and costs of using municipal facilities are more adequately defined.

There are a number of new unique alternatives that have sizable differing financial consequences amounting to tens of thousands of dollars. Many of the alternatives require, by law, that once a financial decision is made it can't be changed, or changed in only one direction. Others are final in that it would be prohibitively costly to change later on in the program. Therefore, the following financial information should be analyzed as a minimum before an equipment decision is made.

> (1) Determine for all debt financing of pollution control investments, the most effective combination of rate and term of the load. Calculate the negative cash flows involved and their net present values.

> (2) Calculate the year-by-year inflows and the present values for each available choice of depreciation.

> (3) Select the management objective by which you would want to judge the financial impact of the investment; for example, lowest short-term profit impairment, least cash drain, long-term profit impairment, etc. Compare the combinations of financing and depreciation values calculated in steps (1) and (2) against the established management objective, and select the combination best suited for your company needs.

> (4) Determine what the municipality's user charge

will be for processing wastes and estimate
the capital expenditure necessary for any
pretreatment facility. Calculate the present values for the treatment expense and a
present lease value for the user charge payment.

(5) Compare the values and year-by-year effects
of step (4), and steps (1) through (3), against
the selected financial management objective.
This will allow you to make a choice between
whether to plug into a municipality's wastewater or invest in a private treatment facility, from a financial point of view.

This analysis presumes that the legal and tax implications of each financial
alternative are fully understood by the analyst in order that present values
and cash flows can be calculated. Likewise, the analysis does not include
the legislative and technical matters which may preclude a poultry processor from being able to have the freedom of choice.

The J.A. Commins and Associates report cited above is divided into five
chapters. Chapter 1 describes the standard depreciation methods and those
which have been established for pollution control facilities. Chapter 2
examines the costs of different methods of financing pollution control equipment. Chapter 3 relates the financing and tax strategies to the normal financial strategies of a company. In other words, how do the incentives
correspond to a company's maximum cash flow strategy or its profit maximi-
zation strategy, etc.

Chapter 4 is a look at the availability of the various financing alternatives
already discussed, both from the federal government and from the five south-
ern states in which the greatest amount of poultry processing takes place.
Some financing alternatives are for practical purposes always available,
while others are dependent upon the source's budget.

The last chapter examines the combination of the first four sections as opposed to the alternative of a user charge system. This analysis sets up a
basis for decision when the costs of the Federal Water Pollution Control
Act become predictable.

PART III.

THE SEAFOOD PROCESSING INDUSTRY

In this section on the seafood processing industry, unlike the previous sections on meat and poultry pollution, a bibliography is provided and reference numbers in parentheses refer to that bibliography.

STRUCTURE OF THE INDUSTRY

An extensive review of the seafood processing industry has been made by workers at the Pacific Northwest Water Laboratory (1). The world marine harvest stands at approximately 50 million tons per year. 90% of this catch is fish, the remainder being whales, crustaceans and mollusks. From 1850 to 1950, this harvest increased at an average rate of 2.5% per year. During the last two decades this increase has jumped to 5% per year (2). Some observers believe that even with modern methods of fishing, the yield can be increased to 5 to 10 times the present value. More conservative analysts estimate a possible increase of 2 to 3 times the present yield (3).

The increased catches of the 1950's and 1960's were due mainly to the intensified fishing efforts of a few nations: Peru, Japan, and the Soviet Union. The annual United States catch, meanwhile, has been steadily declining; since 1962 U.S. fish harvests have decreased 20%. The most common reasons cited for this decrease are low efficiencies, insufficient and expensive labor, and governmental restrictions (4). Based on recent performance, the United States seafoods industry is not expected to expand significantly in the near future.

The annual U.S. catches average approximately 6 billion pounds (5). The fish are utilized as follows: 35% rendered, 30% marketed fresh, 20% canned, 10% frozen, and 1% cured (6). Frozen fish products have been increasingly popular items; a 150% increase in frozen fish sales over the next 15 years has been predicted (7).

The U.S. consumption of fishery products has continued to rise, doubling from 8 to 16 billion pounds from 1959 to 1969. These increasing demands, however, have been satisfied by imported products. This increase in consumption has been almost exclusively due to the population increase; the U.S. per capita consumption of seafood products has remained at approximately 11 pounds per year over the last 20 years (5).

Menhaden, herring, and alewives are oily fishes which comprise the bulk of the industrial fisheries in this country: the rendering of whole fish into meal, oils, and solubles. The meal is used primarily as animal feed and fertilizer; the oil becomes an ingredient in paints, varnishes, resins, and similar materials, is added to animal feed, or is used for human consumption abroad; and the solubles are either fed directly to animals or are dried and processed into meal.

The menhaden fishery is the largest in the United States; the 1968 catch totaled 1.4 billion pounds (5). The industry is located mainly in the middle Atlantic and the Gulf states. Fishing takes place predominantly during the summer and fall months. Since the menhaden fishing areas are largely exploited to the maximum, significant future growth in this industry is not anticipated. Continuous production at levels near those of recent years is expected.

TUNA

Tuna ranks as the number one seafood in the United States. Americans consume over one billion cans of tuna per year (14). Tuna are large migratory fish which feed on smaller macroscopic sea life. Their distribution in the ocean is still largely unknown. The largest part of the tuna harvest takes place off the Pacific Coast.

Most tuna canned in the United States are caught in relatively distant waters. A modern tuna vessel can hold from 150 to 300 tons of fish and has a range of 1,000 miles (15). Because of the length of time in transport, the fish are normally frozen on board the vessels. After the boat arrives at dockside, the tuna canning operation begins with the mechanical unloading of the fish, which are weighed and inspected while they are still frozen.

The annual tuna catch averages approximately 300 million pounds, almost all of which is canned. The U.S. catch in recent years has failed to meet the increased domestic market. Use of scientific methods to determine fish migration should increase future catches and enable the domestic market to expand. A slight upward trend in tuna production has been evident now for the past six years and is expected to continue (16).

SALMON

The only significant commercial anadromous fishery in the United States is the salmon fishery. The five main species harvested in this country are chinook (king), sockeye (red), silver (Coho), pink and chum. The major portion of the catch is canned. The fish are caught fairly close to the canneries and are often stored in the boats without refrigeration.

The total 1968 salmon catch was 301 million pounds compared with the average over the previous five years of 335 million pounds per year (5). The harvesting is centered around Alaska with significant contributions from Washington and Oregon.

The Pacific salmon fishery is now advancing after a general failure which occurred in 1967. The future of this industry is largely dependent on market conditions, pressure from foreign competitors and on future conservation practices. A major expansion of the salmon industry in this country is not anticipated. Continued production at or near current levels is expected (5).

SHRIMP

The shrimp industry is the most important seafood industry of the Gulf of Mexico and South Atlantic areas. It is also significant along the Pacific coast. The season runs from April to early June, and again from August to early October (26).

Shrimp are caught commercially in otter trawls in the coastal waters. The shrimp are separated from the trash fish and stored by various methods. When short storage times will suffice, no preservation methods are used; the shrimp are taken directly to a processing plant or to a wholesale marketing vessel. When longer storage times are necessary, the shrimp are iced in the holds. In some places, notably in the Gulf of Mexico area, the shrimp are beheaded at sea and the heads dumped overboard. The heads contain most of the active degradative enzymes, so this practice retards spoilage. If the shrimp are beheaded within 30 minutes after being caught, the intestinal veins are usually removed with the heads, which is desirable from a quality standpoint.

The shrimp fishery in terms of total value is the most important in the United States. In 1968, the catch exceeded 290 million pounds with a value of approximately 110 million dollars. Currently the most important finished products are frozen and breaded shrimp. In 1968, these two products comprised 92% of the market. Both of these products were successfully developed during the 1950's and markets are apparently continuing to expand. Except in Alaska, the catch areas appear to be fully exploited. Yearly variation in catch seems to be dependent on the survival of the population from the previous year. The Alaskan catch, now less than one-fourth of the national total, could expand substantially with further developments (5). One writer predicted that the Alaskan stocks are capable of producing a catch equal to or exceeding 250 million pounds annually, or five times the existing Alaskan catches (28).

CRAB

The blue crab, comprising 70% of the U.S. crab production, is harvested on the Atlantic coast, principally in the Chesapeake Bay area. The remaining harvest takes place on the Pacific coast where Dungeness crab is the leading species followed by Alaskan king crab. Crabs are harvested from shallow water in baited traps. Rapid and careful handling is necessary to keep the animals alive. Dead crabs must be discarded because of rapid decomposition.

The total crab catch in 1968 exceeded 238 million pounds (5). The catches of the three main species seem to have reached a plateau. Production appears to be determined by the extent of previous years' hatches and the extent of harvesting rather than by marketing conditions. Future harvests of most species should continue at levels dependent on survival of offspring in the fishing grounds. Production of Alaskan king crab may eventually increase slightly due to stricter controls being imposed by the Alaskan Board of Fish and Game (5). The controls established a king crab fishing season from 5 to 7 months long in Alaskan waters. In 1969 all areas were closed on February 15th and not reopened until August.

The tanner crab harvest has been increasing in recent years due to the decreased availability of king crab. Abundant stocks exist off the northern Pacific coast and harvesting of this species should rapidly increase (28).

BOTTOM FISH

The most important bottom fish species are listed by Slavin and Peters (36) as haddock, halibut, cod, ocean perch, whiting (silver hake), flounder, hake, and pollock. Approximately 30% of the industry is located in the North Atlantic region. The major halibut fishery is centered in the Pacific Northwest where the commercial season extends from April through October.

Bottom fish are usually caught in otter trawls. In a typical operation, the fish are spread on the trawler decks, sorted and iced. Perch, flounder and whiting are stored whole, whereas cod, haddock, halibut and pollock are usually eviscerated on deck. The viscera and blood are washed overboard.

In 1968 the bottom fish catch exceeded 490 million pounds, of which approximately 190 million pounds was harvested on the Atlantic coast (5). The total domestic supply of bottom fish fillets and steaks has been steadily declining since the 1940's (5). The major reason for the drop in domestic production seems to have been lower yields in Atlantic coast waters. The halibut production, on the other hand, has been predicted to remain, in the near future, at approximately the 1968 level of 26 million pounds (21). This estimate was based on consumer demand, requirements for growth and limits imposed by the International Pacific Halibut Commission.

SEAFOOD   PROCESSES   AND   POLLUTANTS

MENHADEN

In many cases, the menhaden rendering operations are highly mechanized.
The process, outlined schematically in Figure 34 involves first the harvesting of the fish in purse seines and storage in the holds of the fishing boats.

FIGURE 34:   MENHADEN RENDERING

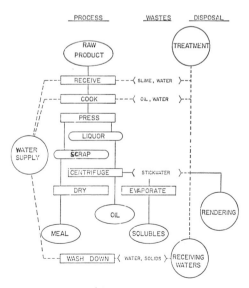

Source: EPA Report 12060-04/70

Ice or refrigeration is used for preservation if the trip exceeds one day. At the plant, the fish are pumped from the holds, washed, automatically sprayed and conveyed into the plant. Cooking is done continuously by steam. The fish are then pressed to remove the oil and most of the water. This press water is screened to remove solids and centrifuged to separate the oil. The remaining water, called stickwater, is discharged or evaporated to produce condensed fish solubles. The solid residual from which the water and oil have been pressed is known as presscake. The presscake is dried to about 10% moisture and then ground for fish meal.

TUNA

The tuna are thawed as shown in Figure 35. The next step, evisceration, is normally conducted by hand in several phases.

FIGURE 35: TUNA CANNING

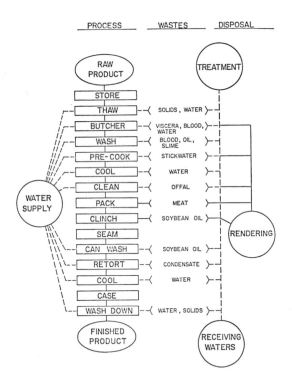

Source: EPA Report 12060-04/70

The body cavities are flushed with water and all adhering viscera carefully removed. The viscera are used for fish meal or pet food and the livers are sometimes recovered for oil and vitamins. After butchering, the fish are steam precooked. The time of cooking varies with the fish size, but it is usually about 3 hours. This cooking removes 22 to 26% of the moisture (15). Following cooking, the fish are cooled for approximately 12 hours to firm the flesh. The meat is then separated by hand from the head, bones, fins and skin.

All dark meat is removed and usually recovered for pet food. The light meat for canning is placed on a conveyor belt and transferred to the "Pak-Shaper." Tuna slices are arranged lengthwise in the Pak-Shaper which then molds the meat into a cylinder, fills the cans and trims the meat after filling. Each machine has a capacity of from 125 to 150 cans per minute (15). Prior to vacuum sealing, salt and vegetable oils are added to the cans. After sealing, the cans are retorted by standard procedures.

SALMON

Canning operations are conducted for the most part employing standard cannery equipment in a conventional manner as shown in Figure 36. After transfer from the holds of the fishing boats, the fish are eviscerated, beheaded and the fins removed. The raw meat, including the bones, is then placed into cans, the cans are weighed, and their weights are adjusted (if necessary) prior to sealing. The cans are then seamed, retorted, cooled and cased prior to shipping.

The principal exception to this standard canning operation is the use, predominantly in Alaska, of the "iron chink." The iron chink performs several functions in one operation, removing heads, fins and viscera mechanically.

SHRIMP

The shrimp are unloaded from the vessels into a flotation tank at dockside to remove the packing ice and then conveyed to a rotary drum to remove surplus water and bits of debris. This is followed by weighing. In Texas and the South Atlantic states particularly, the shrimp are iced after the initial preparation to optimize peeling conditions.

Next the shrimp are peeled (or picked) by hand or machine. Machine-peeled shrimp are used mostly for canning (21). The mechanical peeling process is outlined in Figure 37. The machine-peeled shrimp are paler in color, have a poorer flavor and have a texture inferior to hand-picked shrimp.

FIGURE 36:   SALMON CANNING

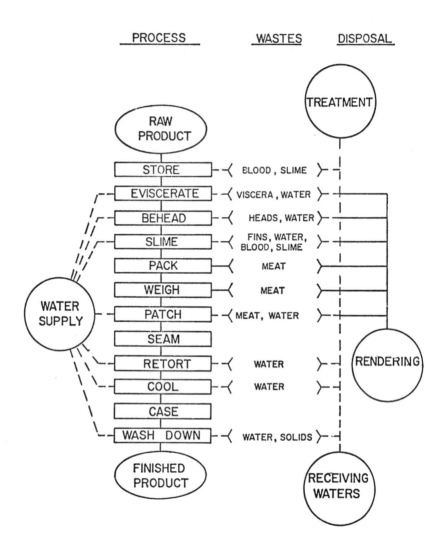

Source: EPA Report 12060-04/70

FIGURE 37:   MECHANICAL SHRIMP PEELING

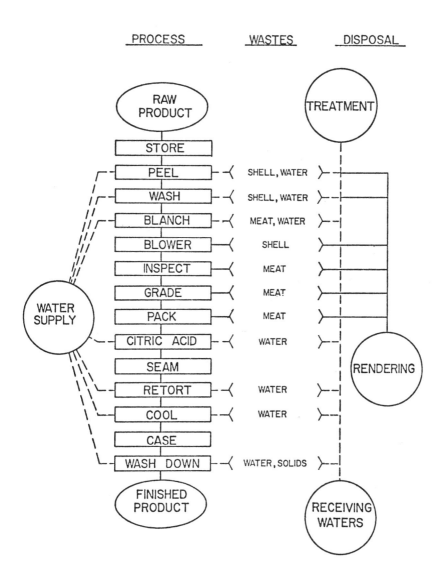

Source: EPA Report 12060-04/70

These disadvantages are offset by the fact that an automatic peeler can handle 500 pounds of shrimp per hour compared to average rates of 100 to 400 pounds of shrimp per day per man for hand picking (26).

After peeling, the meats are inspected and washed. They are then blanched in a salt solution for about 10 minutes and dried by various methods to remove surface water. Again the shrimp are inspected and then canned. Shrimp are marketed fresh, frozen, breaded, canned, cured and as specialty products. An increasing amount are sold breaded or fresh-frozen, whereas the quantities of canned shrimp produced in recent years have been relatively constant. About 40% are sold frozen in the shell (27).

CRAB

At most canning plants, the whole crabs are steam-cooked in retorts for 20 to 30 minutes (32). Pacific Coast Dungeness crab operations differ in that they first butcher the crabs (i.e., remove the backs) and then cook the crabs for 12 minutes or less. Cooked crabs are also marketed in the shell, butchered, or the meats picked from the shell are marketed fresh, frozen, or canned. Figure 38 depicts a frozen crab operation.

FIGURE 38: CRAB FREEZING

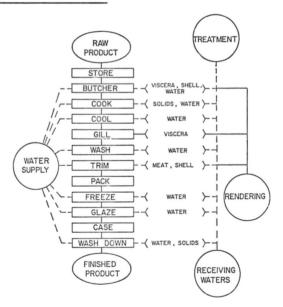

Source: EPA Report 12060-04/70

The majority of the Atlantic blue crab meat is marketed fresh or frozen, while the majority of the Pacific crab meat is canned (33). A large quantity of Dungeness crab is sold in the shell and a large quantity of king crab is butchered at sea (34). Both practices reduce the quantity of butchering waste to be handled at the processing plant site.

Crab canning and crab freezing operations are understandably similar. After cooking, the crabs are water-cooled to facilitate handling. The backs are removed, if they haven't been previously, and the remaining viscera are washed free. The cooking, cooling, and washing waters contain considerable solids and organic pollutants. After cooling, the meat is picked from the shell by hand with a small knife. Mechanical methods have been recently developed to extract the meat from the shell but are not yet widely employed (35). Crab meat quickly degrades in quality and must be chilled, frozen, or canned. Chilled meat can be stored for only a few days and even frozen meat looses texture and flavor qualities rapidly. Canning of crab meat results in the additional wastewater flows of the retort and cooling waters.

BOTTOM FISH

Bottom fish are normally filleted. The typical filleting operation is depicted in Figure 39.

FIGURE 39:   BOTTOM FISH FILLETING

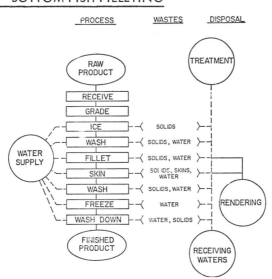

Source: EPA Report 12060-04/70

After unloading, the fish are weighed, washed, and iced in tote boxes. In some larger plants, mechanized unloading methods are used to maintain quality. In small plants, the fish are processed by hand. The fillets are cut on a wooden board next to a sink, washed and immediately iced in boxes for distribution.

Most plants processing fillets use mechanized equipment. First, the fish are washed with sprays of water in large rotating tumblers; then they pass through filleting machines or along hand filleting tables. Filleting machines only operate on certain sizes and shapes, but they are considerably more efficient and economical than hand filleting. The skin is removed from the fillet by hand or machine. The solid wastes from filleting and skinning operations are usually rendered for pet food or animal meal.

The skinned fillets are transported by a conveyor belt to a washing and at times a brining tank. After inspection, the fillets are packed in containers or frozen and then packed. Fillets are marketed frozen (fresh or breaded), chilled, or fresh.

SEAFOOD PROCESSING WASTELOADS

A significant portion of the fishes and shellfishes processed is wasted. The percentage of each species wasted ranges from 0% for fish which are completely rendered (e.g., menhaden) to 85% for some crab (e.g., blue crab). The average wastage figure for all fish and shellfish is about 30%. In addition to these large volumes of solid wastes, significant wastewater flows result from the butchering, washing and processing of the products. The volumes of solids and wastewater vary widely with seafoods and processing methods.

Using the 30% figure, the total annual volume of solid wastes generated in the seafoods industry in the United States is roughly 1.2 billion pounds. A large portion of these wastes is rendered for animal feed. The remainder is taken to municipal or private disposal sites or discharged directly to adjoining waters. The pollutional strength per pound of fish waste has been estimated to be 0.2 pounds of five day biochemical oxygen demand (BOD_5), or approximately one daily population equivalent (8).

As will be discussed later, this figure is highly variable and probably represents only the carbonaceous demand, neglecting the nitrogenous demand which would be exerted somewhat later. Using this figure and assuming that 50% of the fish wastes, as an average are rendered, the population equivalent of this industry can be estimated to be two million people. The population equivalent of solid and liquid fish processing wastes has been estimated by one author to be from 66 to 1,020 per ton of fish (9). For the United States, this represents a population equivalent of 0.23 to 3.6 million. These figures are deceptively conservative, for a major segment of the seafoods production takes place during short seasons, intensifying the problem. The industry is not typified by a constant output month after month.

229

The fish processing waste problem has become serious in certain areas. Waste treatment will be necessary in the future to meet federal and state water pollution control regulations. The purpose of this section is to evaluate the state of the art of fish processing waste treatment and by-product recovery.

In a properly managed menhaden rendering plant, the quantities of wastes produced are small. The only inherently troublesome waste is the fish pumping water. The other wastes result from spills and leakages, both of which can be minimized. The wastewaters from the production of fish meal, solubles, and oil from herring, menhaden and alewives can be divided into two categories: high-volume, low-strength wastes and low-volume, high-strength wastes.

The high-volume, low-strength wastes consist of the water used for unloading, fluming, transporting, and handling the fish plus the washdown water. One author (10) estimated the fluming flow to be 200 gallons per ton of fish with a suspended solids loading of 5,000 mg./liter. The solids consisted of blood, flesh, oil and fat. These figures vary widely; other authors listed herring pump water flows of 250 gpm with total solids concentrations of 30,000 mg./liter and oil concentrations of 4,000 mg./liter (11). The bilge water in the boat was estimated to be 400 gallons per ton of fish with a suspended solids level of 10,000 mg./liter.

The strongest wastewater flows are the stickwaters. In the past, stickwater was often discharged to the receiving waters, but now this practice is generally forbidden by law. One reference listed the average BOD_5 of stickwater as ranging from 56,000 to 112,000 mg./liter, with average solids concentrations, mainly proteinaceous, ranging up to 6% (12). Fortunately, the fish processing industry has found the recovery of fish solubles from stickwater to be at least marginally profitable. In most instances, stickwater is now evaporated to produce condensed fish solubles. Volumes have been estimated to be about 120 gallons per ton of fish processed (13).

It has been estimated that 65% of the tuna is wasted in the canning process (17). Using this figure, the 1968 quantity of wastes generated in the U.S. was calculated to be 190 million pounds. The degree of wastage probably varies somewhat with species. A recent study examined in detail the waste from a tuna canning and by-product rendering plant for a five day period (18). The average waste flow was found to be 6,800 gallons per ton of fish. Organic loadings varied from 500 to 1,550 mg./liter BOD_5. The average daily COD ranged from 1,300 to 3,250 mg./liter and the total solids averaged 17,900 mg./liter of which 40% was organic. The mean values and their expressions in terms of lbs./ton of fish are listed in Table 62.

TABLE 62:   TUNA WASTE CHARACTERISTICS (18)

Parameter	Mg./L.	Lbs./Ton of Fish
COD	2,273	129
BOD$_5$	895	48
Total solids	17,900	950
Suspended solids	1,081	58
Grease	287	15

Source: R.J. Chun, R.H.F. Young and N.C. Burbank, Jr., Paper before 23rd Industrial Waste Conference, Purdue University (1968)

These figures indicate that the five day BOD of the tuna waste was only approximately 40% of the COD value. Due to the high proportion of parti-culate matter in the total solids (leading to low surface-area-to-volume ratios), and to the organic nature of the wastes, a considerable BOD is exerted after five days. In this case, at 22 days, the BOD exerted was 3,520 mg./liter and was noted to still be rising. It is important to realize that the waste exerts a considerable nitrogenous demand (that oxygen re-quired to oxidize the less reduced forms of nitrogen to nitrate) in excess of the five day carbonaceous value.

The quantities and possible uses of salmon wastes have been rather thoroughly researched. One investigating team (19) found salmon processing to produce 34% waste. Similar estimates were reported by other sources: 33% (20), 27% (21), and 30 to 35% (17). The Bureau of Commercial Fisheries (22) listed waste fractions by species as: chinook, 30%; red, 33%; Coho, 33%; pink, 35% and chum, 33%. Using the BCF values of wastage and total catch (5), waste volumes were calculated to be as shown in Table 63.

TABLE 63:   CALCULATED SALMON WASTE QUANTITIES, 1968

Species	Wastage, %	Quantity (lbs. x 10^6)
Chinook	30	7
Chum	33	26
Pink	35	36
Red	33	18
Coho	33	12
Total		99

Source: EPA Report 12060-04/70

TABLE 64: SALMON PROCESSING WASTE STRENGTHS

Process	Flow (mgd)	COD (mg/l)	BOD_5 (mg/l)	BOD_5/raw product (lbs/ton)	Suspended Solids (mg/l)	Total Solids (mg/l)	Volatile Solids (mg/l)
Canning (24)	0.043-0.046	5,920	3,780	65.2-178.2	508-4,780	1,188-7,444	1,048-7,278
Mild curing (24)	0.015-0.066	--	173-1,320	10.2-80.0	44-456	258-2,712	98-2,508
Mild curing and fresh (24)	0.011-0.036	--	206-2,218	3.3-36.0	112-820	484-2,940	84-1,756
Mild curing and fresh (24)	0.014-0.046	--	397-3,082	3.8-18.6	40-1,824	88-3,422	67-2,866
Caviar (24)	---	--	270,000	--	92,600	386,000	292,000
Canning (25)	0.33	--	3,680	--	2,470	--	--

Source: EPA Report 12060-04/70

Referring to Table 63, from 50 to 61% of the waste (depending on species) consists of heads, and collars. Another 11 to 16% is made up of tails and fins. Other waste segments in decreasing order of magnitude are: liver, roe, milt, digestive tract and heart (23).

Claggett and Wong(11) listed the flow from a salmon canning line at 300 gallons per minute with a total solids concentration of 5,000 mg./liter and oil concentration of 250 mg./liter. Other investigators have characterized the wastes from salmon canning operations as shown in Table 64.

The values for all parameters are quite variable, the wastewater strength probably depending on the efficiency of solids removal. The BOD_5 concentrations ranged from 200 to 4,000 mg./liter; suspended solids, 40 to 5,000 mg./liter; total solids, 80 to 8,000 mg./liter; and volatile solids 60 to 7,000 mg./liter. Caviar production often takes place with salmon canning. This process results in extremely strong wastes, but the flows are small.

Jensen (21) estimated that 78 to 85% of the shrimp is wasted in mechanical peeling and 77 to 85% in hand picking. The Oregon State Department of Environmental Quality (17) estimated 78% for hand picking and the Bureau of Commercial Fisheries listed a cleaning loss of 55% (22). The low value from the Bureau of Commercial Fisheries was apparently due to ignoring the blanching loss, which ranges from 30 to 35% of the picked wastes (26). Using a value of 80% wastage, the quantity of shrimp wastes generated in 1968 was calculated to be 233 million pounds.

Shrimp waste has been analyzed and been shown to be predominantly protein, chitin (a complex polysaccharide, not readily biodegradable) and calcium carbonate, as outlined in Table 65.

TABLE 65:   COMPOSITION OF SHRIMP WASTES

	Composition		
Source	Protein, (%)	Chitin, (%)	Calcium Carbonate, (%)
Hand picking	27.2	57.5	15.3
Mechanical picking	22.0	42.3	35.7

Source: EPA Report 12060-04/70

The protein concentration in shrimp waste has been judged satisfactory for animal feed (30). Crawford (31) reported that mechanical shrimp peeler effluents sampled averaged 29,000 mg./liter total solids. The major portion of the crab is not edible and as a result is wasted in processing. The waste consists of the shell and entrails and amounts to approximately 80% of the crab by weight. Large quantities of water are necessary for cooking, cooling, and washing of the entrails from the body.

The wastage of the total crab has been reported as: blue crab, 86% (32); king crab, 80% (21); and Dungeness crab, 73% (22). Using these figures, the solid waste load for crabs for 1968 was calculated to be 194 million pounds, as shown in Table 66. The actual wastes volumes at the processing plants were less, because a significant proportion of the crabs harvested (especially Dungeness) are marketed whole or butchered whole to remove only the backs and entrails.

TABLE 66:   CALCULATED QUANTITIES OF CRAB WASTE 1968

Species	Waste Fraction (%)	Waste Quantity (lbs. x 10^6)
Blue	86	94
Dungeness	73	32
King	80	68
Total		194

Source: EPA Report 12060-04/70

The composition of shellfish wastes is largely determined by the exoskeleton. This exoskeleton is composed primarily of chitin, protein bound to the chitin, and calcium carbonate. The major portion of the wastes consists of exoskeleton materials with varying significant amounts of attached or unrecovered flesh and visceral material included. The Ketchikan Technological Laboratory of the Bureau of Commercial Fisheries reported typical compositions of these wastes as shown in Table 67.

The protein level is considered low compared to visceral fish wastes, thus, this material is considered only marginally satisfactory as an animal feed.

Crab processing wastes, like shrimp, include large volumes of processing washwaters, solid wastes, canning waters (where applicable) and plant cleanup water. No information was found in the literature describing the organic strengths and liquid waste volumes from shellfish processing although currently on-going research may fill this void.

TABLE 67:   TYPICAL CRAB WASTE COMPOSITIONS (29)

| Species | Sources | Composition | | |
		Protein (%)	Chitin (%)	Calcium Carbonate (%)
King	Picking line	22.7	42.5	34.8
Tanner	Leg and claw shelling	10.7	31.4	57.9
Tanner	Body butchering and shelling	21.2	30.0	48.8

Source: Reference (29)

About 35 to 40% of the halibut is wasted in processing (21). The viscera are usually disposed of at sea. The remaining wastes (heads, skins and fins) have been estimated to amount to approximately 12% of the total wastes (37). Using this 12% figure, the halibut wastes in 1968 were calculated to total 3 million pounds. In most other filleting operations, the fish are not eviscerated. The unfilleted portions are discarded or recovered for by-products. Water is run continuously in the spray-washers and during filleting and skinning for bacteriological control. Blood and small pieces of fish flesh are entrapped in this flow. Other waste flows include the packing ice and the cooling waters.

The Oregon State Department of Environmental Quality estimated the solid waste fraction from bottom fish processing to range from 35 to 40% (17). Using the 40% value, the total waste quantity for bottom fish in 1968 was calculated to be 189 million pounds. As noted earlier, cod, haddock and pollock are eviscerated as caught and the wastes dumped at sea. This decreased the estimate of total processing plant wastes to 139 million pounds per year.

Thurston (38) determined the composition of wastes from sole and flounder processing using composites of nonedible parts of 214 fish. The average composition was: moisture, 77.4%; oil, 5.68%; protein, 13.6%; ash, 3.84%; Na, 0.16% and K, 0.22%. Although the nonedible parts of sole and flounder had lower values for protein and ash than did those of other saltwater species, they were judged to be of high enough quality for by-product utilization. The fish averaged 72% waste. The waste flows from bottom fish processing plants include large volumes of wastewater which contains blood, small pieces of flesh, the body portion of the fish after filleting and the skin. Claggett and Wong (11) measured the waste flow from a bottom fish plant and found it to be 450 gpm, with a solids loading of 750 mg./liter. Other investigators (24) have reported organic loadings varying from 192 to 640 mg./liter BOD5 with the average being 74 pounds of BOD5 per ton of fish. Reported bottom fish processing wastewater characteristics are summarized in Table 68.

TABLE 68:   BOTTOM FISH PROCESSING WASTEWATER CHARACTERISTICS

Flow (gpm)	BOD5 (mg./liter)	Suspended Solids (mg./liter)	Reference
105	640	300	(25)
320 – 410	192 – 640	---	(24)
132	1,726	---	(39)
450	---	750	(11)

Source: EPA Report 12060-04/70

TYPES OF WASTE TREATMENT FACILITIES

The liquid wastes resulting from fish processing are most commonly discharged to the adjoining waters. This practice has been restricted in many
areas recently because of the consolidation of plants and intensified enforcement of long-standing and recent water pollution regulations. The
alternative in many cases has been to discharge the wastes to the municipal
sewerage systems. In only one instance did the literature describe a United
States processor having on-site treatment of fish processing wastes before
discharge to a water body (42).

The specific difficulties encountered in the treatment of fish processing
wastes are, in large part, attributable to the characteristics of the wastes.
These are usually: high flows, medium to high BOD_5 and suspended solids,
and high grease and protein levels, compared to domestic sewage. The
frequently short processing season, high peak loadings, and rapid biodegradability of the wastes also contribute to the problem.

Claggett and Wong (43) studied the effectiveness of screening the wastes.
Two specific screen types were tested: rotary and tangential. A 34-mesh
rotary screen made of stainless steel was first investigated. The 4 foot long
barrel section was rated at 100 gallons per minute. Solids were removed
on a screw conveyor and blinding was prevented through the use of high
pressure nozzles.

The tangential screen employed two screening surfaces, each 1 square foot
in area, sized at 20 and 40 mesh. The resulting operating capacities were
35 and 20 gallons per minute, respectively. Both screens were judged successful for salmon canning wastes (43). The results indicated that with the
low investment and operating costs associated with screening, a processor

could expect removals of over 1/2 of the total solids from his wastewaters. Jaegers and Haschke (44) stated that centrifuges can be effectively used to remove fish pulp from the waste streams. Fats and proteins can also be recovered with this method. However, centrifuging entire waste streams would be very expensive when compared to other methods.

In the processing of oily fishes (sardines, herring, etc.), large quantities of fats and greases are present in the wastewaters. Knowlton (45) reported the fat and grease content of sardine canning wastewaters to be from 1,000 to 30,000 mg./liter compared to 50 to 200 mg./liter for domestic sewage. Fats and grease are present as flotables or as emulsions. When the wastes are discharged untreated, serious problems can result if the emulsified grease coalesces and rises to the surface of the receiving waters.

Grease can be removed in clarifiers by two methods: flotation and sedimentation. Limprich (39) reported that the application of 2.5 grams of clay, 2.5 grams of lime and 100 mg. of ferric chloride per liter of waste gave an optimal precipitation with a resulting 75% decrease in BOD_5. A similar procedure was described by Schulz (46) using Al_2O_3, lime, and ferric chloride. Griffen (47) mentioned that high fat and protein wastes can be treated with lime. Chlorination before sedimentation was recommended to prevent the serious odor problems that can result from rapid degradation.

Sedimentation tests of fish processing wastewaters were reported by Buczowska and Dabaska (48). In two hours of quiescent settling, 32% of the suspended solids were removed with a concomitant BOD_5 removal of 25%. About 58% of the organic matter in the wastewaters was in solution or colloidal suspension. Limprich (39) stated that 58% of the suspended matter in fish wastes settled out in two hours. Large volumes of sludge resulted.

TABLE 69:   GRAVITY CLARIFICATION USING F-FLOK COAGULANT

Coagulant Concentration (mg./liter)	Total Solids Recovery (%)	Protein Recovery (%)
5,020	68	92
4,710	60	80
2,390	47	69

Source: EPA Report 12060-04/70

A partially successful gravity clarification system was developed using large quantities of a commercial coagulant called F-Flok (43). F-Flok is

marketed by the Georgia-Pacific Corporation and is derived from ligno-
sulfonic acid. The floc formed slowly, but after formation sedimentation
rates of 4 feet per hour could be achieved. The summary for a large scale
test on salmon wastewater (Table 69) shows a maximum solids removal of
about 70%.

A process developed by H.E. Bode; U.S. Patent 3,248,225; April 26,
1966 involves the provision of starch paste precipitating conditions which
enable the simultaneous precipitation or coagulation of dispersed or col-
loidally suspended nonstarch materials. The following is a specific example
of the application of the process to the alleviation of stream pollution BOD
caused by fish processing waste liquors.

A fish processing waste liquor containing 0.6% of fish waste was used as
the liquid medium for the formation of a 0.6% phosphated starch paste,
made from crude phosphated starch. The resulting blend of phosphated starch
paste and suspended fish wastes was then treated with lime in the proportion
of 1 part of lime per 100 parts of the mixture of phosphated starch paste and
fish wastes. The mixture was stirred for 30 minutes. Upon stopping the agitation an insoluble flock of calcium starch phosphate, carrying with it suspended fish waste solids, quickly settled.

The treated liquor was centrifuged. The centrifuge solids, upon drying,
comprised a blend of edible animal feed ingredients consisting of fish waste
solids, corn proteins, and calcium starch derivative. The calcium enhanced
the feed value of the recovered fish waste material, particularly when intended for poultry feed.

An alternative to the normal sedimentation clarifier is the flotation cell.
The flotation technique relies on the entrainment of minute air bubbles
which float particles to the water surface. The resulting sludge blanket
is continuously skimmed from the surface. Two methods are used to entrain
the air bubbles in the flow, each method having advantages over the other.
The first method uses mechanical aerators to "whip" air bubbles into solution. Dreosti (49) reported that good laboratory results were obtained using
fish wastes with suspended solids levels up to 8,000 mg./liter. Higher suspended solids concentrations produced sludges that did not consolidate well
on the surface.

For optimum results, Dreosti recommended a minimum of air flotation and
short agitation times. Coagulants improved the removal efficiency; however, no mention was made of types or quantities used. The minimum detention time was estimated to be 5 minutes. Hopkins and Einarsson (42)
reported on the results of a similar flotation unit operating on fish wastes

at a flow of 0.065 mgd. The resulting sludge contained 15.5 pounds of grease and 35 pounds of fish solids per day.

The second flotation method involves flow pressurization. The total flow or a part of the flow is pressurized and then passed into the flotation unit which is at ambient pressure. The supersaturated solution begins to release air, forming many tiny bubbles. These bubbles then float the suspended solids to the surface. This method requires pressure pumps and containers and necessitates the recirculation of a portion of the flow, however, greater efficiency is usually obtained than with the whipping method. Three papers (11, 43, 50) describe in detail pilot-scale tests of the flow pressurization method of flotation clarification of fish processing wastes.

Water was pressurized by a centrifugal pump at about 40 psig. Air was added at the rate of about 2% by volume. The pressurization tank had a 1 minute detention time. The recovered sludge was heated and then the protein and oil fractions were removed by centrifugation. All tests were conducted using coagulant aids. The specific aids tested were alum, ferric chloride, F-Flok, aluminum hydroxide, Zetol-A (animal glue), and lime.

In the first tests on salmon processing wastewaters, alum, ferric chloride, and F-Flok were compared. Alum and ferric chloride performed well as coagulants but large doses of F-Flok were necessary to achieve comparable results. The iron in the ferric chloride tended, however, to catalyze lipid oxidation and this coagulant aid was thus judged unsatisfactory. Further tests were conducted and the authors concluded that flotation cells could be used effectively on fish processing wastes. Alum treatment was judged the most promising of the methods used. Feeding tests showed that alum could be included in the recovered solids up to the 1% level and the resultant sludge fed to chickens without altering their growth rate.

A method has been developed (51) to remove fish oils down to the 0.008% level by acidifying the waste stream followed by flotation. This method requires neutralization after treatment. Specially-coated treatment equipment is needed to reduce corrosion.

Little work has been done on biological treatment of seafoods processing wastes. Buczowska and Dabaska (48) did report that the carbon-to-nitrogen ratio of fish processing wastewaters is satisfactory for biological treatment. The biochemical oxidation rate was said to be similar to sewage, but nitrification begins sooner and is more significant. Assuming primary stage removal of reasonable levels of solids, greases and oils, the authors concluded that no special treatment problems should be encountered. Without this pretreatment, several problems can develop. For example, the oil and grease can interefere with oxygen transfer in an activated sludge system (52).

Czapik (53) reported on a trickling filter that clogged due to high levels of solids and oil from a fish processing plant. Anaerobic treatment of fish wastes has been investigated (9). Liquid fish wastes were judged to produce no unusual problems in a digester operation when in-plant screening was employed. Matucky, et al. (52) stated that fish solids and oils digested readily and the resultant sludge dewatered easily. The digester loading rates used by these investigators varied from 0.1 to 0.35 pounds of volatile solids per cubic foot per day.

BY-PRODUCT UTILIZATION

Much effort has been devoted to the development of saleable by-products from seafood processing wastes. From a standpoint of water pollution abatement, however, only one by-product group has contributed significantly to reducing the magnitude of the problem: fish meal and other animal feeds. Other by-products consume only a small portion of the wastes and wastes generated in the processes often are more noxious and less biodegradable than the original waste. If any of these methods were developed into profitable enterprises, however, the revenues realized from these operations could conceivably be used to partially defray the expense of disposing of the remaining wastes.

The use of whole fish and fish scraps for animal feed has been studied thoroughly. The fresh wastes or whole fish are usually processed to a fish meal, fish oil or animal feed (cooked and canned). In addition to meal and oil plants, there were in the United States in 1968 ten plants processing crushed shell for poultry feed, four plants producing animal feeds and two plants producing pelletized fish hatchery feed, all from fish wastes and whole fish (40).

Jones (41) discussed the various species and their wastes that could be used for pet food for several geographic areas of the United States. He concluded that discarded fish and fish wastes will be needed in the future to satisfy increased raw material demands. Several species of under-utilized fishes were listed. However, if all amenable wastes were processed into fish meal or other animal feed at this time, it is questionable whether the market could absorb the increased supply.

Besides fish meal, oils, solubles, and other animal feeds, many products based on fish wastes have been developed and/or promoted in the past. These include protein hydrolyzates, fats and lipids, enzymes, hormones, vitamins, chitin, glucosamine, fertilizers, lime, limestone, pearl essence, glue, caviar and other roe products, shell products and fish protein concentrate. The processes resulting in these products in general fail to reduce significantly the magnitudes of the wastes from which they are made. In most cases, only a very small fraction of the waste is utilized and the remainder must still be handled.

A process developed by A.J. Van Buuren; U.S. Patent 3,339,343; Sept. 5, 1967 involves the purification of polluted air discharged into the atmosphere by certain factories, of which a fish meal factory is a typical example. The most important odorous ingredients of such air are amines.

Various methods have been proposed for removing odorous ingredients from a gas by means of a filter comprising a finely divided surface-active filter material, but generally, the efficiency of these methods has been relatively low. Moreover, the known methods have the disadvantage that the filter material must be periodically removed from the filter to be regenerated; in this regeneration, a substantial portion of the filter material is generally lost, so that the consumption of the filter material is high.

This process has as an object to remove the abovementioned disadvantage and to provide a process for the purification of gases which has a high efficiency and a low consumption of filter material. This process is based on the use of a particular granulated resin as a filter material. This resin is obtained by the condensation of meta-phenylenediamine, to which other substances may be admixed, if desired, with an aldehyde. The condensation is performed in an aqueous medium and in the presence of an acid, and the relative amounts of the meta-phenylenediamine, the other substances, the aldehyde, the acid and the water are chosen in such manner that the volume of the granular resin when dried to a constant weight is at least 25%, and preferably 30 to 70% of the volume of the freshly condensed granular resin in its nondried condition.

Resins of this kind are known from Dutch Patent 81,911, and are commercially available as Centranol W 291. They are used as anion exchangers, i.e., to remove impurities from a liquid medium.

The same resins may also be used, with a high efficiency, to remove impurities from a gas, provided that they are in an air-dry condition. If the resins are humid, the efficiency is considerably lower, since the pores of the resin granules are then filled with a liquid, so that they are inaccessible to the gas to be purified. The behavior of the resins in a gaseous medium is essentially different from the behavior of other anion exchanging resins, which are ineffective to remove impurities from a gas. A further advantage of the resins is that they may readily be regenerated in situ, whereby substantial losses of the filter material are avoided.

Example: 70.983 g. of 40% trimethylamine were placed in a flask having a volume of 4 liters. Distilled water was added to obtain a total volume of 3 liters, and the contents were thoroughly mixed. 10 ml. of the solution were placed in an Erlenmeyer and distilled water was added to obtain a total volume of 50 ml. The mixture was titrated with dilute sulfuric acid (0.0911 N), using bromocresol green/methyl red as an indicator. It was found that 16.57 ml. of dilute sulfuric acid were required for neutralization.

After that, the flask was placed in a glycerine bath and connected at its upper end with a cooling device. By means of a pump, displacing 9 liters of gas in about 27 seconds, the gas in the flask was sucked through a small water separator and through a glass tube comprising 800 ml. of an anion exchange resin which is a polystyrene-divinylbenzene resin which is strongly basic (Dowex 2). The resin formed a layer with a height of about 600 mm.

As soon as the pump was in operation, an amine odor was observed at the outlet of the glass tube, showing that the resin did not absorb any gaseous trimethylamine.

A repeated titration of 10 ml. of the contents of the flask was performed in the above described manner after the experiment; 16.56 ml of dilute sulfuric acid were required for neutralization, i.e., the dimethylamine percentage of the contents was practically unchanged.

CURRENT RESEARCH
ON SEAFOOD WASTE TREATMENT

A variety of research projects on subjects relating to fish processing wastes are presently in progress or recently completed. These projects are briefly summarized below to describe the general trends in research efforts and to provide sources of up-to-date information.

HARVESTING AND PROCESSING MODIFICATIONS

The Oregon State University Seafoods Laboratory (54) is studying the efficiency of the Yanagiya Flesh Separator. The device consists of a revolving stainless steel drum perforated with numerous 1/16 inch diameter holes. A continuous belt is held against a portion of the drum. Whole fish or filleted fish bodies are placed between the revolving drum and the belt and the soft flesh portions are continuously pressed through the drum and thereby extracted. Data show excellent recovery of the flesh portions from the bone structures of the fish. A larger model of this device is being used by one Oregon processor to remove cooked tuna flesh from bone scraps. The recovered flesh is processed as dog and cat food.

Richardson and Amundson (55) have undertaken a five year study of rendering processing of Great Lake alewives. Microbial activity is used to separate the oil and scrap. Proposed uses are fish protein concentrates, fish oils and various oil-based products. The College of Fisheries of the University of Washington (56) has concluded research on the enzyme digestion of shrimp wastes. An effort was made to develop an active digestive system that could operate at high temperatures. Law (57) currently has a USDA grant to study the utilization of marine waste products.

A rapid method of ship-board fish meal production has been developed by a Mexican firm (58). Fresh fish are ground and dried simultaneously in a 240°C. gas stream. The meal is then cooled and packaged. The complete process takes from 6 to 8 seconds as compared to 22 minutes in an alcohol extraction process. One ton of fish meal is recovered from five tons of fish. No reference was made to the applicability of this method to fish wastes, but there is no obvious reason to discount it as a possibility.

A packaged on-board freezer has been recently marketed by a Pennsylvania firm (59). This unit freezes up to 300 pounds of shrimp per hour and maintains freezing temperatures in the storage hold. Utilization of this apparatus could eliminate the use of ice and its resultant wastewater.

Two American ocean vessels have recently been active in the harvesting and processing of fishery products (60). Named the Seafreeze Atlantic and the Seafreeze Pacific, these two ships cost over five million dollars each, and each can handle 50 tons of fish per day. Processing is so complete that "only the skins are wasted." If this venture proves successful, terrestrial accumulation of fish processing wastes could be substantially reduced in the future.

The Bureau of Commercial Fisheries (61) has developed a trap to harvest the sablefish population off the Pacific Coast. The trap has been judged to be moderately successful and further development is planned.

WASTE STRENGTHS AND VOLUMES

The National Canners Association (62) is conducting research on wastewater characteristics from sardines, shrimp, salmon, and tuna processing plants. The wastewater parameters to be measured are COD, BOD_5, total solids, dissolved solids, suspended solids, oil, grease, nitrogen and chlorides. A study on Maine sardine plants has been completed.

WASTE TREATMENT

A Northern California firm (30) has developed a direct-fired gas drier to economically dry fish meal. The drier jet exhausts upward with an adequate velocity to "fluidize" the drying bed of meal. High heat efficiencies have been obtained with this machine (i.e., greater than 95% recovery).

Kempe (63) has proposed research on the efficiency of spray-evaporation of stickwater. This method is considered to be superior to other evaporation methods due to lower cost, simplicity of operation, and faster start-up.

These factors are especially important to the smaller rendering plants with limited capital. Johnson and Hayes (64) have proposed a pilot plant study of the utilization of the chitin fraction of king crab wastes. Matthews (64), of the University of Alaska, is studying the utilization of king crab wastes.

Deyoe (65), at Kansas State University, has proposed research on the nutritive value and economic utilization of catfish processing wastes. Meals produced by various methods would be chemically analyzed and animal feeding tests performed.

BIBLIOGRAPHY ON SEAFOOD WASTE TREATMENT

(1) Soderquist, M.R., K.J. Williamson, G.I. Blanton, D.C. Phillips, D.L. Crawford, and D.K. Law. 1970. Water Pollution Abatement in the U.S. Seafoods Industry. Pacific Northwest Water Laboratory, F.W.P.C.A., U.S.D.I., Corvallis, Oregon.

(2) Holt, S.J. 1969. The Food Resources of the Ocean. Scientific American, 221, 3, 178-194.

(3) _____. 1961 Report of the International Conference on Fish in Nutrition. FAO Fisheries Report No. 1. Washington, D.C. 91 pp.

(4) Wilcke, H.L. 1969. Potential of Animal, Fish, and Certain Plant Protein Sources. Journal of Dairy Science, 52, 409-418.

(5) Lyles, C.H. 1969. Fisheries of the United States...1968. C.F.S. No. 5000, Bureau of Commercial Fisheries, U.S. Fish and Wildlife Service, U.S.D.I. Washington, D.C. 83 pp.

(6) Borgstrom, G. and C.D. Paris. 1965. The Regional Development of Fisheries and Fish Processing. In: Fish as Food, Volume III (G. Borgstrom, ed.) Academic Press, New York, 301-409 pp.

(7) _____. 1969. Computer Projects 73% Frozen Food Poundage Rise During Next Decade. Quick Frozen Foods, 31, 11, 45-46.

(8) Clark and Groff Engineers. 1967. Evaluation of Seafood Processing Plants in South Central Alaska. Contract No. EH-EDA-2. Branch of Environmental Health, Division of Public Health, Department of

Health and Welfare, State of Alaska, Juneau, Alaska, 28 pp.

(9) Nunnalee, D., and B. Mar. 1969. A Quantitative Compilation of Industrial and Commercial Wastes in the State of Washington. 1967-69 Research. Project Study 3F, State of Washington Water Research Center. Washington State Water Pollution Control Commission. Olympia, Washington. 126 pp.

(10) Davis, H.C. 1944. Disposal of Liquid Waste from Fish Canneries, from the Viewpoint of the Fishing Industry. Sewage Works Journal, 16, 947-948.

(11) Claggett, F.G. and J. Wong. 1968. Salmon Canning Waste Water Clarification. Part I. Flotation by Total Flow Pressurization Circular No. 38. Fisheries Research Board of Canada. Vancouver, B.C., Canada. 9 pp.

(12) Paessler, A.H. and R.V. Davis. 1956. Waste Waters from Menhaden Fish Oil and Meal Processing Plants. Proceedings, 11th Industrial Waste Conference, Purdue University, Engineering Extension Series No. 91, 371-388.

(13) Kempe, L.L., N.E. Lake and R.C. Scherr. 1968. Disposal of Fish Processing Wastes, Final Report, ORA Project 01431. Department of Chemical and Metallurgical Engineering, University of Michigan, Ann Arbor, Michigan. 46 pp.

(14) _____. 1963. The U.S. Tuna Industry. Good Packaging, 24, 7, 56-76.

(15) Dewberry, E.B. 1969. Tuna Canning in the United States. Food Trade Review, 39, 11, 37-42.

(16) _____. 1970. Tuna and Tuna-Like Fish Received by California Canneries, 1969. Western Packing News Service, 65, 9, 5.

(17) _____. 1969. A Survey of Waste Disposal Methods for the Fish Processing Plants on the Oregon Coast. Oregon State Sanitary Authority. Portland, Oregon. 77 pp.

(18) Chun, M.J., R.H.F. Young, and N.C. Burbank, Jr. 1968. A Characterization of Tuna Packing Waste. Proceedings, 23rd Industrial Waste Conference, Purdue University Engineering Extension Series No. 132, 786-805.

(19) Magnusson, H.W. and W.H. Hagevig. 1950. Salmon Cannery Trimmings, Part I. Relative Amounts of Separated Parts. Commercial Fisheries Review, 12, 9, 9-12.

(20) Brody, J. 1965. Fishery By-Products Technology. AVI Publishing Co., Westport, Conn. 232 pp.

(21) Jensen, C.L. 1965. Industrial Wastes from Seafood Plants in the State of Alaska. Proceedings, 20th Industrial Waste Conf., Purdue University Engineering Extension Series No. 118, 329-350.

(22) _____. 1944. Operations Involved in Canning, Fisheries Leaflet No. 79. In: Research Report No. 7. Bureau of Commercial Fisheries, Fish and Wildlife Service, U.S.D.I., Washington, D.C. 93-111 pp.

(23) Jones, G.I. and E.J. Carrigan. 1953. Possibility of Development of New Products from Salmon Cannery Waste: Literature Survey. In: Utilization of Alaskan Salmon Cannery Waste, Special Scientific Report: Fisheries No. 109 (M.E. Stansby, et al., ed.). Fish and Wildlife Service, U.S.D.I., Washington, D.C. 7-35 pp.

(24) _____. 1966. Industrial Waste Survey for Port of Bellingham (unpublished). Stevens, Thompson, Runyan and Ries, Inc. 38 pp.

(25) Foess, Jerry. 1969. Industrial and Domestic Waste Testing Program for the City of Bellingham (unpublished). Cornell, Howland, Hayes and Merryfield, Inc. Seattle, Washington. 17 pp.

(26) Dewberry, E.B. 1964. How Shrimps are Canned at a New Orleans Factory. Food Manufacture, 39, 7, 35-39.

(27) Idyll, C.P. 1963. The Shrimp Fishery. In: Industrial Fishery Technology (M.E. Stansby, ed.). Reinhold Publishing Corp. New York. 160-182 pp.

(28) Alverson, D.L. 1968. Fishery Resources in the Northeastern Pacific Ocean. In: The Future of the Fishing Industry of the United States (D. Gilbert, ed.), Publications in Fisheries, New Series, Volume IV. University of Washington, Seattle, Washington. 86-101 pp.

(29) _____. 1968. Preservation and Processing of Fish and Shell-Fish - Quarterly Progress Report. Technological Laboratory, Bureau of Commercial Fisheries, Fish and Wildlife Service, U.S.D.I. Ketchikan, Alaska. 2 pp.

(30) Grimes, E. 1969. personal communication cited in EPA Report 12060-04/70.

(31) Crawford, D.L. 1968. personal communication cited in EPA Report 12060-04/70.

(32) Stansby, M.E. 1963. Processing of Seafoods. In: Food Processing Operations (M.A. Joslyn and J.L. Heid, eds.). AVI Publishing Co., Westport, Conn. 569-599 pp.

(33) Dassow, J.A. 1963. The Crab and Lobster Fisheries. In: Industrial Fisheries Technology (M.E. Stansby, ed.). Reinhold Publishing Corp., New York. 193-208 pp.

(34) Crawford, D.L. 1969. personal communication cited in EPA Report 12060-04/70.

(35) _____. 1970. Extracts Crabmeat Automatically. Food Engineering, 42, 2, 36.

(36) Slavin, J.W. and J.A. Peters. 1965. Fish and Fish Products, In: Industrial Wastewater Control (C.F. Gurnham). Academic Press. New York. 55-67 pp.

(37) Dassow, John A. 1963. The Halibut Fisheries. In: Industrial Fishery Technology (M.E. Stansby, ed.). Reinhold Publishing Corp., New York. 120-130 pp.

(38) Thurston, C.E. 1961. Proximate Composition of Nine Species of Sole and Flounder. Agricultural and Food Chemistry, 9, 313-316.

(39) Limprich, H. 1966. Abwasserprobleme der Fischindustrie [Problems Arising from Waste Waters from the Fish Industry]. IWL-Forum 66/IV. 36 pp.

(40) _____. 1969. Industrial Fishery Products, 1968 Annual Summary. C.F.S. No. 4950. Bureau of Commercial Fisheries, U.S. Fish and Wildlife Service, U.S.D.I. 9 pp.

(41) Jones, W.G. 1960. Fishery Resources for Animal Food. Fishery Leaflet 501. Bureau of Commercial Fisheries, Fish and Wildlife Service, U.S.D.I. 22 pp.

(42) Hopkins, E.S. and J. Einarsson. 1961. Water Supply and Waste Disposal at a Food Processing Plant. Industrial Water and Wastes,

6, 152–154.

(43) Claggett, F.G. and J. Wong. 1969. Salmon Canning Waste–Water Clarification. Part II. A Comparison of Various Arrangements for Flotation and Some Observations Concerning Sedimentation and Herring Pump Water Clarification. Circular No. 42. Fisheries Research Board of Canada. Vancouver, B.C., Canada. 25 pp.

(44) Jaegers, K. and J. Haschke. 1956. [Waste Waters from the Fish Processing Industry]. Wasserwirtsch.-Wassertech., 6, 311.

(45) Knowlton, W.T. 1945. Effects of Industrial Wastes from Fish Canneries on Sewage Treatment Plants. Sewage Works Journal, 17, 514–515.

(46) Schulz, G. 1956 [Purification of Waste Waters from Fish Ponds]. Wasserwirtsch. Wassertech., 6, 314–316.

(47) Griffen, A.E. 1950. Treatment with Chlorine of Industrial Wastes. Engineering Contract Rec., 63, 11, 74–80.

(48) Buczowska, Z., and J. Dabaska. 1956. [Characteristics of the Wastes of the Fish Industry]. Byul. Inst. Med. Morsk. Gdansk. 7, 204–212.

(49) Dreosti, G.M. 1967. Fish Solids from Factory Effluents. Fishing News International, 6, 11, 53, 54.

(50) Claggett, F.G. 1967. Clarification of Waste Water Other than Stickwater from British Columbia Fishing Plants. Technical Report No. 14. Fisheries Research Board of Canada. Vancouver, B.C., Canada. 8 pp.

(51) Aktieselskabet, Aminodan. 1968. Recovery of Oil and Protein from Waste Water. British Patent No. 1,098,716. 4 pp.

(52) Matusky, F.E., J.P. Lawler, T.P. Quirk and E.J. Genetelli. 1965. Preliminary Process Design and Treatability Studies of Fish Processing Wastes. Proceedings, 20th Industrial Waste Conference, Purdue University Engineering Extension Series No. 118, 60–74.

(53) Czapik, A. 1961. Fauna of the Experimental Sewage Works in Krakow. Acta Hydrobiol., 3, 63–67.

(54) Law, D.K. 1969. personal communication cited in EPA Report

12060-04/70.

(55) _____. 1970. Converting the Alewife. The Sciences, 10, 2, 35, 36.

(56) Liston, J. 1969. personal communication cited in EPA Report 12060-04/70.

(57) Law, D.K. 1969. personal communication cited in EPA Report 12060-04/70.

(58) Lopez, J.L.G. 1967. [Fish Meal Manufacturing Machines on Board Shrimpers - Economic Study]. Report No. 35, Mexican Fisheries Bureau. 11 pp.

(59) _____. 1969. Lightweight Packaged On-Board Freezer for Shrimp Trawlers Now on Market. Quick Frozen Foods, 32, 4, 93.

(60) _____. 1969. U.S. Tests Fish Factory Vessels. Canner/Packer. 138, 2, 12.

(61) _____. 1969. Sablefish Off West Coast Sought as Resource for Frozen Packers. Quick Frozen Foods, 32, 5, 107, 108.

(62) Sternberg, R., and G. Brauner. 1969. personal communication cited in EPA Report 12060-04/70.

(63) Kempe, L.L. 1969. Spray Evaporation of Stickwater from Fish Rendering (unpublished). Department of Chemical Engineering, University of Michigan, Ann Arbor, Michigan. 6 pp.

(64) Simon, R. 1969. personal communication cited in EPA Report 12060-04/70.

(65) Deyoe, C. 1969. The Nutritive Value and Economic Utilization of Catfish Processing Waste in Animal and Fish Diets (unpublished). The Food and Feed Grain Institute, Kansas State University, Manhattan, Kansas. 4 pp.

PART IV.

FUTURE TRENDS AND RECOMMENDATIONS

MEAT INDUSTRY

In May 1973 new effluent guidelines for the meat packing industry were issued by the U.S. Environmental Protection Agency. These applied to the following categories of plants:

Segment	Maximum Capacity*
Beef slaughter (only)	>800,000 lbs. lwk/day
Mixed slaughter	>100,000 lbs. lwk/day
Packing houses	>100,000 lbs. lwk/day
Meat processing	> 10,000 lbs. product/day

*The maximum daily production capacity, as determined at the time of application, shall be the highest average level in pounds of live weight kill sustained for 7 consecutive operating days of normal production.

Allowable wasteloads for a packinghouse may require adjustment when normal day-to-day processing is less or greater than would usually be related to the live weight kill. Equations presented in the guidelines can be used to make this adjustment for Schedule A values (see Table 70). They relate BOD_5 and suspended solids effluent limitations to live weight kill and edible products where one of the above situations exists. It should be stressed that manufactured edible products refers to such products as sausage, bacon, hot dogs, etc.

The following process considerations and treatment facilities can be used to achieve the "best practicable pollution control technology currently available," according to the EPA guidelines.

1. Efficient blood collection.
2. Dry handling of paunch.
3. Dry clean-up prior to wash down.
4. High pressure spray system for wash down.
5. Screening and grit removal.
6. Dissolved air flotation.
7. Anaerobic lagoons followed by aerated lagoons or
       activated sludge systems.
8. Disinfection.

Schedule A guidance (see Table 70) is based on effluent BOD5 and suspended solids concentrations of 30 and 40 mg./l., respectively. Processing plant concentrations are slightly lower. Wastewaters from this industry
are readily amenable to biological treatment to these specified quality
levels.

The Schedule B guidance (see Table 70) represents good present day abatement practices.

TABLE 70:   EFFLUENT LIMITATIONS FOR MEAT PRODUCTS INDUSTRY*

Subcategory	Unit	Schedule A		Schedule B	
		BOD5	SS	BOD5	SS
Slaughterhouse	lbs. lwk	0.17	0.23	0.30	0.47
Packinghouse	lbs. lwk	0.26	0.35	0.61	0.87
Processing plant only	lbs. product	0.26	0.26	0.32	0.42

*lb./1,000 units

Source: EPA (May 1973)

POULTRY INDUSTRY

In May 1973 new effluent guidelines were also issued for the poultry processing industry. These apply to poultry processing plants handling greater than 40,000 pounds of live weight kill/day.

The following elements can be used to achieve the "best practicable pollution control technology currently available" for the poultry industry.

1. Efficient blood collection.
2. Dry clean-up prior to wash down.
3. High pressure water spray systems for wash down.
4. Reuse of chiller water in such areas as the feather flume.
5. Grease removal.
6. Biological oxidation by activated sludge or aerated lagoon systems.
7. Disinfection.

The Schedule A effluent guidance (see Table 71) is used based on BOD_5 and suspended solids concentrations of 20 mg./l. and 30 mg./l., respectively. This wastewater is readily amenable to biological treatment to the quality levels indicated. The Schedule B guidance (see Table 71) represents good present day abatement practices.

TABLE 71:   EFFLUENT LIMITATIONS FOR POULTRY PROCESSING
INDUSTRY*

Subcategory**	Unit	Schedule A		Schedule B	
		BOD5	SS	BOD5	SS
Broilers (eviscerating)	lbs. lwk	0.41	0.62	0.59	1.01
Broilers (eviscerating cut-up)	lbs. lwk	0.46	0.69	0.73	1.18
Fowl and duck***	lbs. lwk	0.4	0.62	0.78	1.09
Turkeys	lbs. lwk	0.4	0.62	0.57	0.68

*lbs./1,000 units.
**Figures do not include rendering.
***For plants doing cooking, boning, and dicing, limits may be increased up to 15%.

Source: EPA (May 1973)

SEAFOOD INDUSTRY

The survey of the seafood industry demonstrated that the water pollution problems generated therein are, with a few isolated exceptions, not as critical as those of many other industries. There are two basic reasons for this conclusion. First, seafood processing plants generally dispose of their wastes into estuaries, which results in dispersion and dilution. Soluble pollutant loads are quickly reduced in well-mixed estuarine environments.

Secondly, in many cases the processing plants are located in sparsely populated areas where other industrial wastes and domestic wastes are of limited magnitudes, minimizing the competition for the assimilative capacities of the estuaries. This is not to say that seafood processing pollution problems can be justifiably ignored; rather that it is advisable to attack the problems systematically and develop reasonable solutions in a rational manner.

Based on opinions expressed in the literature, seafood wastewaters are readily amenable to biological treatment and should present no special difficulties from the standpoint of toxicity. The problem with the wastewaters, therefore, remains basically one of economics, not of technology. Economics also seems to be the major concern in the disposal of solid wastes. Solid wastes, unlike liquid wastes, are of potentially significant economic value in the form of by-products. This potential should be recognized and utilized wherever possible in future research and development efforts.

The seafood industry consists of a myriad of processing centers located along the coastlines. The plants are frequently autonomous, intensely competitive, and notably lacking in cooperative spirit. Common problems are seldom handled jointly. Organizations such as the National Canners Association, National Fisheries Institute, Pacific Fisheries Technologists, and others are striving to reverse this trend, but without much success to date. One outstanding exception to this pattern is the current cooperative effort being mounted by the crab processors of Kodiak, Alaska. This undertaking involves the common collection of solid wastes followed by disposal at a single sanitary landfill. Hopefully, this activity is indicative of a developing awareness within the industry of the advantages of attacking in concert the water pollution problems common to all.

The lack of geographic concentration of the industry will tend to influence the type of research undertaken. Solutions which rely on combining the effluents (or solid wastes) from several plants or, the effluent from a single plant with that of a sizeable municipality, will not always be appropriate. Many of the major offenders are remotely located, with few, if any, other industries near at hand, and with only a handful of nearby residents who are most likely employed by the cannery. This situation, of course, is not usually the case, but nonetheless is common enough to warrant consideration.

The diversity of the industry is an added factor which must be considered when planning waste utilization and treatment research. Unlike some of the single-commodity food processing industries, the seafoods processors produce wastes which, while all highly organic and nitrogen-rich (excluding cooling waters), vary from negligible to staggering volumes.

Funding alternatives, both for research and for the ultimate full-scale utilization of the research findings, are an especially important consideration in this case. The industry, as most of the food industries, is typically a low profit enterprise. This fact, compounded by the current stationary production posture and increasing pressures from foreign competitors has already forced many small plants to discontinue operation. Significant increases in expenses, whether for in-house research or water pollution control, are likely to be untenable to many of the remaining smaller processors. Public research and demonstration project funding and treatment facility subsidies (in the form of tax credits or similar arrangements) will probably be necessary to permit the industry to survive in its present form.

It appears that the most urgent research needs in the seafood field lies in three main areas: (a) demonstration scale (solid and aqueous) waste treatment and/or disposal projects; (b) development of in-plant processing modifications (including by-product development) designed to reduce wastage; and (c) production-scale projects demonstrating the technical and economic feasibility of the solutions developed in (b).

To provide the bases for abating the most critical problems now facing a few plants, item (a) should be given highest priority. To make allowance for longer term considerations, items (b) and (c) should also be afforded increased emphasis. In many cases, the basic work outlined in item (b) has already been accomplished (or nearly so), and it only remains to demonstrate the new approach. Work with flesh separators, for instance, has indicated, at least in a preliminary fashion (54), that significant solids recoveries can be realized. Perhaps full-scale demonstration of this concept should be encouraged.

Similarly, the previously-mentioned high speed shipboard meal plant (57) could be applied to fish waste utilization and its effectiveness evaluated. Floating canneries are just now being placed into operation (59). Their advantages from the standpoint of wastes reduction should not be overlooked as their performances are studied.

Before demonstration-scale projects can be intelligently developed the designer must be familiar with the characteristics of the wastewaters with which he is dealing. Definitive studies of seafood processing wastes are scarce, especially for shrimp and crab processing. Further work in this area should be supported.

Most states' water quality standards are phrased in terms such as ...water quality shall not be impaired to the detriment of legitimate existing or foreseen water uses... Since a treatment facility design is based on anticipated efficiencies (in terms of BOD_5 and suspended solids), the level of treatment must be predefined. This requires a thorough knowledge of the effects of the wastes on the aquatic environment, therefore studies of the effects of seafood plant wastes on marine and estuarine environments should be conducted.

In-depth investigations of dissolved oxygen depletion, temperature effects, benthic disturbances, tidal effects, effects on primary and secondary productivity, effects of highly variable and shock loadings, degree of and rate of off-season recovery and many other variables should also be conducted.

The applicability of standard treatment methods is generally well accepted, but has not been sufficiently demonstrated; nor have the optimum operational characteristics been defined for each major type of primary and secondary process. This should be done at full (demonstration) scale for sedimentation, flotation, biological filtration, perhaps activated sludge and ultimately aerobic and anaerobic digestion.

Joint municipal-industrial waste treatment should be utilized whenever practical, since the same advantages inherent in joint treatment of other industrial wastes also apply here: dilution, equalization, the economics of size, etc. Innovative techniques and new treatment methods, while not critical to the immediate solution of the problem, should nonetheless be encouraged.

Solid waste should be considered a resource rather than useless refuse. Direct disposal, either in a landfill or at sea, should only be considered as a last resort, but in instances where deep sea disposal is the only acceptable alternative, perhaps investigations of methods, economics and consequences of deep sea disposal should be carried out.

Another alternative is to avoid concentrating the waste at the plant; i.e., preprocess at sea. Placement of an "iron chink" in a "mothership" which would accompany the salmon fishing fleet is one example. The wastes would be returned immediately to the fishing grounds. The effects of this practice would, of course, require attention.

The manufacture of by-products from solid residues has been extensively researched, especially with regard to salmon. An evaluation of these methods as potential waste reduction techniques leads to the conclusion that only those which utilize all or most of the solids are helpful. Animal feeding and other whole waste utilization methods should be stressed.

Perhaps more basic by-product development work is needed in the crab and shrimp industries, but in general the economic aspects of the operations should be emphasized. Market surveys are needed and transportation alternatives evaluated to determine the economic feasibilities of various approaches.

The seafood industry has a problem: water pollution. It has not generally reached crisis proportions yet. It does, however, require immediate but rational attention. The various avenues of approach should be investigated for each general geographical area and each commodity subsection and the best combination of solutions delineated and implemented in each instance.

COMPANY INDEX

The company names listed below are given exactly as they appear
in the patents, despite name changes, mergers and acquisitions
which have, at times, resulted in the revision of a company name.

INVENTOR INDEX

U.S. PATENT NUMBER INDEX

NOTICE

ENVIRONMENTAL LITERATURE 1973

A Bibliography

by Gary F. and Judith C. Bennett

This book deals with all aspects of pollution and pollution control, it being a bibliography of books, pamphlets, journals (but not of journal articles), and of some audiovisual aids in a field that is now euphemistically named "environmental."

This pollution bibliography is actually the third edition of this work and is about twice the length of the preceding edition, published in June 1969 by the University of Toledo, Ohio under the title, "Bibliography of Books on the Environment: Air, Water and Solid Wastes."

Since that time there has been a substantial increase in the number of primary sources and publications, i.e. journals, books, technical reports, symposia, academic literature and government documents, both domestic and foreign, that contain information about the environment and related subjects.

As in all fields pertaining to the Life Sciences the volume of literature with respect to the number of sources and diversity of contents has led to selective dissemination of information (SDI) on most aspects of environmental information.

This in turn has led to the generation of a multitude of secondary publications (abstracts, excerpts, summaries, card services, "trailing microfiche" publications and many more). The secondary publication is the SDI link for a user's specific information need as he confronts thousands of primary information titles and choices.

Because they fill a practical need, and afford ease of use and reference, such secondary publications have been listed meticulously in this edition.

Title listings of primary publications are complete and are never abbreviated, thus giving a clear indication of what information will be found in the original publication cited. Users of this book have a right to know which references deserve requests for photocopies or inter-library loan. Emphasis is on American publications with a good selection of foreign titles.

Another special merit of this volume is the inclusion of abstracts of meetings and symposium proceedings—all titles which are hard to come by and usually present an arduous and time-consuming task for the librarian. Meeting papers are often changed or augmented considerably, while getting them ready for the printer. Persistent efforts by the compilers in order to verify such information have contributed in a large measure to insure this book's high accuracy and utility.

The literature is divided into categories. It is realized that this division is often arbitrary, for publications that comprise more than one topic are placed into what constitutes the most suitable category in the authors' estimation. The senior author is well qualified to make such selections, he being a Professor of Biochemical Engineering at the University of Toledo, and Chairman of A.I.Ch.E.'s Environmental Division.

To give the prospective user an approximation of the wealth of information available in this book, the table of contents is reproduced here:

Table of Contents

WATER
Wastewater Treatment
Water Chemistry, Analysis and
  Treatment
Hydrology and Water Resources
Nontechnical
Microbiology and Biochemical
  Engineering
The Oceans
Thermal Effects
Symposium Proceedings

AIR
Air Pollution Control
Air Quality Sampling and Analysis
Related Technical
Nontechnical
Odor
Industrial Hygiene
Symposium Proceedings

SOLID WASTE
Books
Symposium Proceedings

NOISE

RADIOACTIVE WASTES
Books
Symposium Proceedings

ENVIRONMENTAL
Technical
Nontechnical
Ecology and Conservation
Law
Bibliographies of Environmental
  Materials
Symposium Proceedings

FILM LISTS

PERIODICALS
Journals
  Wastewater
  Air
  Solid Waste
  Environmental
  General (Less Technical)
  Hydrology, Water Resources and
    Water Treatment
  Biochemical Engineering
Newsletters
Abstracts and Digests
Industrial Media
Environmental Health

ISBN 0-8155-0509-4

134 pages

POLLUTANT REMOVAL HANDBOOK 1973

by Marshall Sittig

The purpose of this handbook is to provide a one volume practical reference book showing specifically how to remove pollutants, particularly those emanating from industrial processes. This book contains substantial technical information.

This volume is designed to save the concerned reader time and money in the search for pertinent information relating to the control of specific pollutants. Through citations from numerous reports and other sources, hundreds of references to books and periodicals are given.

In this manner this book constitutes a ready reference manual to the entire spectrum of pollutant removal technology. While much of this material is presumably available and in the public domain, the locating thereof is a tedious, time-consuming, and expensive process.

The book is addressed to the industrialist, to local air and water pollution control officers, to legislators who are contemplating new and more stringent control measures, to naturalists and conservationists who are interested in exactly what can be done about the effluents of local factories, to concerned citizens, and also to those eager students who can foresee new and brilliant careers in the fields of antipollution engineering and pollution abatement.

During the past few years, the words "pollution", "environment" and "ecology" have come into more and more frequent usage and the cleanliness of the world we live in has become the concern of all people. Pollution, for example, is no longer just a local problem involving litter in the streets or the condition of a nearby beach. Areas of the oceans, far-reaching rivers and the largest lakes are now classified as polluted or subject to polluting conditions. In addition, very surprisingly, lakes and streams remote from industry and population centers have been found to be contaminated.

This handbook therefore gives pertinent and concise information on such widely divergent topics as the removal of oil slicks in oceans to the containing of odors and particulates from paper mills.

Aside from the practical considerations, including teaching you where to look further and what books and journals to consult for additional information, this book is also helpful in explaining the new lingo of pollution abatement, which is developing new concepts and a new terminology all of its own, for instance: "particulates, microns, polyelectrolytes, flocculation, recycling, activated sludge, gas incineration, catalytic conversion, industrial ecology, etc."

In order to have a safe and healthful environment we must all continue to learn and discover more about the new technology of pollution abatement. Every effort has been made in this manual to give specific instructions and to provide helpful information pointing in the right direction on the arduous and costly antipollution road that industry is now forced to take under ecologic and sociologic pressures. The world over, technological and manpower resources are being directed on an increasing scale toward the control and solution of contamination and pollution problems.

In the United States of America we are fortunate in receiving direct help from the numerous surveys together with active research and development programs that are being supported by the Federal Government to help industry and municipalities control their wastes and harmful emissions.

A partial and condensed table of contents is given here. The book contains a total of 128 subject entries arranged in an alphabetical and encyclopedic fashion. The subject name refers to the polluting substance and the text underneath each entry tells how to combat pollution by said substance:

CARBON MONOXIDE
CARBONYL SULFIDE
CEMENT KILN DUSTS
CHLORIDES
CHLORINATED HYDROCARBONS
CHLORINE
CHROMIUM
CLAY
COKE OVEN EFFLUENTS
COLOR PHOTOGRAPHY EFFLUENTS
COPPER
CRACKING CATALYSTS
CYANIDES
CYCLOHEXANE OXIDATION WASTES
DETERGENTS
DYESTUFFS
FATS
FERTILIZER PLANT EFFLUENTS
FLOUR
FLUORINE COMPOUNDS
FLY ASH
FORMALDEHYDE
FOUNDRY EFFLUENTS
FRUIT PROCESSING INDUSTRY
  EFFLUENTS
GLYCOLS
GREASE
HYDRAZINE
HYDROCARBONS
HYDROGEN CHLORIDE
HYDROGEN CYANIDE
HYDROGEN FLUORIDE
HYDROGEN SULFIDE
IODINE
IRON
IRON OXIDES
LAUNDRY WASTES
LEAD
LEAD TETRAALKYLS
MAGNESIUM CHLORIDE
MANGANESE
MEAT PACKING FUMES
MERCAPTANS
MERCURY
METAL CARBONYLS
MINE DRAINAGE WATERS
NAPHTHOQUINONES
NICKEL
NITRATES
NITRITES
NITROANILINES
NITROGEN OXIDES
OIL
OIL (INDUSTRIAL WASTE)

OIL (PETROCHEMICAL WASTE)
OIL (PRODUCTION WASTE)
OIL (REFINERY WASTE)
OIL (TRANSPORT SPILLS)
OIL (VEGETABLE)
ORGANIC VAPORS
OXYDEHYDROGENATION PROCESS
  EFFLUENTS
PAINT AND PAINTING EFFLUENTS
PAPER MILL EFFLUENTS
PARTICULATES
PESTICIDES
PHENOLS
PHOSGENE
PHOSPHATES
PHOSPHORIC ACID
PHOSPHORUS
PICKLING CHEMICALS
PLASTIC WASTES
PLATING CHEMICALS
PLATINUM
PROTEINS
RADIOACTIVE MATERIAL
RARE EARTH
ROLLING MILL DUST & FUMES
ROOFING FACTORY WASTES
RUBBER
SELENIUM
SILVER
SODA ASH
SODIUM MONOXIDE
SOLVENTS
STARCH
STEEL MILL CONVERTER EMISSIONS
STRONTIUM
SULFIDES
SULFUR
SULFUR DIOXIDE
SULFURIC ACID
TANTALUM
TELLURIUM HEXAFLUORIDE
TETRABROMOETHANE
TEXTILE INDUSTRY EFFLUENTS
THIOSULFATES
TIN
TITANIUM
TRIARYLPHOSPHATES
URANIUM
VANADIUM
VEGETABLE PROCESSING INDUSTRY
  EFFLUENTS
VIRUSES
ZINC

ISBN 0-8155-0489-6

528 pages

WASTEWATER CLEANUP
EQUIPMENT 1973

Second Edition

Water pollution is becoming more of a problem with every passing year. Plants engaged in all types of manufacture are being more and more carefully watched by federal, state, and municipal governments to prevent them from pouring their untreated effluents into the nation's waterways, as they used to do. The sewage treatment plants of many municipalities are becoming too small for the burgeoning population, and many communities once served by individual septic tanks are having to build sewers and treatment plants.

Water pollution will be solved primarily by application of techniques, processes, and devices already known or in existence today, supplemented by modifications of these known methods based on advanced technology. This book gives you basic technical information and specifications pertaining to commercial equipment currently available from equipment manufacturers. Altogether the products of 94 companies are represented.

This second edition of "Wastewater Cleanup Equipment" supplies technical data, diagrams, pictures, specifications and other information on commercial equipment useful in water pollution control and sewage treatment. The data appearing in this book were selected by the publisher from each manufacturer's literature at no cost to, nor influence from, the manufacturers of the equipment.

It is expected that vast sums will be spent in the United States during the remaining portion of this decade for control and abatement of water pollution. Much of the expenditure will be for the type of equipment described in this book.

Today's environmental control is taken to mean a specialized technology employing specialized equipment designed to process the discarded and excreted wastes of human metabolism and human activity of any sort.

Next to air, water is the most abundant and utilized commodity necessary for the maintenance of human life. The average consumption of water per person in residential communities in the United States is between 40 and 100 gallons in one day. In highly industrialized communities the average consumption pro head can be as high as 250 gallons per day.

The reuse of wastewater after cleanup is not only becoming a cogent necessity, but it is also becoming more attractive economically. The degree of purity required for industrial water use is in many cases greater or vastly different from that acceptable for potable water.

Special equipment for cleanup of wastewater is therefore an absolute must, and this book is offered with the intention of providing real help in the selection of the proper equipment.

The descriptions and illustrations given by the original equipment manufacturer include one or more of the following:

1. **Diagrams of commercial equipment with descriptions of components.**

2. **A technical description of the apparatus and the processes involved in its use.**

3. **Specifications of the apparatus, including dimensions, capacities, etc.**

4. **Examples of practical applications.**

5. **Graphs relating to the various parameters involved.**

Arrangement is alphabetically by manufacturer. A detailed subject index by type of equipment is included, as well as a company name cross reference index.

ISBN 0-8155-0487-X

372 pages

WASTE DISPOSAL CONTROL

IN THE FRUIT AND VEGETABLE INDUSTRY 1973

by H. R. Jones

Pollution Technology Review No. 1

The fruit and vegetable processing industry is certainly a major industry. As pointed out in a recent report by the National Canners Association ca. 170,000 persons are employed in ca. 1,800 plants of the canned and frozen fruits industry in the United States.

It is estimated that in the U.S. alone (incl. Hawaii) this industry annually:

Processes 26 million tons of raw product.
Discharges 83 billion gallons of wastewater.
Generates 800 million pounds of biochemical oxygen demand (BOD),
And 392 million pounds of suspended solids,
Together with 8 million tons of solid residue.

While these huge wastes are biodegradable, they add enormously to the garbage waste and disposal problem.

This book, largely based on authoritative government reports and surveys, attempts to clarify the ways and means open to the food processor who must keep his polluting wastes down to a minimum.

In the following partial list of contents chapter headings are given, together with the more important subtitles.

ISBN 0-8155-0466-7

261 pages

ENVIRONMENTAL SCIENCE TECHNOLOGY INFORMATION RESOURCES 1973

Edited by Dr. Sidney B. Tuwiner in conjunction with
The Chemical International Information Center
(Chemists' Club, New York)

Environmental science is a new science in many of its aspects. Being a subject of high actuality, it has led to a proliferation of many new publications, stemming from a pressing need for continual updating of the technology and its literature, codes regulating discharges and emissions, etc.

Environmental science is interdisciplinary, involving sociology, law and economics, as well as technology. Some of the problems arising from this fact are discussed here and information retrieval solutions are discussed.

The individual papers give a close look at the many sources of environmental information from the several viewpoints of librarian, editor, and specialist in government sources or industry associations, enabling the user to obtain a broad perspective on environmental information.

Section I includes the proceedings and panel discussions of the Symposium on Environmental Science Technology Information Resources sponsored by the Chemical International Information Center, and held at the Chemists' Club, New York, N.Y. on April 28, 1972.

Introduction — Dr. Sidney B. Tuwiner
Resources and Industrial Cooperation on Environmental Control at the American Petroleum Institute — E. H. Brenner, American Petroleum Institute
The Environmental Protection Agency and its R & D Program — William J. Lacy, Chief, Applied Science & Technology, Office of Research & Monitoring, EPA
Government Sources of Information on Environmental Control — Marshall Sittig, Director of Special Projects, Princeton University
Sorting It Out - Data vs. Information — Steven S. Ross, Editor, New Engineer
Environmental Control Resources of a Large Technical Library — Kirk Cabeen, Director of the Engineering Societies Library

Section II includes selected papers presented at the National Environmental Information Symposium, sponsored by the EPA, held at Cincinnati, Ohio, September 24-27, 1972.

Technical Information Programs in the Environmental Protection Agency — A. C. Trakowski, Deputy Asst. Administrator for Program Operations, Office of Research & Monitoring, EPA
The Environmental Science Information Center — James E. Caskey, Director ESIC (Environmental Science Information Center)
Federal Environmental Data Centers and Systems — Arnold R. Hull, Associate Director for Climatology & Environmental Data Service, NOAA, U.S. Dept. of Commerce
Scientific and Technical Information Centers Concerned with the Biological Sciences — William B. Cottrell, Director, Nuclear Safety Information Center, Oak Ridge National Library
Secondary Technical and Scientific Journals — Bernard D. Rosenthal, President, Pollution Abstracts, Inc.
Environmental Litigation as a Source of Environmental Information — Victor John Yannacone, Jr., Attorney
Scientific and Technical Primary Publications Carrying Environmental Information — D. H. Michael Bowen, Managing Editor, Environmental Science & Technology, American Chemical Society
Applications of Socioeconomic Information to Environmental Research and Planning — William B. DeVille, Director of Program Development, Gulf South Research Institute
Socioeconomic Aspects of Environmental Problems: Secondary Information Sources — James G. Kollegger, President, Environment Information Center, Inc.

Section III is a bibliography of basic governmental, institutional, and organizational documents assembled by the United Nations Conference on the Human Environment, held at Stockholm, Sweden, June 5-16, 1972.

Introduction
Basic Documents Received from States Invited to the Conference
Basic Documents Prepared Within the United Nations System
Basic Documents Received from Other Sources

ISBN 0-8155-0467-5

218 pages

FEEDS FOR LIVESTOCK, POULTRY
AND PETS 1973

by M. H. Gutcho

Food Technology Review No. 6

Food fads, health claims and high prices notwithstanding, meat remains Western man's most preferred source of high quality protein.

The trend in modern livestock production is toward rearing animals with a rapid rate of growth. Feed efficiency in poultry and cattle has been increased 50%, and 40% in swine, with a corresponding weight gain, over what was considered normal 15 years ago.

Since estrogens and antibiotics are no longer accepted components of feeds, new accessory factors are of great importance. Many processes in this book are concerned with just such growth-promoting compositions, making the natural nutrients easier to digest and to assimilate.

Among the fastest selling animal feeds in a gaining market are those for pets. In the U.S. a pet population of 55 million dogs and cats eats 3 million net tons of food every year. Formulations for dog and cat food are therefore included in this book, as are some for birds, tropical fish, fur bearers, and laboratory animals.

The book describes 396 patent-based processes and formulations. A partial and condensed table of contents follows. Numbers in ( ) indicate the number of processes per topic.

ISBN 0-8155-0496

389 pages

TEXTURED FOODS
AND ALLIED PRODUCTS 1973

by M. Gutcho

Food Technology Review No. 1

This book deals primarily with the preparation of meat-like foods from readily available protein, such as soy protein, peanut protein, and wheat gluten. Techniques employed by the textile and plastics industries have been borrowed and applied to plant protein.

Processes have been developed for spinning protein into odorless, tasteless filaments, which provide the necessary texture for simulated food products, or as meat extenders. Fibrous textures can also be obtained by nonspinning techniques, such as thermoplastic extrusion.

This new category of food has been designated by the Food and Drug Administration as "textured protein products." These sources of protein, when used as meat, in order to be acceptable to the consumer, must simulate the texture, chewiness, flavor, and appearance of a natural meat product.

Textured plant protein has gained acceptance as a meat extender, especially in school lunch and geriatric programs, which permit a 30% addition of plant protein to meat items. The book reviews 78 U.S. patents, most of them issued quite recently. Numbers in ( ) indicate a plurality of processes per topic. Chapter headings are given, followed by examples of important subtitles.

ISBN 0-8155-0463-2

Date Due